Classroom Testing: Construction

CLASSROOM TESTING: CONSTRUCTION
by
Charles D. Hopkins
Richard L. Antes

INDIANA STATE UNIVERSITY

F E. PEACOCK PUBLISHERS, INC.
ITASCA, ILLINOIS 60143

F. E. Peacock Publishers, Inc.
Itasca, Illinois 60143
Library of Congress Catalog Card No. 78–61879
ISBN 0–87581–238–4

Contents

Preface

Classroom Testing: Construction is the first of a series of books about special topics specific to testing in the classroom. The purpose of this series is to provide in-depth studies rather than broad, general treatments of topics, thus allowing teachers and preservice teachers to focus on their own present needs. The "how-to" thrust of this presentation is directed toward the practical aspects of building tests for classroom use and the contribution that measures generated by such tests can make to strengthen classroom instructional programs.

The material is organized and based on contemporary measurement theory and techniques that have withstood the test of time. A minimum of theory is presented, but we feel that a firm foundation of theory underlies the text material. The integration of measurement and ongoing evaluation as well as terminal evaluation and further decision making requires an understanding of a certain amount of test theory, and it is included when deemed necessary.

The practical orientation allows the use of the book in pre-service courses that devote a portion of time to test construction but more importantly Classroom Testing: Construction develops a desktop resource for the in-service teacher. The preparation of this book has been guided by the tenet that the preparation of good tests by classroom teachers supports teaching in the classroom and integrates the element of measurement into the educational process. The validity and usefulness of evaluations of students and programs and decisions upon which those evaluations are based rely on proper measurement. We hope that these basic positions are reflected not only in the material but more importantly in the classroom programs of those who study from and/or use Classroom Testing: Construction.

The true measure of the worth of the endeavors of manuscript preparation, publication, and study of a book on testing lies in the impact that is felt in the education, not of teachers who study it, but those who are in classes that they teach. If that influence is felt in the day-to-day learning activities, then we feel that a contribution has been made to the instructional process of education. Since all measurement is only approximate the measure of worth must remain unknown as all true measurements must be.

C. D. Hopkins
R. L. Antes

1 Use of the Teacher-Made Test

The assessment of student learning has always been a part of the teaching-learning process. Students, parents, teachers, administrators, and others in the community need information about the extent of individual and/or collective student learning. If teachers are to be successful in their efforts to foster learning in students, they need ways to determine the effectiveness of their teaching and indications of what students learned. Placement of students for future instruction and development of effective school programs also depend on information collected from and about students. The information needed is, for the most part, collected in the classroom by many observational procedures, including administration of **tests**[1] —both teacher-made and **standardized.** Other information is collected in the classroom by the use of nontesting procedures and by the observation of students in other school settings.

Since valid decisions about student placement and school curricula depend on valid data, the importance of collecting sound information cannot be overestimated. **Observation** of all kinds, including test administration, must be conducted to collect data about students. **Direct observation** depends on objective techniques and devices to select data and make objective interpretation of the collected information. Construction of tests also must be given special consideration to generate interpretable data. If these procedures are followed, decisions based on the collected data will aid in further education of students.

For a test to fulfill its purpose—the generation of valid information—careful attention must be given to the planning and actual

---

[1] The first time a glossary word is used in the book it will be in **boldface type.** As indicated, the word **test** is denoted in the glossary.

construction of the test instrument to be administered to students. Much, but by no means all, of the needed information concerns student achievement. Information about students' emotional, psychological, social, and physical development is equally important. All of this information is used to plan the school program and supplementary school activities and is the basis of individual students' programs. The test is by no means the only, or even the best, way to collect all data from students. However, many of the considerations given to the characteristics of test instruments and their use are applicable to other observational procedures and devices to aid observation.

Importance of Testing

Since the student is the object of primary concern in education, testing procedures must be judged by how well they support the learning process. Preparing students to function in a modern world involves a host of persons who rely on test data when helping students to reach their potential. These persons include students, parents, classroom teachers, other school personnel, and many community persons who rely on test data to aid in making important student and school-related decisions.

STUDENTS

The importance of testing lies in the importance to which test results are put. Students use these results in two widely differing ways. First, they use test scores to determine how successful they have been in meeting certain requirements for satisfactory completion of desired learning. Second, they use test sessions and the results of tasks they are asked to perform to direct study for the rest of the course.

The student uses test score information to help make a **summative evaluation** of performance on material covered by the test. Comparison of a test score either to a set of absolute standards or to performance of peers allows each student to gain insight into how well s/he performed on the test.

A student may also use the results of a test session to find out what the teacher expects from students. The kinds of tasks presented on the test direct student study for following units. Since a problem, question, or item on a test may present a task requiring simple recall of a fact or a more complex task requiring understanding, application, analysis, synthesis, or evaluation, the kinds of tasks asked for on a particular test point up to the student what is important in that class and how to study for that course in the future. For example, teachers create situations for application of learned facts and knowledge on tests, such as verbal problems in algebra, laboratory problems in physics, and design problems in shop courses. If educators want students to know how to apply knowledge, then students should be confronted with a situation in which they are called upon to apply knowledge in the test session. This kind of test structure not only measures the learning but also directs further study beyond accumulation of facts.

Since most teachers do not limit their expectations to simple recall, they need to reflect their higher-level expectations in their tests to direct students to meaningful study. Tests direct student attention and study to the kinds of knowledge and the behaviors that are asked for on the tests. Hills says:

> that whoever controls the tests and evaluations in a school really controls the curriculum. If you want to control what is learned, get control of the tests—not the textbook, the choice of teachers, the size of class, the syllabus of the course, or any of the other things that curriculum developers talk about.[2]

The teacher reveals to the student what is important through the kinds of tasks which s/he is asked to perform on tests, and what is learned is, to a large extent, a function of the collection process.

PARENTS

Test results are important to parents because they communicate information about student progress. Parents can be informed of student progress in many ways. A meaningful explanation to parents should include more than a report at the end of an instructional period or a semester or year. A complete system for informing parents of their child's progress should have many reports, including student's performance on tests throughout the instructional period.

Parents usually feel that they understand what scores on tests mean when they are provided a frame of reference for interpretation. Since a **raw score** on a test has little meaning, a way of interpreting the test score should be provided[3] or a written note about performance sent to the parents.

[2] John R. Hills, *Measurement and Evaluation in the Classroom* (Columbus, Ohio: Charles E. Merrill Publishing Company, 1976), pp. 275–76.
[3] Charles D. Hopkins and Richard L. Antes, *Classroom Testing: Administration, Scoring, and Score Interpretation* (Itasca, Ill.: F. E. Peacock Publishers, 1979).

CLASSROOM TEACHER

Test results are important for teachers to direct future learning experiences. If the teacher has administered a test based on the content which was covered and requires behaviors asked for in instructional objectives, then s/he has a means of determining how well students have met objectives. If the overall performance is less than satisfactory, the deficient part of the performance can be identified. Explanation of the deficiency could be: (1) that the objectives were beyond the reach of the students, (2) that the students were not motivated, (3) that the instructional program was not effective for this set of students, (4) other possible sources, or (5) a combination of two or more of the preceding. The need to investigate for reasons of the deficiency is pointed up by low test scores.

Support of learning also comes through the use of the test results to identify specific points of difficulty. Certain diagnostic factors can be utilized if each test paper is scanned and noted for any specific difficulties that a student has. Incorrect answers may fall largely in one topic studied, or a similar kind of error (e.g., in computation) may be apparent in several problems. Any test administered to a class can be used in a general way to diagnose or identify student difficulties with content or behaviors; however, a truly diagnostic test must be constructed in a particular way.

SCHOOL/COMMUNITY

Test results are used by other school personnel and other members of the community for several purposes. Curriculum specialists and school administrators have special needs for results of classroom tests. Although some teachers feel that they are personally judged by student performance on tests, this is not the purpose of supplying these persons with test results. Too many factors beyond the control of the teacher affect test scores; therefore, test results cannot point out good teachers and should not be used to form judgments about them. If everything were constant except for different teachers, some inference about the effectiveness of a teacher might be made from test scores, but that situation is not likely to be found in a real school setting. Rather, test results should reflect program effectiveness and indicate to administrative persons how instructional materials and procedures have affected student learning.

Community leaders, school board members, and taxpayers believe that schools should be accountable to the community and show

how the money that has been spent is reflected in student learning. Test results should be a factor in **accountability.** However, test results too often have been the only factor considered in accountability studies, so that public attention is focused on a limited scope of objectives. Although test results should be part of any accountability investigation, many objectives do not fall under the scope of testable outcomes, and they too should be considered. Student population characteristics should also be considered when deciding whether or not the schools have given value received for the educational funds they have spent.

Role of Testing in the Classroom

Five important elements of the educational process are:

1. **Student needs**
2. **Instructional objectives**
3. **School program**
4. **Collection of information**
5. **Assessment and appraisal**

Relationships between and among these five elements can help place the role of testing in proper perspective. A formal **needs assessment** or an informal needs identification forms a basis for classroom activities. When the *needs* of the students have been identified, certain *instructional objectives* are written to reflect those needs. These objectives are written with the assumption that if they are reached, then student needs have been met. Using the set of objectives for guidance, school officials set up a *school program* of activities with the idea that the program will move students toward attainment of the listed objectives. Certain steps must be taken to ascertain how well those goals have been met. *Information* is collected from students. The role of testing—a data-collecting procedure—is to supply a portion of this information. Items in tests are written to require students to use knowledge and skills stated in the specified set of objectives. Information is also supplied by nontesting procedures, such as direct observation, ratings, rankings, and **anecdotal records.** All collected information is then organized and used to make an **evaluation** of how well the school program has moved students toward goal fulfillment and, in turn, met the needs of the students.

Administration of tests is a **measurement** procedure while *appraisal* of program effectiveness and student *assessment* are evaluative procedures. As was pointed out previously, the two procedures of measurement and evaluation are closely related but at the same time serve education in two different ways. For our study of test construction the reader should keep in mind that a measuring instrument is being constructed and that the test results will be used to make evaluations and, in turn, important decisions. A commonly used measuring device—the thermometer—provides important information but does not in itself make decisions. Decisions are made by using available information. For a low reading from a thermometer you choose different clothing than you would choose if the thermometer gave a high reading. The instrument measures and reports, but you make evaluations and decisions based on the reading. A test score is similar to a thermometer reading in that the score is not useful in and of itself. All measures, including test scores, must be interpreted and judgments made about what each means before decisions can be made.

WHAT IS MEASUREMENT?

When the term *measurement* is used, the idea of quantification comes to mind. Educational measurement is concerned with quantifying those personal characteristics which are important to students and educators as they deal with the process of education. When the classroom teacher thinks of educational measurement, s/he usually thinks of achievement testing.

In what ways can classroom testing be considered a measurement process? First, the instrument (the test) is a measuring device. It serves the classroom teacher who wants to measure achievement in the same way that a thermometer serves the meteorologist or physician to measure temperature. Although these two instruments approach measurement differently, both of them generate values that indicate differences of some characteristic. Second, the differences reported in test scores reflect different quantities; thus, test administration is a process of quantification. Third, the constructor of a classroom test must give attention to the same set of characteristics for measuring devices that a physical scientist must deal with when building measuring devices for physical characteristics.

Since classroom measurement produces results which are the bases for important decisions about students and their instruction, testing, including the construction of the test, should become an integral part of classroom procedure. When the classroom teacher views testing as a process of measurement, the importance of testing becomes almost self-evident. The number value established by the test must correctly identify differences that exist among the students being tested. In technical terms this means that the teacher needs a good rule (a good test) to make number assignments to achievement. Other data-collection techniques and devices need the same good rules and careful control.

Norm-referenced[4] tests approach measurement of student achievement in much the same way that scientific devices measure physical properties. Classroom tests which are to be **criterion-referenced**[5] use measurement in a somewhat different way, but the principles of test construction do not differ greatly. Criterion-referenced measurement is not intended to separate the scores of the students or to order the students according to the amount of the attribute being measured. Rather, the score on each student's paper is compared to a specific predetermined score which has been set for a standard as a minimum level for acceptance of satisfactory performance. A major difference in construction is found in the level of difficulty of the items which are written for the two reference systems used for interpretation of the scores. For the criterion-referenced test, the items are of an easier difficulty level because the test measures at the level of minimum acceptance. For the norm-referenced test, where each student is given the opportunity to reveal the highest level of achievement, the items are written at a medium level of difficulty.

WHAT IS EVALUATION?

When the term *evaluation* is used, the idea of judgment comes to mind. When the classroom teacher thinks of educational evaluation, s/he usually thinks of student appraisal and judgment of program effectiveness. The information generated by achievement tests and non-testing procedures is used to form judgments about how well students met the objectives set for them. Does the information indicate goal attainment completely or partially—and to what degree?

The judgment can be made about one student. How well did this student meet objectives set for all class members and those set for him/her specifically? A valid answer to this question is important because future assignments and placement for instruction will be based on the evaluation. If the evaluation is made during a course of study and direction in the course for the student is guided by the appraisal, the judgment would be **formative evaluation.** If the appraisal is made at the completion of a course of study, it is known as summative evaluation.

Judgment about the effectiveness of school programs is made in an overall appraisal about how well all students met their goals collectively. How well did the class as a whole meet objectives? A valid answer to this question is important when considering how to continue the program. Formative evaluation can provide feedback for an ongoing

[4] Ibid, chapter 8.
[5] Ibid, chapter 7.

program and suggest changes within a course of study. Summative evaluation can be made at the end of a study to direct development of the program for future students. This essential ingredient of instruction allows the teacher to use information about a class of students to make appraisals of the value of particular learning experiences and the effectiveness of the organization of the classroom activities.

RELATIONSHIP TO DECISION MAKING

Since decisions are made at different levels of school organization, the use of measurement results and evaluations in decision making is different at the classroom level and the school level. It must be kept in mind that although decisions are made at different levels, the student data are always gathered at the classroom level.

Classroom Level

The relationship of classroom testing to decision making must be viewed through the instructional process. Instruction is considered effective if behavioral changes (cognitive, affective, and psychomotor) result from the instructional process. At the classroom level the teacher is concerned about students individually, and test scores are used largely to supply information about individual student behavior changes, primarily in the cognitive domain. In addition, the teacher uses the set of student scores as an indication of program effectiveness for that specific class.

Evaluation at the classroom level is a process of appraisal which involves the use of test data and other information collected by nontesting procedures to judge how well individual students met objectives. Has the set of activities in the school program served to move each student to meet objectives? The answer is usually given in terms of the degree of attainment but may be dichotomous, such as pass/fail.

At the classroom level the test scores provide a large portion of the data as input for the evaluative procedures which, in turn, provide input for decisions about future instruction for individual students and program development in general. Since these important decisions rely on a wide information base, classroom testing becomes an integral part of classroom instruction.

School Level

Testing at the school, school district, state, regional, or national level serves much the same purposes that it does for the classroom teacher. One exception is that the individual student per se is not the primary concern of schoolwide testing and evaluation systems. If a score from schoolwide testing is used for an individual student, the use will be at the classroom level as teachers and curriculum personnel consider each student individually.

Scores from schoolwide testing programs may not reflect a total score from each student. **Item sampling** allows a score for a test to be a composite of part scores from several students. In this way long tests can be administered without any individual student taking all of the test. When item sampling is used, a total test score does not exist for each individual and the identity of any one student is necessarily lost. Therefore, interpretations about individual student progress cannot be made when item sampling is used.

Sets of scores from schoolwide testing programs allow curriculum persons and administrators to look at the general effectiveness of programs. This can be done schoolwide and also, in terms of effectiveness, for certain geographical and cultural divisions. If educators are to be students of students rather than students of subject matter, achievement tests must support efforts to build appropriate curriculum for schools and, in turn, for students.

Purpose of Teacher-made Tests

There are many specific uses of test scores. Educators use test scores as an aid to diagnose specific learning difficulties, motivate study and learning, place students for instruction, select students for special programs of remediation or acceleration, plan an ongoing program, plan future programs, and report assessments of student learning to students and parents. Common to all of these specific uses are two strands which permeate testing and explain the purpose of teacher-made tests:

1. **They measure student progress.**
2. **Scores from the tests communicate important information to the teacher, student, parents, and school officials.**

Teacher-made tests can be constructed to measure how well a specific set of objectives has been met—something that standardized tests are not expected to do.

It can then be said that the major purpose of any classroom test is to measure how well an individual student has met a well-defined set of objectives. If good testing procedures are followed, differences in classroom test measures (the test scores) reflect differences in some aspect of student achievement. Furthermore, test results can indicate program effectiveness by reflecting the teacher's objectives and instructional emphasis.

MEASURING STUDENT PROGRESS

The two major classes of characteristics which teacher-made tests can measure are achievement and skills. Since these are, by their nature, very different, the approaches to their measurement employ widely differing methods.

Achievement

Tests to measure cognitive achievement, are, in general, of the paper-and-pencil variety, especially for the content subjects. Popularity of the paper-and-pencil test rests on the ease with which it can be administered within the classroom setting. It also seems appropriate for a cognitive medium to be used for measurement of learning of content which, by its nature, is cognitive.

By varying the test-item tasks and the behaviors needed to respond, the paper-and-pencil test can serve a wide range of measurement situations. Uppermost in the mind of the person preparing and administering a test is the importance of measuring progress toward stated instructional objectives, both general and specific. For each test task, comparison must be made between the behavior asked for in the objective and the behavior required by the item on the test. Tasks which ask the student to identify what happened on twenty-five dates between 1860 and 1865 are probably not able to measure student progress toward the following general objective: The student will understand economic, political, and societal aspects of the Civil War period. To measure this objective, different behaviors must be involved when students respond to tasks. Therefore, an item must be written to elicit the behavior stated or implied in the objective.

Classroom teachers should rely heavily on their own paper-and-pencil tests to measure achievement in subject-matter content, but they should not be slaves to that means of measurement. Oral testing, although time consuming for both student and teacher, can be used effectively for some topics. Other methods of collecting information should be considered and used if any of them could better generate the kind of data needed. Nontesting procedures which can be considered include direct observation, anecdotal record, written assignment, conference, and **unobtrusive observation.** A well-rounded program of data collection should involve as many of these as needed.

Skill Development

The assessment of the level of skill development can utilize some of the same methods of data collection as those used in measurement of achievement. Appraisal of skill development utilizes many techniques and reserves paper-and-pencil testing for measuring in the cognitive domain. The paper-and-pencil test is able to measure cognitive knowledge about a skill but will probably reveal little about how well the skill itself is performed.

Assuming performance skill from cognitive tasks is, at best, risky. Probably the best way to assess the level of skill development is to ask the student to actually exhibit the skill. Assessment can be made in terms of the procedures used and the product which was the result of the process. For example, the student could be asked to take a paper-and-pencil test for knowledge about how to install a zipper in a skirt. Although certain knowledge is needed, other factors are involved in actually sewing the zipper into the garment. Motor development, techniques of stitching, and other sewing processes are needed to construct an acceptable final product. Information about this skill could include a test over knowledge of the skill and an opportunity to actually install a zipper. Chapter 8 gives attention to this important area of performance testing for classroom use.

COMMUNICATION

The second function of teacher-made tests is important because, through utilization of test results, change within students can be identified and/or needed change in programs can be analyzed. Communication of test results is necessary if the time spent for testing is to be used constructively. The method of reporting will depend on the audience and the use to be made of the reported information. Parents, administrators, and prospective employers as well as students make decisions based on test scores.

Student and Parents

When reporting to students and parents, the teacher should keep in mind that the individual student and his/her parents are concerned about total classroom performance only as context for interpreting that particular student's test score. The teacher should be aware that a raw score has little meaning in and of itself and that the test score can communicate student standing only when a means of interpretation is provided.

Possessing the information from test results, the student or parents can decide courses of action based on how well s/he did on tests and other information from nontesting procedures. Awareness of student strengths and weaknesses allows an objective approach to decisions about future courses of study and pursuit of a particular trade, occupation, or profession.

Classroom and School

Teachers and school officials are interested in how the class as a whole performed as well as how each individual met expectations. School programs are changed according to how groups of students achieve. Certain parts of the program can be augmented while other parts may receive less emphasis. New topics may be introduced into the instruction, and old topics reorganized, based on how well classes as a whole met objectives.

School records are also transmitted under special arrangements to prospective employers or schools of higher education to allow them to determine whether or not a student meets employment or admission standards. In these cases, recorded scores of tests need to be interpreted in the context of some model of standards or relative performance.

Interpretation of Student Performance

Student performance in the broadest sense can be broken into two divisions according to two questions:

1. What does a student know?
2. What can a student do?

The kind of question asked can give direction about how to plan for performance interpretation.

Also to be considered in interpretation is the frame of reference to be applied for the interpretation. Either a reference group or a set of standards serves as means to interpret student performance.

NATURE OF PERFORMANCE

Within the classroom setting, students are asked to accomplish many actions. These actions involve doing, making, achieving, fulfilling, executing, carrying out, completing, consummating, recalling, understanding, applying, analyzing, synthesizing, evaluating, organizing, valuing, and a host of other actions. The total of these actions makes up the nature of classroom performance. Since the performance is so varied, no single framework can be presented to explain classroom performance. The wide variation in types of performance also is the reason why classroom measurement and evaluation are topics of debate and continued discussion.

In general, performance can be divided into two parts—(1)

the actual act of performing and (2) the results of that act. When this division is made, the study of performance is better explained in terms of procedures and products, the procedures being the process of the performance and the product being the result of the performance. This can be explained, for example, by dividing the actions used in constructing a soaring plane (procedures of construction) in a technology class and the result of the actions (product—the plane itself). The sum of the two parts constitutes the performance. The flying of the soaring plane can also be divided into the actual actions of flying (procedure) and the degree of success in flying (product). For other acts, such as a classroom speech, the performance is not easily divided into procedure and product; however, the two parts are distinguishable and can be considered separately. Decisions about how to appraise performance must be made within a complex arrangement of many contributing factors (see Chapter 8).

CRITERION-REFERENCED AND NORM-REFERENCED TESTS

When judgments are to be made of student performance, some point of reference must be set as a basis for the appraisal. Historically, two methods of interpreting test performance have been used. Before the days of formal interpretation, teachers made appraisals without clearly established guidelines that structured their evaluations. They were able to make these decisions because they were teachers and no one questioned whether they could or could not do it.

Later teachers set up standards (usually percentage of right answers) as a framework for interpretation, and few, if any, questioned this practice. For example, given a percentage correct scale of 95 and above—A, 88 to 94—B, 80 to 87—C, 70 to 79—D, and below 70—F, the teacher could, in addition to making statements indicating satisfactory or unsatisfactory work, make statements about the degree associated with the satisfactory classification. Interpretation to such absolute standards was first used to report school achievement and is an early example of criterion-referenced interpretation.

A second way to interpret performance is by comparison to one of several possible distributions of test scores which is used as a model. This interpretation can be made with statements like "a score of 65 is considered to represent good performance because only 10 percent of the scores in the comparison distribution are greater than 65" or "a score of 38 is a poor score because only 8 percent of the scores in the comparison distribution are less than 38." Interpretation to such comparison distributions is referred to an norm-referenced interpretation.

The set of scores for the classroom or a set of scores from an external **norm group** are two distributions which could be used for interpretation. When this type of interpretation is used, the relative position of each score to all the other scores is important to establish how students have performed. Test performance is reported in relative terms, but the report does not tell specifically what the student knows.

Each type of interpretation is important in its own right, and neither should be used to the exclusion of the other. When a well-defined body of knowledge is to be tested, criterion-referenced interpretation probably is better. If the test is designed to reveal differences in performance and each student is to be offered an opportunity to show maximum achievement, then norm-referenced interpretation probably is better. Scores from a criterion-referenced test tend to be very much the same, while scores from a well-constructed norm-referenced test should differ widely.

The major difference between the two ways of referencing is in interpretation of the scores; however, certain differences in construction of data-collecting devices must be considered. A norm-referenced test is more likely to have complex tasks. Criterion-referenced tests are more likely to have items to which all or nearly all of the students make a correct response. Norm-referenced tests usually test large bodies of content. Criterion-referenced tests usually test smaller bodies of knowledge.

Concluding Statement

The key role that collection of information has in the process of education makes the construction of tests and testing procedures an integral part of the process of education and of classroom activities. Most data for evaluation must be gathered in the classroom during the regularly scheduled school hours; however, some opportunities allow for unobtrusive observation. Whether or not some long-range objectives have been reached cannot be directly investigated until long after the student has left the classroom. For example, one objective for social studies courses could be that the student become a responsible citizen by voting in all elections. Since the student must reach voting age before feedback can be gained about attainment of this objective, some indirect approach must be utilized for information at the classroom level. Results from test or nontest procedures can be utilized to predict goal attainment, and assumptions can then be made about future behavior.

The best way to view behavior is in a natural, real-world setting where student behavior is not contaminated by any procedures or devices of observation. However, only occasionally will classroom teachers have the opportunity to collect large amounts of data from students in an environment which is a natural setting.

Some objectives allow the teacher to create near-natural conditions. Vocational, business, art, music, home economics, language, and physical education classes have many objectives which allow observation under natural or near-natural conditions. Skill development in elementary school classes also can be observed under natural conditions. Whenever possible, teachers should use these opportunities to collect information.

When natural conditions can not be created, teachers may use paper-and-pencil tests in lieu of the ideal conditions. These tests are given with the assumption that performance on the test is the same as performance would be in a real-world setting. The rest of this book is devoted to presenting ways to help the teacher construct tests which meet this assumption as nearly as possible. All efforts to do this are directed toward making valid tests, or more specifically making tests which generate valid data. Without **validity,** tests and test scores make little, if any, contribution to furthering individual or collective student learning.

2 Planning Teacher-Made Achievement Tests

The teacher-made achievement test is an instrument which proposes a sequence of tasks—items, clusters of items, or any performance—to which a student is to respond. The results of these tests are used as measures of student achievement, and construction of an achievement test is a time-consuming task that teachers often face. When using a test, the teacher should begin to plan for test construction prior to instruction because carefully planned achievement tests are essential to measurement of relevant student learning outcomes. Since a good testing program supports the teaching-learning process, the quality of instruction and the amount of learning depends to some extent on how well the teacher plans for and carries out classroom achievement testing. In this chapter, attention focuses on the factors to be considered and decisions to be made in planning for an achievement test.

Learning Outcomes Stated as Instructional Objectives

Learning outcomes occur as a result of the instructional program carried out in the classroom. The desired learning outcomes, stated as instructional objectives, are determined by the classroom teacher prior to beginning instruction and give direction to a classroom program. These instructional objectives may be written to cover a course or subject-matter area, a specific unit of instruction, or other subdivision, such as an assignment, and serve as guides to measurement as well as teaching and learning.

If the purpose of a test is to measure desired learning outcomes, the objectives must be clearly defined. The description of what to measure is found directly or indirectly in the statements of instructional objectives as developed by the classroom teacher. The teacher should incorporate broad goals previously set by the local school system into his/her classroom program. These general objectives may have been arrived at through joint efforts of curriculum specialists, state departments of education, and/or committees composed of personnel from various educational organizations outside the community. A teacher should peruse any information available concerning goals, purposes, and objectives prior to firmly establishing classroom instructional objectives. However, these instructional objectives to guide educational activities should be tailored to each classroom based upon the special needs of students in that class as well as the specific nature of the course and unit of instruction.

OBJECTIVES

Instructional objectives provide direction for the educational program and set goals for student learning. Another way of stating this is that objectives pertain to the goals to be reached by students by the end of the learning experience. The objectives, or goals, act as guides for evaluating student learning and program effectiveness. Program effectiveness refers to each teacher's evaluation of how well the instructional objectives are being reached and what changes need to be made in the ongoing, day-to-day instructional activities that support the attainment of those objectives.

The importance of instructional objectives was emphasized by Victor H. Noll and Dale P. Scannel when they wrote:

> Definition of goals comes first—as it must if teaching is to have purpose and direction. To try to teach and evaluate without defining objectives is like starting out on a journey without knowing where you want to go. It may be pleasant to wander around for a while, but it is doubtful that any sort of progress can be made without some direction.[1]

Sets of goals which reflect the concerns of those using them have been developed for various audiences. These aims range from the general, such as those at the national, state, and schoolwide level, to the specific, such as classroom objectives set for a course, unit, or daily lesson. For example, general goals or objectives expressed at the national

[1] Victor H. Noll and Dale P. Scannel, *Introduction to Educational Measurement* (Boston: Houghton Mifflin Company, 1972), p. 166.

level reflect concerns of broader society for the education of citizens. Two examples of sets of general objectives are *Cardinal Principles of Secondary Education*[2] and *Elementary School Objectives.*[3]

Objectives at all levels have a function in education, but instructional objectives must be specific to a given classroom, a subset of that classroom, or an individual. Instructional objectives vary in degree of complexity, depending on student experiential level, maturation level, content studied, and presentation of the subject matter. Our concern is with instructional objectives which guide learning and can be used to assess the effectiveness of instruction; therefore, each test item should relate to one or more of the instructional objectives established for the classroom.

Instructional objectives may be stated with either a nonbehavioral or a behavioral orientation. Nonbehavioral objectives deal with general learning outcomes and focus on learning in a broad sense. Since these objectives are stated in general terms, audiences, including educators, may not understand what a particular objective requires on the part of the student. The following are illustrative of nonbehavioral objectives:

1. **Comprehend the basic needs of animals.**
2. **Understand measurement to the nearest half-inch.**
3. **Understand the background of the American Revolution.**

These objectives are general and may be ambiguous because such words as *comprehend* and *understand* can be interpreted in many ways, depending upon an individual's orientation to the topic and his view of needed understanding of the content by the student. Nonbehavioral objectives deal with general ideas which cannot be easily measured, although they may be converted to a behavior orientation for classroom use by writing in more specific terms.

A behaviorally stated objective uses an action word to specifically express what the student will be doing to successfully complete the objective. The condition that exists while the behavior is being performed and the criteria to be met to complete the objective are also stated. The focus is on student behavior. The following are illustrative behavioral objectives:

[2] National Educational Association, Commission of Reorganizing Secondary Education, *Cardinal Principles of Secondary Education,* Bulletin No. 35 (Washington, D.C.: U.S. Office of Education, 1918).
[3] Nolan C. Kearney, *Elementary School Objectives* (New York: Russell Sage Foundation, 1953), pp. 35–41.

1. **Using ten minutes of class time, the student will write a two-paragraph essay acceptable to the teacher concerning the basic growth-related needs of animals.**
2. **The student will demonstrate knowledge of measurement by using a sixteen-foot steel tape to measure the classroom and report the measures accurately in feet and inches.**
3. **The student will write from memory fifteen important events which contributed to the colonies' declaration of independence and the resulting American Revolution.**

These objectives are explicit because they give direction for a specific student action. In addition, each indicates who will perform a particular action, the conditions under which the action will be observed, the product to be created, and the minimum level of acceptance for goal attainment.

Both nonbehavioral and behavioral objectives are valuable to the teaching-learning program, and neither should be used to the exclusion of the other. It is also important to keep in mind that all objectives cannot be stated in behavioral terms, nor can the outcomes of all learning be directly measured by a test. Nontesting procedures, such as direct observation, checklists, scorecards, rating scales, unobtrusive observation, and anecdotal records, are employed in collection of data to be used in evaluation of learning outcomes that can not be measured through a testing device. The teacher must choose how to state objectives based upon knowledge of student needs and the learning outcomes which are to take place.

The teacher may choose other ways of specifying objectives, such as stating them in general learning outcomes and then listing the specific types of behaviors desired under each outcome. For example:

General outcome: **Students will understand the concept of set as related to the four mathematical processes.**

Specific outcomes: 1. **Learn to associate a number with a set of objects.**
2. **Be able to draw an array for a given number.**
3. **Join sets in addition and separate sets in subtraction.**
4. **Join sets in multiplication and separate sets in division.**
5. **Solve fractional problems using parts of sets.**

Educators must be able to identify student needs and to develop sets of objectives which, if reached, will meet those needs. It is important that a teacher state objectives which direct his/her class in its pursuit of learning. Teacher-made tests should be based on those objectives and reflect classroom activities; therefore, classroom teachers usually better understand objectives that they develop than objectives that are developed outside the classroom. Student learning should be enhanced with the integration of objectives into each individual classroom.

DETERMINATION OF LEARNING TO BE DEMONSTRATED BY STUDENTS

The determination of what is to be measured and the development of items that call forth desired learning outcomes or behaviors are crucial in assessing achievement. A myriad of learning outcomes can occur as a result of the instructional program carried out by classroom teachers. These learning outcomes can be classified in a **taxonomy** to help teachers determine instructional objectives which relate to the expected student behavior. Taxonomies for the cognitive, affective, and psychomotor **domains** provide the teacher with a common reference for classifying student behavior in instructional objectives. Each domain is subdivided into categories arranged in hierarchical order from simple to complex. The cognitive domain is concerned with intellectual outcomes, the affective domain with interests and attitudes, and the psychomotor domain with motor skills. An instructional objective may involve more than one domain or classification of behavior, but cognitive behaviors are most closely related to achievement; therefore, they are presented here. The summary outline of the condensed version listing behaviors in the cognitive domain consists of six major levels arranged in hierarchical order moving from "knowledge" to "evaluation."

Condensed Version—Cognitive Domain[4]

1. **Knowledge**
   - **1.10 Knowledge of Specifics**
   - **1.11 Knowledge of Terminology**
   - **1.12 Knowledge of Specific Facts**
   - **1.20 Knowledge of Ways and Means of Dealing with Specifics**
   - **1.21 Knowledge of Conventions**
   - **1.22 Knowledge of Trends and Sequences**
   - **1.23 Knowledge of Classification and Categories**
   - **1.24 Knowledge of Criteria**
   - **1.25 Knowledge of Methodology**

[4] Benjamin S. Bloom et al., *Taxonomy of Educational Objectives: The Classification of Educational Goals, Handbook I: Cognitive Domain* (New York: David McKay Company, Inc., 1956), pp. 1–43.

    1.30 Knowledge of the Universals and Abstractions in a Field
    1.31 Knowledge of Principles and Generalizations
    1.32 Knowledge of Theories and Structures

2. Comprehension
    2.10 Translation
    2.20 Interpretation
    2.30 Extrapolation

3. Application

4. Analysis
    4.10 Analysis of Elements
    4.20 Analysis of Relationships
    4.30 Analysis of Organizational Principles

5. Synthesis
    5.10 Production of a Unique Communication
    5.20 Production of a Plan or Proposed Set of Objectives
    5.30 Production of a Set of Abstract Relations

6. Evaluation
    6.10 Judgments in Terms of Internal Evidence
    6.20 Judgments in Terms of External Evidence

The subcategory of knowledge indicates that students are to recall facts or remember previously learned material. Its twelve divisions further separate knowledge into what is to be remembered. Comprehension, the second subcategory, involves the use of material in a form different from the way it was learned. The grasp of meaning and the intent of the material can be demonstrated by changing information from one form to another, that is, by restating it in different words or using it in a different way. The third subcategory, application, calls for the ability to use abstractions, principles, and learned material in new situations. Emphasis is on remembering and using principles and generalizations in real-world situations. Analysis, the fourth subcategory, is the ability to break material into its component parts so that the organizational structure is understood. The fifth subcategory, synthesis, is the ability to put parts together or to form an element not clearly there before. The sixth and last major subcategory, evaluation, involves the ability to make value judgments and to combine elements of other categories from the cognitive domain.

    Learning outcomes based on the six major subcategories of the cognitive domain encompass objectives that have a mathematical or verbal orientation emphasizing problem-solving and intellectual tasks. The emphasis and the relative importance of learning outcomes are to be decided by the teacher. Since most classroom tests overemphasize the subcategory of knowledge, often to the exclusion or near exclusion of other important divisions of the cognitive domain, the taxonomy is a place to check that relevant areas of student behavior are considered.

When building classroom tests, teachers should be sure that they require behaviors on the test which reflect the behaviors asked for in the instructional objectives. The subcategories of comprehension, application, analysis, synthesis, and evaluation should not be overlooked in building classroom tests. The complete taxonomies for the cognitive,[5] affective,[6] and psychomotor[7] domains are available and should be consulted as needed.

Criterion Referenced and Norm Referenced

Criterion-referenced classroom achievement tests compare a student's performance to an established standard as determined by the teacher or by school policy. A norm-referenced classroom achievement test compares each student's performance to class performance or some external reference system. A teacher must decide whether to measure only learning outcomes that all students must acquire (criterion referenced), to measure the complete range of expected values (norm referenced), or a combination of both.

The decision to use criterion-referenced or norm-referenced approach has implications for test planning. A criterion-referenced test is oriented to the assessment of mastery in a well-defined content area using specified behaviors. A high level of mastery can be expected if the instructional program was developed from the instructional objectives and the test items adequately sample the content and behavior specified in the instructional objectives. If students have met the standards set by the teacher, then scores will cluster at the high end of the measuring scale. A norm-referenced test is built to maximally discriminate among students possessing different amounts of a characteristic, but at the same time it can be built to measure specific learning outcomes. A good norm-referenced test will be moderately difficult, and if student learning varies widely, the distribution of test scores will reflect that variability.

The type of referencing used for the interpretation of the test scores will affect the way a test is constructed; however, the writing of test items per se is not extensively affected by the reference system used. Test items for criterion-referenced tests tend to be easier than items

---

[5] Ibid.

[6] David R. Krothwohl et al., *Taxonomy of Educational Objectives: The Classification of Educational Goals, Handbook II: Affective Domain* (New York: David McKay Company, Inc., 1964), pp. 95–193.

[7] Anita J. Harrow, *A Taxonomy of the Psychomotor Domain* (New York: David McKay Company, Inc., 1972), pp. 44–99.

on norm-referenced tests, but the item-construction considerations remain the same. The following presentation explains the differences between the two referencing systems in terms of whether the test is to be criterion referenced (mastery) or norm referenced (open ended).

MASTERY TESTS

A mastery test is a particular type of criterion-referenced test which measures student attainment of a set of learning outcomes for a limited scope of content or clearly defined skill development. Mastery objectives are chiefly concerned with the taxonomy subcategories of knowledge, comprehension, and application. The predetermined acceptable level of performance is usually part of the objective statement and is expressed as a percentage level of correct responses or as the number of correct responses required to exhibit mastery. For a true mastery test the expected correct response rate is 100 percent. In practice, the criterion standard for satisfactory performance (minimum acceptance level) is usually set at less than 100 percent. The standard for acceptable performance should be stated in the behavioral objective and set at a level deemed appropriate for that objective in that course. For example, the student may be expected to complete the objective by exhibiting a minimal level of 85 percent, or some other percentage, correct. The same procedure can be used for a mastery test which covers several objectives if enough items are written for each objective and student responses are scanned for weakness on each specific objective. Specific examples of objectives illustrating the use of percentage correct as a mastery standard follow:

1. **Given a list of twenty words, the student will be able to divide the words into syllables by rewriting them with 85 percent accuracy.**
2. **Given a list of ten words orally, the student will write vowel sounds in each with 90 percent accuracy.**
3. **Given a list of fifteen words, the student will be able to write plurals with 100 percent accuracy.**

When teaching is for mastery, students not meeting criterion (minimal level of acceptance) restudy the material and must pass criterion on a new test before proceeding to new learning. Since all students are expected to meet the specified level of attainment, mastery tests do not go beyond what every student is expected to know; therefore, they have a relatively low ceiling. The age and ability level of the students in a classroom guide the teacher in setting a ceiling level that all students can meet.

Mastery learning is most appropriate for subject-matter areas where the content has been relatively stable or is sequential in nature. The basic skills and knowledges in primary and elementary school subjects, such as arithmetic, reading, and spelling, have stable content or are organized sequentially. At all levels of the educational process there are bodies of content where it is important for students to know all or nearly all of that content. Many prerequisite skills and knowledges may be necessary for progressing to the next instructional level, and it becomes important that the test items correlate with instructional objectives. Mastery learning is not intended to place a limit on learning, but it does place a ceiling on the scale used to measure the learning.

OPEN-ENDED TESTS

Classroom teachers sometimes must construct tests which measure student performance in such a way that the ceiling for the test is above the range of the highest-scoring student. The term *open-ended* has been applied to designate a test which allows measurement for the full continuum of true achievement. An open-ended test assesses outcomes in situations in which all students are exposed to the same instruction but achieve at different levels. Many factors, including range of student ability, the content studied, student age, motivation, and other personal characteristics, can affect the level of achievement. The instructional approach related to open-ended testing assumes that differences exist in potential and that the test is constructed to measure each student's actual achievement level. The test has an upper limit which will probably not be reached by the highest-achieving student (open ended) and a lower limit that probably will not be reached by the lowest-achieving student. When measuring achievement of students at all levels, the test must allow for a wide range of possible scale values. Open-ended test scores are best interpreted through a norm-referenced procedure that measures each student's level of achievement over a broad range. This approach gives each student the opportunity to score at his/her true level of achievement, and places no ceiling on the measures.

It is possible within the open-ended approach to develop objectives which the teacher expects each student in the class to obtain (master) even though there may be other objectives that no student may be able to fully meet. Those objectives all class members are to meet usually refer to knowledge and skills in a specific subject area. Students may be expected to master prerequisite knowledge (terms, concepts, and skills) necessary to further learning and then be encouraged to go as far as possible in developing application and critical-thinking skills. Varying degrees of achievement along a continuum of learning occur if the test items are adequately written and selected.

Gronlund approaches criterion-referenced testing as mastery learning and developmental learning. The mastery outcomes (minimum essentials) are concerned primarily with simple knowledge outcomes. Developmental outcomes (performance beyond the mastery of minimum essentials) are concerned with complex types of achievement.[8] The division of the criterion-referenced test into measuring mastery or developmental learning supports the discussion above concerning the open-ended test in which prerequisite knowledge (mastery of objectives) may be included within the open-ended test (norm-referenced) format. Mastery items incorporated in an open-ended test must be evaluated in a way that makes it clear whether or not mastery has been obtained. A certain criterion for the number of correct responses for a mastery item is expected. Developmental learning corresponds with open-ended testing: members of a class have an opportunity to go beyond a minimal level of essentials (mastery), and the test opens the complete range of values for possible student scores.

There is need in the classroom for both mastery and open-ended tests. When the content is fixed, instructional objectives should be stated in behavioral terms and the mastery approach should be utilized. Many other objectives can be best measured by the open-ended test, keeping in mind that good norm-referenced measurement produces measures which have meaning beyond each student's relative standing in the class.

The discussion of open-ended (norm-referenced), mastery, and other criterion-referenced tests has pointed up some of the similarities and differences in interpretation of test scores. Figure 2.1 presents a com-

Characteristics	Open-ended	Mastery
Purpose	Measure complete range of student attainment	Measure mastery of minimum essentials
Objectives	General or specific	Highly specific and detailed
Learning outcomes covered	Broad range	Limited range
Representative learning outcomes	Many items	Few items
Type of test items	Selection-type and supply-type	Primarily selection-type items
Difficulty of tasks	Medium difficulty	Relatively easy

Figure 2.1 Comparative summary of open-ended and mastery tests.

[8] Norman E. Gronlund, *Preparing Criterion-Referenced Tests for Classroom Instruction* (New York: The Macmillan Company, 1973), pp. 8–20.

parative summary of various aspects of mastery and open-ended tests. Prior to test construction, these factors as well as others should be given consideration.

Selecting Tasks

Effective achievement testing requires the selection of tasks for the student and item types which best measure achievement. Choosing the tasks or items to be placed on a test is determined by the content studied, the instructional emphasis, and the kind of information needed to assess student progress. Because of the interrelatedness of these components, special attention must be given to task selection.

When the test maker delays task selection until the last minute, s/he may not have time to choose the kind of tasks required to collect needed information. If the selection of tasks is not given careful consideration, the test may not measure the desired learning outcomes. Items should be written in rough form as a part of the teaching component of the teaching-learning process as content is introduced and covered during classroom instruction. The decision concerning the type of tasks to be included in the test must be made far in advance of when the test will be administered. The teacher selects those test items that call forth the learning desired from students. This process raises the question, "What kind of items should be selected?"

WHAT KIND OF ITEMS?

The content studied in the class and the behaviors asked for in the instructional objectives may preclude the use of some kinds of test tasks and suggest other kinds of tasks to be presented to the student. Classification of item types is based upon the demand placed on students as they respond to assigned test tasks. Classification of items includes: (1) the problem-type item, which presents a perplexing situation to the student and asks that it be solved; (2) the supply-type item, which requires the student to create a verbal response; and (3) the selection-type item, which provides alternatives from which the student is to choose a response. As many as three different item types may be used on a particular test if more than one type is needed to obtain the information sought. Items for teacher-made tests of achievement are further categorized as follows:

> **A. The problem-type item**
>   **1. Mathematical problem**
>   **2. Technical problem**

B. **The supply-type item**
   1. **Completion**
   2. **Short answer**
   3. **Extended response essay**
   4. **Limited response essay**
C. **The selection-type item**
   1. **True-false**
   2. **Multiple choice**
   3. **Matching**
   4. **Classification**

Problem-Type Item

Mathematical situations and technical situations form the basis for two common problem-type items. A mathematical test problem consists of any mathematical task that uses a story to present students with the task of solving a problem. The structure of the task may require the student to make a variety of decisions, such as the approach to be used in solving the problem. An item that includes only the basic facts of addition, subtraction, multiplication, and division is not a problem-type item. Of course, students should not have seen the problem previously.

The **technical problem** is similar to the mathematical story problem, but there are important differences. A technical problem is written for the kind of limited, specialized study that would be found in the physical sciences, vocational courses, technology, engineering, and business. Thus, the technical problem must be structured with these special requirements in mind so that the student can solve the problem based on the information provided. The problem-type item is used to measure interpretation, analysis of relationships, use of principles, ability to draw conclusions, and evaluation. In addition to these cognitive aspects some of the technical problems require skills in the psychomotor domain.

Supply-Type Item

A supply-type item requires the student to create a response within the structure provided. Specific supply-type items are used in the following ways:

1. Completion items require the student to complete a statement by filling in a blank(s) with a response in the form of a word or series of words with a common association. This type item can be used to measure knowledge of facts, definitions, terminology, vocabulary, and basic concepts. Completion items seem to be most useful in measuring the behavior related to the recall of facts.

2. Short-answer items require the student to respond to a task in a short phrase or sentence. This type item is useful in measuring

knowledge of facts. In general, this type of item measures the same behaviors as the completion item, but it also allows more freedom in the response. The use of the short-answer item is a step into the more complete response required by the essay item.

3. Extended-response essay items present tasks with a narrative and/or a question and require the student to prepare well-developed discourses. The nature of the task is unrestricted, and the student must make a decision concerning the coverage and depth to be given in the response according to the amount of time allotted. The task asked for is so extensive that closure cannot be made and is not expected. This type of item is most appropriate for measuring written expression and skill in organizing a logical presentation of a topic with a wide scope. The student may need to exhibit behaviors in several levels of the cognitive domain. For example, the extended-response essay item may require that the student explain, relate, compare, contrast, interpret, or summarize. The language arts writing class, English units, or any other class devoted to development of writing skills could find use for the extended-response item.

Some teachers have found use for the extended-response essay item as learning experiences for students. An in-class assignment not presented as a test could give the student an opportunity to check knowledge and a chance to fill in gaps. This use should not be presented as a testing situation to the student but rather as what it is—a learning experience. Classroom measurement procedures hopefully serve as a learning experience if follow-up is given in later classes to discuss test items and expected responses. The use of the extended-response item as a learning experience does not imply that other measurement procedures cannot be designed to include a component of student learning.

4. Limited-response essay items present tasks which are appropriate for use in achievement tests for content subjects. Although the student creates a complete response, this type of essay item should have well-defined boundaries. The scope of the expected answer should have definite limits so that the area of concern is "fenced-in" for the examinee. If it is not "fenced-in," the respondent will not know when required material has been adequately covered. A fence not only "fences-in" but also "fences-out" and gives the writer direction about what not to include in the response. Without this orientation the person responding is placed in a position of having to guess the nature of the task being presented.

Selection-Type Item

In selection-type items the student is required to choose from alternatives. These alternatives may be presented as part of the item, or they may be implied from the test directions. Specific selection-type items are used in the following ways:

1. True-false items are presented as declarative statements, and the student indicates whether the statement is true or false. True-false items are helpful in measuring student knowledge of specific facts, knowledge and understanding of principles and generalizations, and soundness of conclusions. Contrary to what some people believe, true-false items can be used to measure understanding and comprehension as well as knowledge.

2. Multiple-choice items are presented through a question or incomplete statement which serves as a premise, and the student selects the correct or best response from a series of alternatives. Measurement at the level of comprehension and application is facilitated by use of multiple-choice items. They may be used for measurement of behaviors at all levels and are applicable in measuring knowledge of facts, cause-and-effect relationships, logical reasoning, critical analysis, value judgments, and ability to discriminate.

3. Matching items require the student to identify relationships among a set of premises and a set of responses. For example, this type of item can measure for association of names with events, dates with events, names with places, capitals with states, and other combinations of related information. These involve the use of factual knowledge, which is probably the most important characteristic measured by this type of item.

4. Classification items require the student to categorize according to an exhaustive set of divisions. This type of item can be presented as a series of words, incomplete sentences, or complete sentences. The responses of the student are thus limited to a particular set of classes. This type of item can be used to measure the ability to associate by categories and to relate kinds of factual knowledge.

Determining which kind of item to use depends on many considerations. Figure 2.2 provides a comparison of test characteristics that may be helpful in determining the type of item to include in the test. The purpose of the test and what is to be measured are important to selection of the item type. For example, if a measure of written expression is desired, the extended-response essay test would be useful.

The time required for preparation of test items must also be considered. Ease of scoring is a factor, since it takes longer to score supply-type items than selection-type items. The number of students being tested presents another practical consideration. When a large number of students is being tested or the test is to be used again, the selection-type test may be best.

The teacher's skill in preparing the different types will influence the type of item used. We hope that the use of this book will

Characteristic	Selection	Completion and Short answer	Essay	Problem
Item preparation	Tedious, difficult	Relatively easy	Difficult	Relatively difficult
Number of items	Many	Many	Few	Few
Items	Specific	Specific	General	Specific or general
Test time use	Reading, thinking	Reading, thinking	Thinking, writing	Reading, thinking, writing, problem solving
Responses	Symbol (letter or such)	One word or short phrase	Expressed in student's words	Expressed in solution
Responses	From provided alternatives	Brief	Extensive	Relatively brief
Scoring	Objective	Semi-objective and reader's judgment	Reader's judgment	Semi-objective and reader's judgment
Scoring	Easy	Relatively easy	Time-consuming	Relatively time-consuming
Scores	Value determined largely by the test constructor	Value determined largely by the test constructor	Value established by reader of responses	Value determined by reader of responses
Cognitive domain	Knowledge, comprehension, application	Knowledge	All levels	All levels
Freedom of response	Restricted to given options	Very little	Very much	Much
Guessing	Permits, occasionally encourages	Little	Very little	Very little
Bluffing	None	Some	Permits, occasionally encourages	Very little
Implications for study	Study for facts and higher uses of knowledge	Study for facts	Study for facts and higher uses of knowledge	Study for facts, specific procedures

Figure 2.2. Comparison of test characteristics.

help you to improve the items you have used in the past and add to your repertory of types of items. A detailed discussion of each type of item mentioned in this chapter will be found in Chapters 4, 5, and 6. You may wish to read these chapters before you finish this one.

DIFFICULTY LEVEL OF ITEMS

Although an experienced teacher is able to estimate the difficulty of items being used for the first time, the difficulty is usually determined after the test is administered and the items are scored. The proportion of students who responded incorrectly to a test item determines the difficulty level of that item. Deciding on how difficult items should be depends on a variety of factors, including the purpose of the test and the ability, age, and grade level of students. Items that have been used previously should be listed in a **test-item file.** This file should have information concerning previous student responses that indicates the difficulty of the items. Chapter 7 includes a discussion of item analysis for true-false and multiple-choice items which covers the discrimination power as well as the difficulty level of these types of items.

As indicated earlier the items on a mastery test will be relatively easy because classroom instruction emphasizes the minimal skills and knowledge to be mastered. Nearly all students are expected to respond correctly to each item. In this situation the items are selected to determine whether or not the learning was mastered; therefore, each student either meets or does not meet the minimum requirement set by the behavioral objective. Open-ended tests should have items of medium difficulty to allow that they measure the various levels of student achievement along a continuum from low through high achievement.

Some educators believe that a multiple-choice or true-false test should contain items of varying degrees of difficulty so that each student can respond to the tasks from easy to difficult until the upper limit or capability is reached, thus establishing a ceiling for each student. This principle may be useful for standardized testing but has little, if any, use in teacher-made tests.

The concept of difficulty has more meaning in a selection-type test containing true-false or multiple-choice items than in a supply-type test composed of essay items. In an essay test, responses have degrees of correctness while the true-false or multiple-choice item has either a correct or incorrect response. This indicates that the students set the level of difficulty for objectively scored items while the scorers determine the difficulty level of essay test items.

For selection-type tests where some items can be answered correctly by blind guessing, some allowance for correct guesses must be given when determining the difficulty of an item. For example, on a five-response, multiple-choice item 20 percent (about one out of five) correct can be expected by blind guessing alone. For a true-false item the expected correct responses from blind guessing is 50 percent. On a five-response, multiple-choice item answered by 100 students, the ideal rate is 60 percent, midway between 20 and 100, which represents total correct responses. On a true-false test item answered by 100 students, the ideal average correct responses is 75 percent correct, which is midway between 50 and 100.

The ages and ability levels of students direct the teacher in estimating the difficulty level of items for students. The appropriate difficulty level of items for an average class at any one grade level will not be appropriate for a high-achieving or low-achieving class. In a practical sense the difficulty level of tests given in the elementary school may vary from time to time. For example, a test constructed to be easy will help to instill a feeling of accomplishment and self-satisfaction for slower-learning students or those possessing less capability. On the other hand, a test considered to be difficult will challenge the more capable students and give them a feeling that they have not reached their maximum potential. A teacher in touch with students can determine when either of these types of tests will be beneficial for a particular group of students. A teacher should skillfully explain to students the rationale for differences in test difficulty since they are partners in the teaching-learning process.

Test as a Sample

Any test represents only a sample of what may be an unlimited number of items that could be included. A test for a unit of work or one six-week grading period will inevitably cover fewer concepts than a test over a semester, an entire course, or a year of work. However, even in a six-weeks test the possibilities for test items are probably uncountably large. The teacher must select a sample of test items that represent the subject matter covered and the behaviors expected of students. The assumption is made that a student will get about the same proportion of items correct in the sample as s/he would if the total population of possible items could be included. For example, in a six-weeks test in mathematics it would be impossible to administer a test including all the problems that could be created for the concepts covered during that period; therefore, a sample of items must be drawn from that infinitely large population that can be represented as follows:

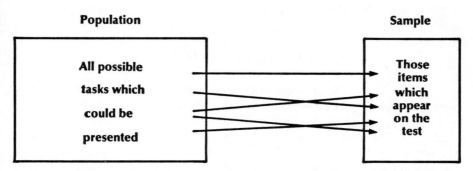

The test maker is presented with a lesser problem if the possibilities are finite; however, the teacher must develop any sample so that it represents the content and behaviors to be tested. Even in a spelling test covering 180 words to be learned in a unit of study, the population of words is too large to present in its entirety for one test. If the teacher presented one word each thirty seconds, the test would take over ninety minutes—much too long for a spelling test. Rather than give all the words, the teacher could include a portion—say 20 or 25—of the 180 on the test, assuming that the student will get the same proportion of words correct in the sample as s/he would get if all of the 180 words were included. This approach can be represented as follows:

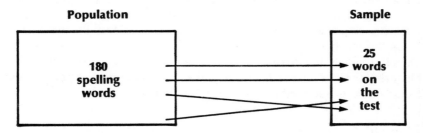

Practical considerations restrict the number of items a teacher can include on any one test. The length of time available for testing will limit the number of items to be given at a particular setting. Different types of items demand different amounts of response time. For example, it is generally agreed that, on the average, a student can respond to about one multiple-choice item per minute and about two true-false items per minute. The reading level of the student also restricts the type and number of items which can be included in the test. Because of these limitations, the teacher must select test items that provide an adequate sample of the desired learning outcomes and also allow each student sufficient time to demonstrate his/her knowledge of the content. Construction of a test that fulfills these demands is guided by a table of specifications which is discussed in the next section.

Table of Specifications

A valid achievement test must be balanced for content and include test items that are related to instructional objectives and behaviors expected of students. Without a definite plan to guide the construction of a test, the teacher has no assurance that the relationship between objectives and items is established within the test. A table of specifications, if used properly, supports the establishment of the desired relationship. By building a table of specifications from the general format (See Figure 2.3) before beginning instruction the teacher will be able to more effectively coordinate his/her selection of teaching materials and resources, assignment of outside readings, and use of class time with the instructional objectives that form the basis for the program and the test. The table of specifications in its final form bridges the two elements of school program emphasis and test emphasis.

A blueprint is used widely in the fields of engineering and construction. It is a detailed plan or outline that is used to guide construction workers in building a stable and functional physical structure. To measure achievement, a detailed plan that measures the learning outcomes stressed during the unit of work or course of study is also needed. This is the purpose of a table of specifications. It serves as a blueprint for tests, displaying the scope and emphasis of a test. In this way it helps the teacher who is building a test in much the same way that a blueprint serves the person who is building a physical structure. Each blueprint or table of specifications guides construction of something and assures that its intended function will be attained.

BUILDING THE BLUEPRINT

The table of specifications is a two-way table or chart listing the behaviors for a unit across the top, or horizontal, axis and the content areas down the side, or vertical, axis. Cells are formed by drawing vertical lines for behaviors and horizontal lines for the content topics. Figure 2.3, a framework for all tables of specifications, exhibits the basic elements needed. Each cell is divided to provide one space for emphasis expressed as a percentage of the overall coverage and one space for the number of items for that cell. Based on the percentages the number of test items for each cell is then determined. Totals for each content area (last column) and for each behavior (bottom row) are included in the table. The total percent for the last column and bottom row will be 100 percent, and

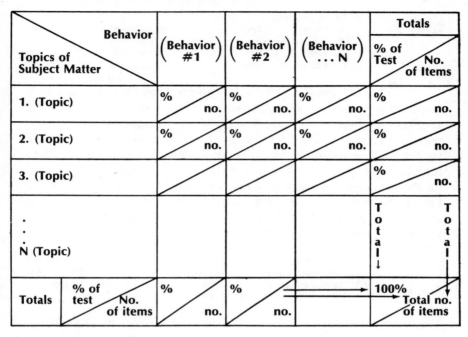

Figure 2.3. General format for a table of specifications.

the number of items in the last column and bottom row will be the number of items on the test (see the bottom right cell).

A table of specifications should be constructed for each test, whether it is a quiz, six-weeks test, a midterm test, or a final examination. There should not be more than three behaviors or more than five subject-matter topics included in the table. The number of subdivisions for a unit of work should ensure adequate, detailed content coverage. A list of subject-matter topics for the course content in arithmetic for a primary grade may be as follows:

Major Topics

1. Sets
2. Numbers and numeration system
3. Operations and fractions
4. Sentences
5. Geometry
6. Measurement

Since the table of specifications displays the scope and emphasis of a specific test, each of the major topics listed above may be further subdivided for a particular test. For example, the major topic of measurement for a third-grade test could be subdivided as follows:

6. Measurement
   A. Money   **30 percent**
   B. Linear measure   **20 percent**
   C. Time   **30 percent**
   D. Liquid measure   **20 percent**

From this point the teacher determines the emphasis which has been devoted to topics studied. For the test on measurement the emphasis has been expressed relatively by percentages and listed to the right of the topics. Figure 2.4 is a table of specifications made specifically for the unit on measurement. The percentages of the test devoted to topics are given in the row totals. For example, the subtopics to be covered for the measurement unit reflect the percentages 30, 20, 30, 20 for the four subdivisions. The percentages for desired behaviors to be exhibited are indicated in column totals. For example, the behaviors to be exhibited on this test are listed as follows:

1. Knowledge (recall of facts)   **50 percent**
2. Understanding (comprehension)   **30 percent**
3. Application (ability to apply   **20 percent**
   knowledge and understanding)

The emphasis which has been devoted to the behaviors studied is determined. For this test the emphasis has been expressed by the percentages 50, 30, and 20 and listed in the column totals.

The percentage of items to be written for each cell is determined and entered in the cell. Then the table is checked to make sure that the entries total the correct amounts for both the rows and columns. The total number of items for the test is placed in the lowest cell of the right-hand column. The percentages for each cell can be transformed into the number of items by multiplying the total number of items by the cell percentage.

Selection Tests

For selection-type tests (classification, true-false, multiple-choice, and matching items) and supply-type tests composed of completion and short-answer items, the number of items assigned for each topic is based upon the importance of a topic. The amount of emphasis and amount of class time devoted to each topic provide guides to each topic's relative importance. When one point is provided for each correct response, the importance of each topic is reflected in the total test score by the number of items written on that topic. For example, if four topics have the following proportions of relative importance, Topic A—.30, Topic B—.20, Topic C—.30, and Topic D—.20, each figure becomes

Behavior / Topics of Subject Matter	Recall (Knowledge)	Under-standing (Compre-hension)	Apply (Application)	Totals (% of test / No. of items)
1. Money	10 / 4	5 / 2	15 / 6	30 / 12
2. Linear measure	10 / 4	10 / 4	0 / 0	20 / 8
3. Time	20 / 8	10 / 4	0 / 0	30 / 12
4. Liquid measure	10 / 4	5 / 2	5 / 2	20 / 8
Totals (% of test / No. of items)	50 / 20	30 / 12	20 / 8	100 / 40

Figure 2.4. A table of specifications for a unit test on measurement.

the percentage of items to be written for a topic (30, 20, 30, and 20 percent respectively). In the event that forty total items comprise the test, Topic A would have 12 items, Topic B would have 8 items, Topic C would have 12 items, and Topic D would have 8 items. Thus, the weighting by numbers of test items is based on the importance of each topic in relation to all topics on one test.

Essay Tests

Although the amount of emphasis on topics reflects their relative importance, weighting for essay tests may be more difficult than for other types of tests. First, the number of topics to be covered on an essay test is determined; then the relative importance of each topic is expressed as a percentage. Next, the items are written and points assigned to each item based on the proportion of time to be devoted to each task on the test. The following example relates the three topics to be covered on a test with the items, suggested time, and points to be given.

Topic	Importance	Task	Time	Points	Totals
A	30%	Item 1 Item 2	3 12	6 24	30
B	40%	Item 3 Item 4 Item 5 Item 6	5 5 5 5	10 10 10 10	40
C	30%	Item 7 Item 8	10 5	20 10	30
Totals	100%	8 items	50 min.	100	100

USING THE TABLE OF SPECIFICATIONS

The table of specifications becomes the guide to item writing by specifying the number and nature of items relating behavior and subject-matter outcomes. The teacher will find that behaviors for some items will relate to more than one cell; when overlapping occurs, the teacher must decide to which cell the behavior should be assigned. The stated proportion and number of items per cell are guidelines, and adjustments should be made when necessary.

The main purpose of the table is to serve as a guide in building a test with a high degree of content validity. The relationship of test items to content and behaviors is clearly revealed to the teacher and other interested persons. High content validity is established when test items call forth behaviors and measure subject-matter topics to the same degree they are listed in objectives and presented in instruction. Content validity is largely established through careful planning of the test content to reflect instructional emphasis.

For Norm-Referenced Tests

The previous discussion concerning the table of specifications applies in its entirety to norm-referenced tests. The third-grade unit test on measurement is an example of how the table would be used for a norm-referenced test. The broad coverage of the table is very helpful, probably essential, in building valid norm-referenced tests.

For Criterion-Referenced Tests

The major difference between norm-referenced and criterion-referenced testing lies in the amount of content covered. For a criterion-referenced test the learning outcomes covered are usually more narrow in scope. The representatives of the behaviors and content can be viewed readily from the table for criterion-referenced tests. For a very limited amount of content covered and one behavior domain, the value of a table is less than for other tests; however, a table of specifications with only two to four cells is useful in building a test that will generate valid data.

Validity and Reliability

The most important characteristic of an achievement test is validity. A useful instrument for measuring student achievement must (1) be consistent in what it does (reliability) but more importantly, (2) measure consistently what it is intended to measure (validity). Thus reliability becomes a condition for validity but reliability alone does not establish validity. A test constructed to measure some characteristic is valid to the degree that it accurately and consistently measures that characteristic. For example, a test constructed to measure student achievement in mathematics should produce accurate scores which consistently reflect each student's level of achievement in mathematics.

VALIDITY

There are three types of validity: content, criterion related (includes concurrent and predictive), and **construct.** Content validity is established for a test by comparing the content coverage and behaviors exhibited on the test to classroom instructional emphasis and behaviors called for in the objectives. Concurrent validity (criterion related) compares the test scores to an external criterion of actual present performance. Predictive validity (criterion related) compares the test scores to an external criterion of actual performance sometime after the test scores have been obtained. Construct validity compares student performance on a test with behaviors considered important to describe a particular psychological theory. Although each type of validity is important in specific tests, the primary concern for classroom achievement testing is content validity, which is discussed next.

The degree of content validity in a classroom test relates to how well the test measured the subject-matter content studied and the behaviors which the test tasks require. A test will have high content validity if the items are representative of the population of possible tasks. This is accomplished by constructing a test from a table of specifications.

A test will have content validity to the degree that it provides a balanced sample of the total number of possible items based on the subject-matter content and behavioral outcomes to be measured. If the test consists of the first twenty-five items that the teacher thought of, this would probably not be a **representative sample** of items. A classroom teacher knows what content has been covered and what behaviors are expected, and when these two factors are incorporated into selection of items by using a table of specifications and a representative sample of items to be included in the test, an instrument with high content validity is assured.

Validity is specific to a particular use, and a highly valid test for one purpose may have low validity for another purpose. For example, a classroom test that is valid for measuring mathematics achievement for one teacher may not be as valid for a teacher who did not construct the test, particularly if the content covered and behaviors expected were different. This principle applies for standardized tests and tests developed for school districts when one test is used in classrooms which have different emphases.

RELIABILITY

A test is reliable to the degree that it measures whatever it measures consistently. Therefore, reliability is a necessary, though not sufficient, condition to establish validity since to be valid a test must measure something specifically. For a classroom, teacher-made achievement test, reliability can be determined by splitting the test into two equivalent parts—odd-numbered and even-numbered items—and comparing student scores on the two halves. The two scores for each student should be nearly the same if the test is reliable. The extent of agreement among all the pairs of scores of all students indicates the degree of the test's reliability.

Reliability can be reduced because of several reasons. Sources of lack of agreement for pairs of scores could come from student differences on characteristics such as motivation, attitudes, physical health, and emotional state. Other sources of difference may come from environmental conditions during testing, such as temperature, lighting, noise level, and interruptions. Some of these conditions are not controllable by the teacher; however, consideration should be given to each one, and optimum conditions should be created within the student and the situation to support high reliability.

Another source of lack of agreement can be the test instrument itself. Items which do not discriminate levels of achievement do not support high reliability. Items should be written clearly, and answers should be definite; otherwise, ambiguity will result in student guessing, which lowers the reliability measure. In general, these differences are controllable by the teacher. If good testing practices are followed, these differences will probably be kept to a minimum, thus increasing measures of reliability. All of the considerations regarding test construction given later in this book deal with reducing test-induced differences in test scores.

The lack of agreement between pairs of scores reflects **error** in measurement, where error is considered to be the variation observed among measures. An illustration will clarify how error occurs. Suppose that six elementary-school children are asked to measure the length of the teacher's desk using a twelve-inch ruler marked to the nearest sixteenth of an inch. The six independent measures for the students are: student A—$34\frac{1}{8}$ inches; student B—$34\frac{1}{4}$ inches; student C—$33\frac{7}{8}$ inches; student D—$34\frac{1}{8}$ inches; and student E—$34\frac{1}{16}$ inches. In this example the measurement error is a result of the discrepancies among the measures. However, in testing, measurement error does not refer to mistakes in measurement; rather it refers to discrepancies which result from uncontrollable factors. The error in the students' measures of the desk may be caused by lack of precision in marking off twelve units or reading the scale, distractions which break the attention of students from the task, or by other factors. These factors are controllable up to a point. Teachers must take advantage of all possible control of variation when building and administering tests. Error may not influence the meaning of measurement, but it can influence the precision of measurement. Reducing and controlling error as much as possible lead to reliable measures.

Several available methods of estimating reliability involve correlating two sets of data. For the classroom test, the split-half reliability is the most often used method of estimating reliability. The test is divided into two parts—one part made up of the odd-numbered items and the other part made up of the even-numbered items. Each part is scored for correct responses, and the two sets of scores are compared by using a correlation procedure. The Pearson product-moment correlation method is a widely used technique for estimating test reliability and is expressed as a reliability coefficient *r*.

Computation of *r*

The computation of *r*, using raw scores to estimate the relationship between the even-numbered and odd-numbered items for a classroom test, is illustrated as follows:

$$r = \frac{N\Sigma XY - \Sigma X\Sigma Y}{\sqrt{[N\Sigma X^2 - (\Sigma X)^2][N\Sigma Y^2 - (\Sigma Y)^2]}}, \text{ where,}$$

r = **Pearson product-moment correlation**
Σ = **means to add**

X = score on even-numbered items
Y = score on odd-numbered items
$(\Sigma X)^2$ = sum of X scores squared
$(\Sigma Y)^2$ = sum of Y scores squared
ΣX^2 = sum of squared X scores
ΣY^2 = sum of squared Y scores
ΣXY = sum of the products of paired X and Y scores

Student	Scores on the Even-numbered Items (X)	Scores on the Odd-numbered Items (Y)	Squared X²	Y²	Product of (X)(Y)
Charles	15	12	225	144	180
Daniel	19	22	361	484	418
Dave	13	15	169	225	195
Elaine	15	15	225	225	225
Lynne	16	12	256	144	192
Rich	18	20	324	400	360
Stacy	12	14	144	196	168
Susan	10	9	100	81	90
	118	119	1804	1899	1828

$$r = \frac{N\Sigma XY - \Sigma X\Sigma Y}{\sqrt{[N\Sigma X^2 - (\Sigma X)^2][N\Sigma Y^2 - (\Sigma Y)^2]}}$$

$$r = \frac{(8)(1828) - (118)(119)}{\sqrt{[(8)(1804) - (118)^2][(8)(1899) - (119)^2]}}$$

$$r = \frac{14624 - 14042}{\sqrt{(14432 - 13924)(15192 - 14161)}}$$

$$r = \frac{582}{\sqrt{(508)(1031)}}$$

$$r = \frac{582}{\sqrt{523748}} = \frac{582}{723.70} = +.80$$

Scoring the even and odd items separately and correlating the two sets of scores indicates the degree that the two halves of the test provide the same score value. The correlation of +.80 represents the amount of agreement for the two halves of the test in the example. To determine the reliability for the total test, the half-test reliability is converted by using the Spearman-Brown formula (split-half procedure) to predict the increase in reliability of the total test. The correlation for the two half-tests is +.80 (odd and even items); therefore, to estimate for a full length test, the Spearman-Brown formula is used as follows:

$$r = \frac{2r_{oe}}{2r_{oe} + 1}, \text{ where,}$$

r = reliability of the long form as administered
r_{oe} = reliability of the odd and even divisions

$$r = \frac{(2)(.80)}{.80 + 1}$$

$$r = \frac{1.6}{1.8}$$

$$r = .89$$

Interpretation of Correlation

The correlation coefficient *(r)* indicates the degree of relationship of two sets of measures. A positive correlation indicates that the two sets of scores are related such that high values on one set of scores are associated with high values on the other set of scores, middle with middle, and low with low, as illustrated in the following scattergram.

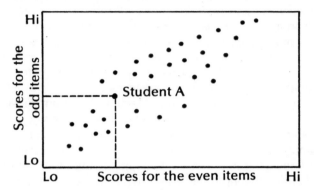

Each of the dots represents the student's two scores on the two halves of the test. The closer the dots are to a formation of a line, the closer the relationship and the higher the coefficient of correlation *(r)*. It is possible to get negative values for *r* through the correlational procedure, but this is unlikely to happen when investigating for test reliability. Reliability coefficients range from about 0.00 to nearly +1.00, which represents perfect reliability. Since test reliability refers to the consistency with which a test measures whatever it measures, it is important to have a high correlation coefficient. The reliability coefficients for good classroom achievement tests are expected to exceed +.70; therefore, the reliability coefficient for the example is sufficient. The closer to +1.00 the better. For any reliability coefficient to be meaningful, it must be compared with coefficients generally obtained for the particular type of test.

Individuals who build standardized tests usually demand reliability coefficients in excess of +.90, but measures of some other attributes may have acceptable reliability even if estimates fall below

+.70. The question arises, How may the teacher increase reliability on classroom tests? The reliability will generally be greater for:

1. **A long test rather than a short test**
2. **A test over homogeneous material rather than heterogeneous material**
3. **A group of students with a wide ability range**
4. **A test made up of well-written and relevant items**
5. **Scoring error is not included in any of the scores**
6. **Scores obtained in optimum testing conditions where each student is motivated**

Improvement of Instruction and Learning

Since tests direct student study as well as measure student achievement and provide feedback to the student regarding the amount of learning, the ultimate purpose of careful test planning is the improvement of learning. The tasks presented on a test point up what the teacher feels is important and direct how students study for that class.

The teacher has the opportunity to determine effectiveness in guiding student learning and in meeting the instructional objectives. When a test reveals that the objectives were not satisfactorily met, the teacher may wish to reteach the material in another manner or from a different approach. Through good testing the teacher can increase the quantity and quality of learning by enhancing teaching. Teachers who are knowledgeable in a content subject and approach testing as a way to further student learning are aware of the importance of tests serving their purposes. Therefore, they will need to look carefully at the validity and reliability of the tests which they use in their classrooms and plan the tests to support valid measures in student test scores.

3 General Considerations

In the preceding chapter the importance of careful planning for teacher-made achievement tests was emphasized. However, other general considerations also affect the validity of test results, and for a test to have maximum effectiveness, they also must be given attention. The validity of a teacher-made test depends on how well all aspects of the instrument have been properly developed and planned. It would be absurd to carefully plan a test and then provide a haphazard organization of poorly written items and directions. This chapter discusses the general considerations which are necessary to build a test of maximum effectiveness for measuring the specific behaviors and achievement requested in the instructional objectives.

Test Directions

Test directions must be clear and concise but at the same time provide enough information so that each student in the classroom will be able to complete the tasks presented. The teacher must empathize with students and meet their needs by writing test directions in an easily understandable way. Students who have learned to read should be able to take the test without oral directions; therefore, the meaning of directions provided will be identical for all students, and each is given the opportunity to perform at his/her highest level of achievement. The reading level of directions should reach the lowest reading level represented in the group being tested.

The subject-matter coverage, age, and grade level of students provide guides to suitable vocabulary and wording of test directions. Whether or not the directions are satisfactory can be determined by asking students similar to those who will take the test to read the directions and complete some of the items. The feedback will confirm the level and clarity of directions necessary for the students being tested and indicate where changes, if any, are needed. If the teacher deems it necessary, s/he can use an established system of determining the reading level of a narrative to check the reading level of the directions and test items.

GENERAL DIRECTIONS

Before the students are to take a classroom test, the teacher should explain the purposes of testing as they pertain to the area of study, the progress of individual class members, and the class as a whole. This eliminates the need for a written explanation in the directions each time a test is administered to the class.

General directions are usually placed on a separate cover page that does not show test items. A cover page is especially helpful when students are to begin work at the same time and the test can not be placed in the hands of all class members at the same time. Until time to begin the test, the focus should be on reading and understanding the general directions. Figure 3.1 provides an example of a cover page and the directions for a test which combines objective and essay items. A separate page for test directions is usually used for a six-weeks test, a mid-term test, or final examination for upper elementary, junior high, or senior high school students, but it may be also needed for younger students.

Test directions for each of the item types on tests for elementary school students should precede the section where each is used. Since there are many nonreaders in primary school groups and some in intermediate and secondary grades, verbal directions may be necessary. Although the directions are read or explained by the teacher for each test for young students, the written directions with sample items are included in tests for early grades primarily to provide an experience for later testing, when the students will be expected to read directions. Students will gradually become aware of how to use written directions and sample items when they are presented on tests and pointed out by teachers. The teacher should work through sample items with the class to avoid misunderstandings of how to respond and to show how to record answers for the items or tasks. Before the first regular test is administered, the teacher could have a practice session during which students are asked to work through a simulated test. The purpose of this exercise is to orient students to testing procedures; students should understand that this is not a regular test with the purpose of measuring achievement.

Upper elementary, junior high, and senior high school stu-

Name _____ Course _____

Date _____ Section _____

GENERAL DIRECTIONS: DO NOT turn the page until you
(1) have provided the information requested above,
(2) have read and understood the directions below,
and (3) have been directed by the teacher to begin
the test.

This mid-term examination consists of 50 multiple-choice items, each worth one point and three essay
items, each worth 10 points. You have 2 hours (120
minutes) to complete the examination.

SPECIFIC DIRECTIONS

Part I. Multiple-choice items. Read each item
carefully and decide which alternative (A, B, C, D)
best completes the statement or answers the question.
Respond to all items on the answer sheet provided by
marking A, B, C, or D like this: A Ⓑ C D

If your pay is $52 a month, how much will you earn
in a year?
A. $600
B. $624
C. $656
D. $784

Part II. Essay items. Read each item carefully
and prepare an outline of the points you are going to
make in your response. Write your outline and answer
on the three sheets of paper furnished, using one
sheet for each response.

Score: Part I _____ Test _____
       Part II _____
       Total _____

Figure 3.1. Example of a separate direction page.

dents customarily record responses to items on a separate response sheet. Responses for young and inexperienced students are best recorded on the test page. If students of any age or grade level are exposed to a type of item which has not been used before, then sample items are necessary to orient them to the new task. Special caution may be in order for some classes of older students since they may feel that they know what to do and thus will either fail to read the directions or just give them a brief glance.

Students can be assisted in planning their use of test time by a written statement regarding the amount of time to be given for the total test and an allocation for each subdivision. The relative importance of divisions can be given by points for each subdivision as a guide to how much time should be devoted to each part of the test. The amount of time available for different item types may vary according to student ability and reading skill, but students should, on the average, be given one minute or more for each multiple-choice item and a half-minute or more for a true-false item. The teacher should specify the amount of time s/he feels should be devoted to each essay item. Some students will select the order in which they respond to items according to the item type and the time allotted.

The weight or point value assigned for each item should be clearly understood. The weights or values of essay items and points to be assigned in a total test are generally proportional to the amount of time that is allotted for response to each item. In many classroom situations it is understood that all items, except essay items, are to be assigned one point in value unless otherwise specified at the time of testing. The understanding the teacher has with students will determine whether or not the point values for items should be included in the written directions.

In most classrooms students are given time and directed to respond to all items and to guess at the response to selection-type items even when they are unsure of the answer. In this way any knowledge or understanding of an item should be reflected in the final test score. For a rigidly timed test or a speed test the teacher may feel that some control for guessing is needed. If this question about the effects of guessing is strong enough, the teacher may want to investigate the possible use of a **correction for guessing.**[1] Although standardized test makers find a need to make a correction for guessing for part of their testing proce-

[1] Charles D. Hopkins and Richard L. Antes, *Classroom Measurement and Evaluation* (Itasca, Ill.: F. E. Peacock Publishers, Inc., 1978), pp.173–176.

dures, it is unlikely that classroom teachers will need this for their tests.

For most classroom tests students are given ample time to finish a test except when speed of response is an important factor. In general, teachers are more interested in whether a student can or can not do something rather than how quickly it can be done. If a strict time limit is imposed on a test and a large proportion of the students will not be able to finish, the teacher might consider a correction for guessing. If a correction for guessing is used, the directions (oral or written) must explain what the correction is and what it does.

The test directions should be placed in the test so that a clear distinction is made between items and directions. Students' attention should be attracted to the directions by the spacing and indentation of test format.

SPECIFIC DIRECTIONS

Specific directions should be written for each different type of item on the test. Problem-type items require a mathematical response in the form of a number or symbol or technical answer to a complex situation. Multiple-choice items require the student to select the alternative which best completes the statement or answers the question posed. True-false items ask the student to decide whether the item is true or false. Matching items instruct the student to make an association between pairs of elements. Classification items request the student to identify a class to which a thing belongs. Completion items ask the student to furnish a word or series of words to complete a sentence. Short-answer items call for the student to create a response in the form of a word, a symbol, or a short phrase. Essay items demand a fully developed response from the student. Directions for other types of items include information and guides necessary for the student to complete the tasks and record the responses as expected. Specific directions are necessary to make the task clear and to tell the student exactly what is to be done in response to an item.

Problem-type Item

The following directions, examples, and solutions for the mathematical problem and the technical problem illustrate specific directions for these types of items. Directions for the mathematical problem vary and must be written in terms of each problem or set of problems presented. Instructions for the technical problem are customarily an integral part of the item.

Mathematical Problem

A. Directions: Read the statement and work the problem in the space provided using the example as a guide. Underline your response.

Example: John works as an apprentice mechanic in his uncle's garage. He earns $1.20 an hour and is paid time and a half for overtime. During a busy week last summer, he worked the usual 40 hours at regular pay and 10 hours overtime at time and a half. What was John's pay for that week's work?

Solution: hrs. × wage = earnings
40 × $1.20 = $48.00
10 × $1.80 = $18.00
            $66.00   **$66.00**

B. Directions: Use formulas to solve these problems. Write the formula first, and then work the problem in the space provided. Be sure to show all steps clearly since credit is divided 2 points for the formula, 2 points for procedure, and 2 points for the correct answer.

Example: Find the area of a triangle with a base of 5.6 inches and a height of 8.2 inches.

Solution: $A = \frac{1}{2}\,bh$ or $A = bh/2$
$A = \frac{1}{2}\,(5.6 \times 8.2)$
$A = \frac{1}{2} \times 45.92$
$A = 22.96$ sq. inch.

C. Directions: The following problems can be solved by using a formula that has been used in class assignments. Write the formula that should be used for calculation of the answer. Solve the problem. Be sure to show each step of calculation in the space provided. Credit will be·

1. Correct formula   2 points
2. Correct procedure   2 points
3. Correct answer   2 points
         TOTAL   6 points

Example: An 18-inch pulley turning at 100 rpm is driving a 6-inch-diameter pulley. What is the rpm of the smaller pulley?

Solution: $\dfrac{D}{d} = \dfrac{r}{R}$ then $rd = DR$, and $r = \dfrac{DR}{d}$

$r = \dfrac{18 \times 100}{6}$

$r = \dfrac{1,800}{6}$

$r = 300$

D. Directions: The following problems are best solved in two steps. For each one clearly show the two step procedure which you used to work to solution. Credit will be:

1. **Correct procedure**   **4 points**
2. **Correct answer**   **2 points**
      TOTAL   **6 points**

Example: How much money will you have to lend to get $24.00 interest at 6% if you lend it for 6 months?

Solution: $\$24 \div \dfrac{1}{2} = 24 \times \dfrac{2}{1} = \$48$ interest for one year

$$\frac{\$48}{.06} = \$800 \quad \text{or} \quad \frac{\$48}{\%_{100}} = \frac{\$4800}{6} = \$800$$

Or

$$\frac{48}{1} \times \frac{100}{6} = \frac{4800}{6} = \$800$$

E. Directions: Write the numeral missing in each row of the following table.

Example: To change a measurement in	To a measurement in	Multiply the number of
8. feet	inches	feet by (12)
9. miles	yards	miles by (1760)
10. yards	inches	yards by (36)

Technical Problem

The directions for a technical problem are part of the item. When the problem is outlined for the student, the specific directions should clearly state what the student is expected to do to complete an acceptable response to the proposed problem. They should also explain how the student should report the solution and the measuring units to be used in the solution.

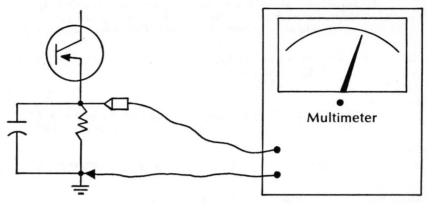

Example: Use the schematic to represent a check of emitter bypass capacitor. Explain how a signal-tracing probe can be utilized to check for open emitter bypass capacitors.

Selection-type Item

The following directions and examples for selection-type items illustrate specific kinds of directions that should be used for these types of items. Specific directions for the true-false and multiple-choice items are written for a set of items. Specific directions must be written for each matching and each classification item based upon the task presented in each item.

Multiple-choice

Directions: For each of the items select the best alternative and mark it on the response sheet like this:

A   B   C   Ⓓ

Example: The galaxies most distant from earth that have been identified are about how many light-years away?

    A. two million
    B. one billion
    C. five billion
    Ⓓ ten billion

True-false

Directions: Read each of the following statements. If the statement is true, mark the "T" to the left of the sentence. If the statement is false, mark the "F."

Example: Ⓣ F   The largest optical telescopes collect light with mirrors.

Matching

Directions: On the line to the left of each phrase listed in column A, write the letter of the term listed in column B which matches. Each of the terms in column B may be used once, more than once, or not at all.

Example:

		Column A Phrase	Column B Term
(E)	1.	A star pattern in the sky	A. perihelion
(C)	2.	A cluster of a large number of stars	B. ellipse
(G)	3.	A star located close to the celestial pole	C. galaxy
			D. aphelion
(B)	4.	The shape of the path a planet makes as it goes around the sun	E. constellation
			F. spectrum
			G. Polaris
(A)	5.	Closest approach of a planet to the sun	H. Aquarius

Classification

Directions: For each pair of words write S on the line between them if the words in a pair of words mean the same thing (synonyms). If the words in a pair of words mean the opposite (antonyms), write an A on the line between them.

Example: encourage   (A)   discourage

complain   (S)   grumble

liberal   (A)   stingy

Supply-type Item

The following directions and examples for supply-type items illustrate specific directions for these types of items. Specific directions for completion or short-answer items are written for the set of items on a test. Specific directions for essay items may be needed for each item; however, if one set of directions will cover all essay items on the test, use just one set.

Completion

Directions: Read each incomplete sentence below, and complete the meaning correctly according to the article you have just read.

Example: Father sat on the _____ (stool) _____ .

Short Answer

Directions: Write the response to each riddle on the line.

Example: We grow on branches and are found on trees.
<u>(leaves)</u>

Directions: Write a response to each question, using only the space provided by the line.

Example: Why do bananas grow only in the tropics?
The tropics have the long growing season that
bananas require.

Limited-Response Essay

Directions: Carefully read each essay item to understand the proposed task. Write a response to the essay item in the space provided. You may wish to outline your response before writing.

Item Arrangement

Depending upon the rationale employed, there are different ways to arrange items for a test; however, the primary concern is to arrange the items in such a way that students will feel most comfortable when taking the test. In a short classroom-achievement test which uses only one item type, the arrangement of items is usually random, except that a few easy items may be placed at the beginning to ease test anxiety. A longer test containing two or three item types covering several subject matter topics and behaviors has potential for a logical organization, which is convenient for students taking the test and the teacher when scoring. There is one general format based on principles that make it efficient and helpful to students. The item arrangement is systematically based on three factors: (1) item type, (2) subject-matter content, and (3) level of difficulty.

ITEM TYPE

Arrangement of items into sections by item type requires the fewest sets of directions. The directions are easier to follow when all items of the same type are grouped together, because the student can keep the same mental set when responding to all questions of one item type. Furthermore, the items should be presented to students in a simple-to-complex order. In other words, simpler or easier item types should be presented first, followed by increasingly difficult types of items. This kind of sequence should also be used when more than one type of item is used. The hierarchical arrangement based on overall complexity of item types is as follows:

1. **Classification**
2. **Matching**
3. **Completion**
4. **True-false**
5. **Short-answer**
6. **Multiple-choice**
7. **Essay, limited-response**

Arrangement by type also facilitates scoring since the responses for each item type are recorded in the same way.

SUBJECT-MATTER CONTENT

The cells of the table of specifications provide a guideline for grouping subject-matter content within the item types. An example of subject-matter content grouping for the table of specifications for a unit test on measurement in Chapter 2 (Figure 2.3) includes the topical areas of: money, linear measure, time, and liquid measure. This grouping may be helpful for identifying student strengths and weaknesses in content areas. During testing this grouping helps students direct their thoughts because they are better able to concentrate on one subject topic before they must change their frame of reference to consider another subject topic. In other words, they can concentrate on one set of items at a time rather than having to reorient their thinking after each item. The subject-matter content arrangement assists the teacher in discussion of the subject areas when s/he returns test papers, and appraises students' understanding of the subject-matter content.

Closely related to subject-matter content grouping is grouping by behaviors. All items measuring the same instructional objective, such as knowledge of terms, recall, understanding, application, or other category of the taxonomy, could be grouped together. Depending upon the use to be made of the test results, the teacher may prefer this type of grouping to subject-matter content grouping. An example of grouping by behaviors for the table of specifications for a unit test on measurement includes the areas of recall (knowledge), understanding (comprehension), and applying (application).

LEVEL OF DIFFICULTY

Arranging items for a subject-matter topic in ascending order of difficulty provides a convenient format for both student and teacher. The teacher must use his/her knowledge of the students' level of development and other factors to judge the degree of difficulty of items. If the teacher selects previously used multiple-choice and true-false items, s/he should have an **item analysis** of each of those items. The item analysis will give the levels of difficulty for past administration, thus providing an index of difficulty for each item. Other advantages of the process of item analysis will be discussed later.

Test items should be grouped by item type according to the hierarchy of complexity of item types, within item type by subject-matter content (in some situations by behaviors), and within subject-matter content by an ascending level of item difficulty. If circumstances do not allow this organization, adjustments can be made.

Editing the Items

Writing test items is an ongoing process. Items should be written daily in rough form as subject-matter content is introduced in class and studied. The initial drafts of items can periodically be rewritten for clarity and conciseness to eliminate ambiguity. Any imperfections that should be corrected can be attended to at this time. In addition to the teacher's review of the pool of items available for a test, it is most helpful to have a colleague review them. Each reviewer should work through the items as an actual test situation, keeping in mind the subject matter content, age, and grade level of the class the test is being prepared for. A scoring key should be provided for the reviewer to check the agreement of responses and keyed answers. The advantage of having a competent colleague review the test is that s/he should provide the teacher with high-level feedback concerning deficiencies in individual items.

If a colleague is not available, the teacher must rely totally on his/her judgment about the quality of each item. In this event the teacher should review the items twice. At least a few days to a week should elapse between these two reviews. The purpose of a second review is to check the correct response as well as to look for imperfections which can be corrected prior to test reproduction.

When constructing the test, the teacher should assign each item to a cell of the table of specifications. The total for each cell should agree with the number specified by the table. Although some items, especially essay items, may be associated with more than one cell in combinations of behaviors and content topics, it is necessary to assign each item to one cell so that it can be related to its proper place in the table.

The overall coverage of the table of specifications can be checked, and items for the test can be selected from the pool of items to satisfy the tabled values. If the teacher pays close attention to the table when selecting items and pencils tally marks on the table to keep a running tabulation, s/he will be able to keep an ongoing check on the balance (adequate sampling) while assembling the items. In assessing the items individually and collectively, the teacher must consider additional factors and points which will be discussed later in this chapter (see pp. 61–63).

Test Item File

Writing test items can be a time-consuming and arduous task. This is another reason for writing rough draft items as subject-matter

Front Side of Card

COURSE:										
OBJECTIVE:										
ITEM:										
TEST DATE:										
ITEM NO:										

Reverse Side of Card

ITEM RECORD											
		Upper					Lower				
Date	A	B	C	D	Omit	A	B	C	D	Omit	P D	D
Comments:											

Figure 3.2. Test item card.

content is covered in class; however, each newly constructed test does not have to be composed of all new items. A teacher should develop a pool of items for use in future tests. A convenient method for accumulating an item pool is to write each item on a five-by-eight-inch card. A collection of items used becomes the test-item file. Figure 3.2 presents a suggested format for an item card. The front side of the card provides space for the course name, the objective (subject-matter content, behavior, learning outcomes), the item, the test date, and item number.

During the review and editing of items, the cards can be shifted as the items are rewritten, replaced, or changed. The card procedure makes it easy to arrange items by type, subject-matter content, and level of difficulty. The newly written items and the items selected from the test-item file are placed in the order they are to appear on the test, typed into a test, and duplicated.

By revising and improving the items as they are used and by using the test-item file system, a teacher should soon have a good supply of items to use on future tests. Teachers may also wish to pool their resources. Teachers who share items may be the same colleague(s) who collectively review and edit items. This approach is based on the idea that none of us is as smart as all of us. The item writer is close to the items, and small, but important, points may be inadvertently overlooked without outside assistance in reviewing test items. Item analysis and item review are helpful in determining the effectiveness of items and in improving them for the item file. The end result of this process is better items and, therefore, better tests. (Figure 3.2 also provides a layout of the reverse side of the item card, which is used for item analysis. Item analysis is discussed in chapter 7.)

Test Reproduction

The general and/or specific test directions are brought together with the test items and arranged in a systematic order in preparation for test reproduction. If the proper attention is paid to the details of test format and reproduction, the items will be presented to students in a readable manner.

The spacing of items on the test should visually focus student attention on one item or task at a time. Double-spacing between items and generous borders help provide items which are uncrowded and clear. Regardless of type, an item should never be split between pages, although it may be necessary to place some kinds of tasks on facing pages. For example, an interpretive exercise may have material too long for one page, requiring that all items be placed on one page and the introductory materials (graphs, charts, and so on) on the facing page.

When multiple-choice items are used, the alternatives for each item should be listed in a vertical column beneath the stem of the items as follows:

10. When the shadow of an object consists of an umbra, the source of the light is

    A. from an extended source.
    B. striking the object in parallel rays.
    C. from more than one source.
  *D. from a point source.

For short-answer and completion items, ample space should be provided for words or phrases to be written:

14. The tax on imported goods is called _____ .

15. The immediate cause of the war with Spain was _____
_____ .

The amount of space for the response can provide a clue to the length of the word. This may be avoided by providing a line of the same length for all short-answer items and another constant length for all completion items. Since it is helpful to many students to be able to determine the approximate length of the word by the length of the line or space provided, there may be situations, for example, at the primary level, where younger students can be directed by deliberately indicating the length of the word by the length of the blank.

To facilitate student choices the categories for classification items should be clearly indicated. The list of categories for the items must be clearly distinguishable from the items themselves. The two lists for matching items should be clearly distinguishable and the columns identified.

All items in a single test should be numbered consecutively throughout all parts or sections of the test. In this way the test has only one (1), one (2), one (3), and so on. If each section begins with a new series of numbers starting with (1), the same number appears more than once. When a separate answer sheet is used, this becomes very confusing for students who skip items the first time through the test and return to those items later. There also may be confusion when the test is returned and the items are discussed as a learning experience if there are multiple numbers for items.

Responses may be recorded on the test page or booklet to aid primary school students and some special classes at the higher grades in recording responses. More space for written responses is needed for very young children since their writing may be large. Lined paper may be helpful for young students in making some responses.

The test should be carefully proofed and reviewed before the pages are run off. Then enough copies should be prepared so that each student has a copy of the test. This will allow each student to progress at his/her own rate. The test pages are usually reproduced by the direct master technique of spirit duplication or mimeograph; however, an offset process may be used when a large number of copies is needed. Spirit duplication should be limited to one side of the paper since the process may allow print to come through the paper if a second run is made.

Very young students can be permitted to mark the responses directly on the item itself. The extra work for the scorer is justified because the difficulties that might arise in transferring responses to an answer sheet are eliminated. As students get older and have more test experience, a column down the left side of the page can be added for the response record. The next step is to use a separate response sheet.

For very young children the following item is appropriate.

Father came to get his two _____.

A. sheep
Ⓑ. boys
C. coats
D. books

The item below could be used for older children.

A B Ⓒ D What is another name for 6?

A. 2^3
B. 3×3
C. $\sqrt{36}$
D. 3^2

The following item is appropriate for students who can use an answer sheet without making errors in recording.

Which of the two testing procedures—criterion-referenced measurement (CRM) or norm-referenced measurement (NRM)—would be most beneficial to a teacher who has organized classroom activities on an individual basis?

*A. CRM
 B. NRM
 C. Either would work equally well.
 D. Neither could be used.

Guides to Construction

The planning stage for the development of a classroom test sets the direction for the actual test construction. Directions for item writing are furthered by considerations already discussed in this chapter. Decisions of construction have been made about the difficulty level of items and the type(s) of items to use, and a table of specifications indicates how many items are needed for (1) each subject matter topic and (2) behaviors to be exhibited by the student. A large number of possible items should be contained in a test file, and items should have been written in rough (or final) form during the period of instruction. A test developed from a large item base (pool) has a better chance of doing its job than a test which is constructed at the last minute with little opportunity to select and refine the items. The next step is to write the items as they will appear in the final form of the test.

No set of rules can be developed that, if followed, will guarantee how an item or set of items will perform when they are actually used on a test. Item writing remains much of an art to which science makes some, but limited, contribution. This section is intended to present some general help in writing items. By adding the ingredients of originality and creativity, along with a good working knowledge of the subject matter, teachers at all levels can build tests made up of good items.

Construction of test items is attended to in detail in the next three chapters as the problem, supply, and selection-type of items are given individual attention. General considerations which apply to all three item types—problem-type, supply-type, and selection-type—are presented in this section. Directions for construction are presented as guides to be followed with an eye to development of the art of item writing rather than as a set of rules to be learned and then implemented. Hopefully the teacher's item-writing ability will continue to develop with the experience of preparing classroom tests. (Chapters 4, 5, and 6 discuss these item types in greater detail.)

Consideration of the following points is essential to production of a valid test instrument.

1. Write items in preliminary form during the instructional period. Ideas for specific items should be recorded, and rough drafts of items should be written as they are conceived in the context of ongoing classroom activities. Testing has a better opportunity of becoming an integral part of the classroom program when the teacher considers testing as a continuing aspect of instruction and learning. If item writing is concentrated into a short time period just before test administration, the task becomes burdensome for the teacher, and the quality of the items is likely to be lowered. Poorly prepared test items are harmful because

evaluation and decisions will probably be based on invalid data, and students may become confused about what knowledge and behaviors are important.

2. Use the test's table of specifications to maintain a relationship between items on the test and the set of educational objectives. Only when the test items are tied to the objectives can test scores be useful in judging the extent to which goals have been reached.

3. Base each test item on an important point, idea, learning, or skill. An item which deals with trivial information or one which is obscure or insignificant reveals little about what important things the students have learned. Furthermore, if these kinds of items do appear on tests, future study may be directed to learning trivial information or obscure and insignificant points which have little relationship to basic understanding.

4. Write items which require specific knowledge about the content studied. Items which can be answered from general knowledge cannot reflect knowledge learned in study of a defined body of content. Although generally applicable knowledge is important and its acquisition is to be encouraged, tests over a fixed domain should measure within the scope of study.

5. Present each task as straightforwardly as possible. The simplest item form should be used to test the concept or learning being measured. As the behavior becomes more complex, the type of item will need to be expanded to encompass the larger scope of the behavior (recall, understanding, application, analysis, synthesis, and evaluation).

6. Review items from other sources. New ideas about how to present items can be gleaned from other classroom tests and standardized tests. The quality of classroom tests should increase as teachers try new ideas and evaluate their effectiveness in collecting the needed data.

7. Check use of language. (a) Observe good language expression. Rules of grammar must be followed to avoid a breakdown in communications and to convey the intent of the writer. (b) Use simple and precise language. Build a test with vocabulary appropriate for the age and ability level of students who are to be tested. If the student cannot understand the task being presented because of inappropriate vocabulary, s/he cannot receive credit even if the answer is known. (c) The suggestions in (a) and (b) can be used to avoid ambiguity in (i) presentation of the task, (ii) instruction about how to respond, and (iii) alternatives for selection.

8. Use original, not textbook, language. Students who meet tasks in tests the same way that they first met them in study can answer the items through recall. If the intention is to write an item to test a

higher-level behavior, then the item has failed. Textbook language or items lifted verbatim from the book contribute little to good tests.

9. Avoid clues or suggestions that would help a student who lacks the knowledge to answer an item with a correct response. Selection-type items are especially susceptible to these clues, but essay items must also be written so that the unknowing student is not given unintended direction to the correct response.

10. Ask fellow teachers to serve as editors to review and take the test. They may be able to pick up clues or ambiguity in items or directions that have escaped your notice. Give them your keyed responses so that they may check their responses with your responses. Disagreement is cause to look at the item for possible defects.

The above guides to construction are common to all items presented in the next three chapters. These guides should be considered when studying each item type in the following chapters. Keep in mind that a guide may apply to one item type more than to others.

4 Problem-Type Items

Some writers have made a distinction between items that require only recall of knowledge to answer correctly and items that require recall plus use of the knowledge at a higher level of cognition. Those items which require the *use of knowledge* to answer correctly have been considered to be **problem-solving** items. The latter situation could, in the broadest sense, be considered a problem-solving case since the student is presented with a new set of circumstances and asked to derive the answer. In this frame of reference a large portion of tasks on good tests would be classified as problem solving.

Although we have no quarrel with that approach, we use the term *problem-type item* to refer to the mathematical problem or technical problem. This item type is a somewhat involved situation created for an in-depth investigation for interpretation of data, development of relationships, use of principles, drawing of conclusions, analysis, or evaluation. The dissimilarity between our problem and the other types of items used to measure beyond the recall level is a difference in degree rather than kind. Certain problem-solving tactics are necessary in all tests that require the student to go beyond mere recall of facts to make correct choices.

The problem-type test item has much in common with the essay item. Problems serve quantitatively oriented learning areas in much the same way that essay items serve nonquantitative learning areas. A problem is typically presented by giving (1) a set of conditions to structure a situation, (2) descriptive information, (3) quantitative data, and (4) instructions about what answer(s) are to be derived. Some technical problems may omit the quantitative data. The demands made on the student range from a very simple situation to extremely involved circumstances.

Probably the simplest of all problems is the one presented in algorithmic form where the question to be answered is implied in the presentation of the data. For example, if the student were given the following problem, the **algorithm** gives the conditions, the information in the form of data, and implied instructions about what answer is expected.

647 ÷ 25 = ☐

[**The preceding problem in algorithmic form is the special case** $a \div b$**, the division algorithm that eventually gives the largest whole number** q **such that** $q \times b \le a$**. If** $q \times b = a$**, then** q **is the missing factor. If** $q \times b < a$**, then** q **is the quotient, and there is a remainder. So** $a = (q \times b) + r$**, where** r **may or may not be zero (0). (All of this is implied in the algorithm.)]**

The algorithm is a very convenient way to present some kinds of problems since it sets up a numerical process that can be applied again and again to reach a solution to a problem and relieves the teacher of writing extensive directions each time. The algorithm is especially useful for objectives that require the student to make computations but do not require application of the mathematics.

Presentation of an example for the "extremely involved circumstances" is not included here since it would be necessary to base it on some special area of study. Because certain technical knowledge of that special field would be needed, it would not be generally understood by readers from other disciplines. Each reader will be left to develop specific items of that type for her/his tests as needed. The discussion in the rest of the chapter should help direct the writing of complex problem-type items for all subject areas.

Although other organizational schemes are possible, in general, the student's approach to solving problem-type items follows the following set of steps:

1. **Identify the problem by recognizing a clear question (either stated or implied).**
2. **Sort out and organize the needed information and data.**
3. **Set up a procedure for arriving at the solution.**
4. **Complete the sequence, and report the results and conclusions in the form of a number, symbol, or other response.**

Although the problem and the above solution steps are directed specifically to mathematics and the physical sciences, nearly all fields of study can use the problem to collect information about a student's level of functioning. Problems are particularly relevant for testing student understanding of principles by requiring the student to use new data with a new set of circumstances. In this way the teacher can find out how well a student can take a set of learned principles and apply them.

As with all types of items the problem type has been used by some teachers to the exclusion of other types of items. Some mathematics teachers have made problem tests their sole source of data. Rarely, if ever, will one item type be appropriate for collection of all data. While encouraging those who do not use the problem at all to consider it, we want to encourage those who use it exclusively or rely on it too heavily to use other types of items. The guidelines remain—decide what kind of information is needed and then choose a procedure that can generate the needed data. If it is decided that a test is needed, then choice of the proper testing procedure, including the appropriate item type, must be made. There is a great repertory of testing and nontesting procedures, and teachers should use a variety of data-collection procedures in the classroom.

Mathematical Problem

There is an ongoing debate over what the thrust of mathematics teaching should be, but there seems to be little doubt that students should learn to compute and be able to deal with both theoretical and applied mathematical situations. Except for the basic facts of addition, subtraction, multiplication, and division, any arithmetic or mathematical task could be considered to be a problem-type item unless the student has seen the exact same problem before. Problems can relate to objectives that ask for behaviors of understanding and all higher divisions of the cognitive domain.

ADVANTAGES

Problem solving is the basic skill in mathematics. Learning to solve problems is the principal reason to study mathematics. These two arguments may be reason enough to support the use of problem-type items on mathematics tests. Other advantages are:

1. Mathematical problems can be used at all levels of the educational process. A kindergarten child can be asked the following:

How many boxes of milk will be needed for lunch today?

This problem situation can test to see how the concept of one-to-one correspondence has been developed.

An elementary school student can be asked the following:

How much fencing would be needed to make a puppy cage which is to be four feet long and three feet wide?

This tests for concept of perimeter and addition skill (possibly for multiplication skill depending on how the student attacks the problem).

A class of advanced secondary students or college students can be asked to:

Find an algorithm suitable for minicalculator computation that can compute the length and direction of [vector] V directly from a, b, and θ (figure 1).[1] [This problem could be presented in an even more basic form by reconstructing the problem as it developed in biomedical engineering.]

This problem involves the use of many principles used in higher levels of mathematics, and the ones used are a function of the logical approach used by the student.

2. Problem tests (the test as a whole but not individual items) are relatively easy to prepare when compared to objective tests. Since fewer items are needed, the task of building the test is reduced considerably in both time and effort.

3. The student can be tested on how s/he can apply principles to new situations. Involving the student in application of principles engages him/her directly in the process of problem solving, hopefully fostering its transfer to real-world situations.

4. Near-natural situations can be created to give information about how the student would be expected to perform in a real-world situation. Although the classroom continues to be an artificial environment, the problem allows creation of situations based on natural circumstances.

5. Conditions can be set up to make the problem item relevant to on-the-job performance and to make predictions about future performance. For technical subjects, especially vocational ones, the problem allows the instructor to obtain feedback about how a student would function at a later time when s/he assumes a position after formal schooling.

6. Problem tests rate high in objectivity. The task can be clearly defined, and reasons for giving credit or "taking off" from the total points allotted for the item can be explained to students. Both procedure (the process) and product (the result) can be clearly observed, scored, and evaluated.

7. The mathematical algorithm, the most highly structured

[1] John H. Staib, "The Cardiologist's Theorem," *The Mathematics Teacher 70*, 2 (January 1977): 36–39.

problem situation, allows the teacher to diagnose computational difficulties.

8. The problem controls for student guessing or bluffing answers to test tasks. Since the student must create the response, guessing is reduced to a minimum. The highly structured situation allows only a limited number of ways of proceeding to solution, and each can be judged objectively in terms of efficiency and the result.

9. Solving problems on a test can be a learning experience. Using learned principles in new ways generalizes the learning into new and unique circumstances and directly supports the instructional component of classroom activities.

10. Presentation of problems on tests allows the testing session to become an integral part of the total classroom program. Facility in problem solving is an acknowledged aim of social science and physical science programs as well as mathematics instruction. Inclusion of problems on tests in these subjects supports the integration of the testing program with the instructional program.

LIMITATIONS

The following limitations of the mathematical problem type of item are connected to possible small samples and built-in scoring difficulties.

1. The relatively small number of problems, especially complex ones, that can be worked in a testing session may result in low content validity if the problem test is used exclusively. This should not be a limitation if the problem is used when appropriate and in conjunction with other types of items.

2. There may be more than one way to solve a problem. While an item may appear to have only one solution, knowledgeable students may uncover alternate solutions. While these may be clearly correct, an alternate solution may raise questions: (1) How efficient is the process? and (2) How important is efficiency to the total problem? Judgment of the relative importance of procedure and product must be made when reading student responses and setting rules for scoring responses.

3. The response may be correct in some aspects and incorrect in others. A logical and correct rationale may be followed to develop a procedure, but the answer may be wrong because of an error in computation. All-or-none scoring should not be used for problems because information from a partially correct response is lost if credit is given when only the answer is considered. The teacher must decide the relative importance of the procedure and the correct answer.

4. The use of an incorrect answer in computation may cause one or more subsequent answers also to be incorrect. Adjustment in the scoring procedure should be made so that the student is not penalized more than one time for an error in responding to the task.

5. Considerable time may be needed to score the student responses. This limitation is formidable for complex problems and when students miss several problems. Diagnostic use of the scores and procedures is also time consuming, but it should not be considered a limitation.

6. Individual complex problems may be difficult to construct. Although a problem-type test may generally be easier to construct than objective tests, each problem is likely to be more difficult to write than individual objective items.

GUIDES TO WRITING

The special characteristics of individual mathematical problems require that the item writer give attention to the following specific points when preparing the tasks.

1. Provide enough information and direction so that students clearly understand the problem. A familiar algorithm can accomplish this purpose for many problems. If an algorithm can not be used, then it may be necessary to give detailed directions for a set of problems or one complex problem.

Example A

Directions: $a \cdot b = \boxed{}$ $\quad 4 \cdot 2 = \boxed{8}$

$43 \cdot 27 = \boxed{}$ $\quad 76 \cdot 30 = \boxed{}$ $\quad 14 \cdot 19 = \boxed{}$

$55 \cdot 11 = \boxed{}$ $\quad 23 \cdot 32 = \boxed{}$ $\quad 78 \cdot 96 = \boxed{}$

Example B

During summer vacation Rich and Dan agreed to paint their neighbor's garage. One side of the garage is eight meters long. The boys mark a point on the side which is four meters from each end. Each one starts at one end and paints toward the center mark, four meters from each end. Can we be sure that each painted the same area of that side if each paints to the center mark? [No. This would be true only if the side of the garage were rectangular.]

Other modifications of this item could be presented. If the second sentence is changed to read, "One side of the garage is rectangular and eight meters long," then the answer is "yes." The manner of asking the question and the expected answer would vary with the purpose of the task and the age and experiential background of the students. The task should *not* be presented in the first form for any age if the answer "yes" is expected. For an expected "yes" response, the qualifier "rectangular" should be included to relieve the item of any ambiguity so that a student who visualizes that the side could be or such is not penalized.

2. Any computational problem should indicate the degree of precision expected in the answer. Indicate how to handle rounding of approximations and decimals or fractions in answers.

Example A

Directions: In the following set of exercises for figuring z-scores from the raw scores, use the mean and standard deviation values to the nearest hundredth of a raw score unit.

Example B

Directions: The proportions which you report for the ratios should be given in decimal fractions to the nearest hundredth of a point.

Example C

Directions: For this set of problems use the usual rules which this class has for rounding, approximation, and reporting fractional parts of the final answers. [This direction would be used only when the rules are clearly presented in instruction and would be used to test how well the student has remembered the ground rules.]

3. The units for reporting the answer(s) must be clearly specified.

Example A

Directions: Total elapsed time should be reported in minutes and seconds.

NOT: **143 seconds**

CHANGE TO: **2 minutes, 23 seconds**

Example B

Directions: When reporting the perimeters, give your answer in either feet and inches or meters and centimeters, depending on the units used in each problem.

4. For primary-school students, mathematical problems of computation should be grouped according to process or other characteristic. Other situations may occur in later grades where this division should

also be made. If both addition and subtraction problems are to be computed, list the addition problems together and the subtraction problems together (see Example A). Do not mix these through the test because the student may become confused even though each problem may be clearly marked as to the process to be used. Problems which require square root extractions should be separated from those which require the division process (see Example B). Separate as follows:

Example A

ADDITION

$14 + 24 =$ [ ]　　$28 + 21 =$ [ ]
$87 + 23 =$ [ ]　　$47 + 14 =$ [ ]
$92 + \ 8 =$ [ ]　　$76 + \ 9 =$ [ ]

SUBTRACTION

$42 - 31 =$ [ ]　　$76 - 45 =$ [ ]
$44 - 15 =$ [ ]　　$34 - 16 =$ [ ]
$99 - 67 =$ [ ]　　$17 - 18 =$ [ ]

Example B

SQUARE ROOT

$\sqrt{225}$　　$\sqrt{625}$　　$\sqrt{725}$
$\sqrt{1457}$　　$\sqrt{900}$　　$\sqrt{12345}$

DIVISION

$25\overline{)725}$　　$31\overline{)930}$　　$45\overline{)901}$
$30\overline{)627}$　　$10\overline{)1000}$　　$61\overline{)327}$

5. If a particular algorithm is to be used, it should be indicated. The problem could be presented in algorithmic form.

Example A

For the following division problems, use the subtractive algorithm for division to arrive at the answer.

$48 \div 24 =$ [ ]　　$57 \div 15 =$ [ ]
$83 \div 20 =$ [ ]　　$29 \div 11 =$ [ ]

Example B

43	16	11	63	99	13	20
×27	×10	×11	×24	×71	×76	×30

6. When using regular "everyday" words to present a mathematical situation, make sure that the connection between the structured situation and the real world is genuine and not false or ambiguous in any way.

Example

A teacher may want to build some background for permutations. Rather than saying, "Create a permutation for the three letters in TEA," a teacher may present a problem on a test without using the word permutation since it was not used in instruction. The problem might be presented as, "What words can you make from the letters in TEA?" Although the teacher is expecting to get TEA, ATE, EAT, ETA, AET, and TAE, the student could be confused in one or more ways. Since ETA, AET, TAE are not words, should they be listed? ETA is a Greek word, so it might be considered as a special case. Should the word TEA itself be listed? The directions should be written so that it is clear to the student that the task is to arrange the letters in TEA in all possible ways.

7. Check "GUIDES TO CONSTRUCTION" on page 61.

EXEMPLARY ITEMS

Examples of problems for use at different levels are provided as further guides to writing mathematical problems, but the reader must extend the list with ideas beyond those which are given here as models to make problems relevant to a particular area of instruction. Methods books, curriculum materials, colleagues' tests, and teacher manuals are rich sources of ideas for problems. Your own creativeness is also needed for your specific class of students. Knowledge of your subject matter, examples from other sources, and creative schemes are needed to write problems which will give valid measurements in your tests. The grade level of the school which could use the items is not listed because of the great differences in school programs. You can select the appropriate level according to the group which you do, or expect to, teach.

Elementary School Subjects

1. **Directions: Perform the multiplication for the following exercises:**

   $16 \cdot 4 = \boxed{}$ $(32)(7) = \boxed{}$ $38 \times 5 = \boxed{}$

   $23 \times 7 = \boxed{}$ $78 \cdot 3 = \boxed{}$ . . . .

   . . . .

2. **Directions: Perform the indicated process for the pairs of numerals. [This situation could be used without violating guide number 4 if one of the knowledges to be tested is that of knowing the symbols for the four basic processes.]**

   $12 + 16 = \boxed{}$ $8 \times 73 = \boxed{}$ $23 - 9 = \boxed{}$

   $505 \div 5 = \boxed{}$ $42 \div 3 = \boxed{}$

   $(16 + 3) - (7 - 2) = \boxed{}$ $27 \times 12345 = \boxed{}$

   . . . .

3. Directions: Mark names for five (5) like this

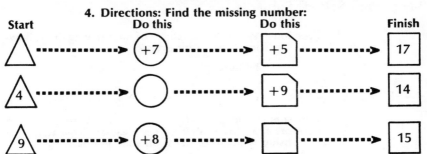

$8 - 4$ $11 - 6$ $4 + 2$ $\boxed{3 + 2}$ $10 \div 2$
$2 \div 10$ $\sqrt{25}$ $(14 + 1) - 10$ $\dots$ $\dots$
$\dots$ $\dots$ $\dots$ $\dots$

[This exercise can be leveled for many classes by adjusting the level of difficulty for the terms in the list.]

4. Directions: Find the missing number:

Start	Do this	Do this	Finish

△ ············> (+7) ············> +5 ············> 17

⁴△ ············> ◯ ············> +9 ············> 14

⁹△ ············> (+8) ············> ☐ ············> 15

5. In each exercise below, each of the letters A, B, C, D, E is to be replaced by one of the digits 0, 1, 2, 3, 4, 5, 6, 7, 8, 9. The letters may be replaced by different digits in different exercises. Two letters together (AB, CE, or such) represent a 2-place numeral.

ADDITION   SUBTRACTION

```
 47      47     DD          64      ABC
  4       D      E           A       42
 --      --     --          --      ---
 A1      CC     80          C8      153

 CC      E4                 BB       7A
  C      3C                 B2       AB
 --      --                  -       --
 60      87                  4       14
```

6. Two rectangles are placed as shown so that a larger rectangle is formed. Find the areas of both smaller rectangles and the area of the larger one in square units. ☐ ☐ ☐

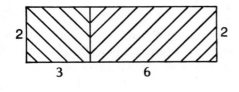

Is the larger area the sum of the other two? _____
Write a number sentence to represent the relationship among the three areas. _____
What property of rational numbers does this number sentence illustrate? _____

7. The farmer put 60 carrots in bunches of 5 carrots. How many bunches did he make?

8. A jet plane carried 42 passengers in one section and 102 passengers in another section. How many passengers were aboard the jet?

Secondary School Subjects

1. Directions: Write the equations of lines having the following pairs of intercepts:

	X-intercept	*Y*-intercept
A.	−3.0	2
B.	0.5	3
C.	4.0	2

2. Write some of the points ( ), ( ), ( ), ( ) whose ordinate is 6 more than twice their abscissa values. Now write the relationship which represents all such points.

3. Directions: Find the midpoint of the line joining:
   a. points (5,−9) and (−13,19)
   b. points (16,0) and (0,9)
   c. points − − − − − − − −
   d. − − − − − − − − − − − −

4. Directions: For premises 1 and 2, form an inference or conclusion for step 3. Show the relationship for each syllogism with a Venn diagram.

   1. $p \rightarrow q$ 1. Every element of p is an element of q.
   2. $q \rightarrow r$ 2. Every element of q is an element of r.
   3. ∴   3. ∴
                     In the space below show the relationships with a Venn diagram.

5. Directions: Using the graph paper provided, draw graphs for the following inequalities. Use the guidelines set for drawing graphs in this class.

   1. $x + y > 6$ 2. $y \geq x - 4$ 3. $3x - 2y < 6$

Technical Problem

The technical problem is presented here as the complex situation written for a limited and specialized study. Technical problems are widely used in tests for physical sciences, vocational courses, technology, engineering, and business. Other disciplines at the secondary level use the technical problem to a lesser extent. Elementary school classes rarely study a topic in sufficient depth to warrant the use of the technical type of problem, but some uses have been found in special materials, especially in science. However, the problem-type test usually works better at the secondary or higher levels because students at these levels tend to have stronger motivation to work through an involved test situation to a successful solution. The student has a personal interest in the special study, is usually a major in the subject, is preparing for a special job on completion of the course or series of courses, or has formed a special interest in the topic.

The versatility of the technical problem rests in the wide scope of possible situations which can be provided. The technical problem is not to be confused with the performance test, which is used to see how well a student will perform a specific skill. The technical problem could be used to generalize on-the-job performance in a wide scope, while performance tests are more for special skills and talents.

Since each technical problem is specific to a special content area, coverage here will be limited because (1) the scope of the book does not allow coverage of all possible uses, and (2) our knowledge in most of those special areas is limited. Exemplary items, although included, are not intended to be exhaustive even to areas which can use the technical problem.

ADVANTAGES

Because of the similarity of the mathematical problem and the technical problem, their advantages tend to be much the same. The technical problem can test students for application of principles, control for guessing and bluffing, rate high in objectivity, and allow for learning during testing. Presentation of technical problems on a test also allows the testing session to become an integral part of the ongoing activities of the classroom. Other advantages include the following:

1. The technical problem allows an in-depth investigation that encompasses many related factors and allows the student to exhibit knowledge of the interrelatedness between and among those factors.

2. The technical problem can be used to judge how a student will attack a problem when one of several procedures could be used. It may be that the final answer is not really of great importance to this type of problem, and judgment of a student's performance may be primarily in terms of how the student reached a solution rather than the solution itself.

3. The technical problem is the most direct way to measure many outcomes and provides an adequate data base to make inferences about student competency and to predict future performance.

LIMITATIONS

The limitations of technical problems are similar to those of mathematical problems: both use a small sample, and responses are difficult to score. The small sample may result in low content validity. There may be more than one solution, or the response may be partially correct, thus requiring much time to score and possibly lowering reader reliability. Other possible limitations follow.

1. The major limitation of the technical problem is the difficulty of setting up a situation that includes the necessary aspects within clearly defined limits. Since the problem is so broad in scope, much thought is required to include all information needed for solution.

2. The technical problem can not be used extensively with large classes. Even though an individual scorer tries to be objective in reading, and scoring procedures are standardized for a set of scorers, some variation in scoring can be expected because of the subjective decisions which remain in every case of scoring of a technical problem. This difficulty, coupled with the great amount of time needed to score a technical problem, makes it less useful with large classes than with small classes or individual students.

GUIDES TO WRITING

The special characteristics of the technical problem require that the item writer give attention to the following specific points when preparing tasks.

1. Be sure to include enough information and direction so that the student understands the scope of the problem and that parameters are clear. In addition to reading the words, the student must internalize the content of the problem.

Example

Mike Mechanic ran an exhaust gas analysis on his V-8 engine and found everything okay in the left tail pipe of a dual exhaust system. He got very erratic readings on the right pipe. All of the readings were extremely lean. How do you diagnose the problem? Explain your repair schedule.

2. Indicate the degree of precision and units for reporting answers for computational parts of the problem.

Example

During the computation approximate all values to the nearest hundredth, and report your final answer in square feet to the nearest unit.

3. Check GUIDES TO CONSTRUCTION on p. 61.

EXEMPLARY ITEMS

Examples of technical problems for use at different levels are provided as further guides. Knowledge in the technical subject being tested and creative schemes are necessary for writing problems specific to each subject area.

Elementary School Subjects

The elementary school teacher will rarely find use for the true technical problem because study is not sufficiently specialized at this level. A somewhat technical problem could be devised for laboratory situations in some topics of science and possibly in some other elementary school subjects.

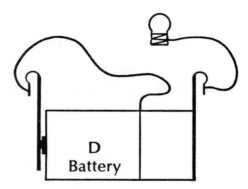

1. Use the picture above to represent an electric setup. If the battery and bulb are good, what must be done to make the bulb turn on? Explain the principle of electricity which told you how to turn on the light bulb.

2. **The pointers for pulley A and pulley B are both set at zero (0). Explain how the ratio of revolutions for the two pulleys could be established.**

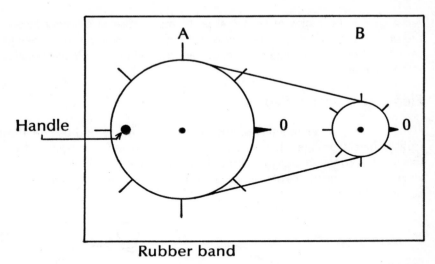

Rubber band

[This problem could be made more difficult by leaving off the scale for each pulley. The student then would need to develop some way of scaling the turns.]

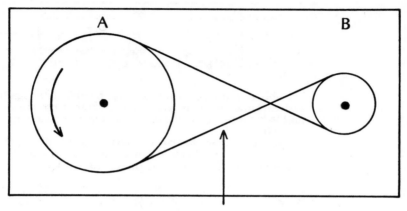

Rubber band

3. **Pulleys A and B (above) are connected by a driving belt as shown. If pulley A moves in the direction indicated, show on the diagram which way pulley B will move. [This problem can be extended to 3 or more pulleys with many variations.]**

Secondary School Subjects

1. **The furniture-maker is confronted often with the problem of adjusting the lengths of the four legs of a stool, table, or chair so that they all rest solidly on the floor. Explain how you could trim the length of the legs and cut off the bottoms so that all legs rest flat on the floor.**

2.

Ignition Secondary "Scope" Pattern

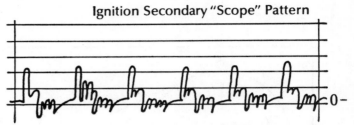

The above reading indicates possible trouble in the ignition system. How do you diagnose the problem from this reading? What replacement(s) do you suggest to overcome the difficulty?

3. Using the diagram below, connect light A with switches S_1 and S_2 so that light A can be turned on and off by either switch S_1 or switch S_2 (three-way switch).

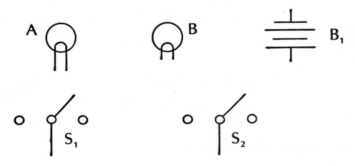

4. It is sometimes necessary in drafting to draw some special views of an object to show certain features more clearly. Through a series of 4 or 5 drawings and associated narrative extend drawing (a) to include a fourth view which is an auxiliary view showing the true size and shape of the inclined surface.

(Not included in the task presentation.)

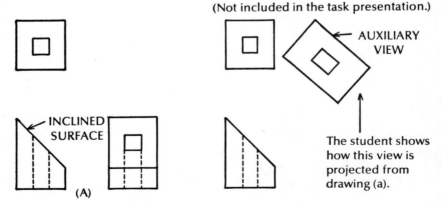

The student shows how this view is projected from drawing (a).

5. The following information for three customer accounts is taken from duplicate sales invoices. Your task is to record the sales in a Sales Journal and to post to customer accounts in the Accounts Receivable Ledger. Select forms that you need from the table at the back of the room.

A. Record in a Sales Journal these sales:

May	2	Kroftie Brothers, Jasonville, Ind.	$642.50
	5	Sullins and Jessell, Linton, Ind.	$432.09
	8	Allied Manufacturing, Marshall, Ill.	$173.60
	10	Sullins and Jessell	$973.24
	12	Allied Manufacturing	$ 43.60
	15	Kroftie Brothers	$493.14
	22	Kroftie Brothers	$132.90

B. Post from the Sales Journal to the debit side of the customers' accounts in the Accounts Receivable Ledger. Use terms "Net, 30 days" for all customers.
C. Find the total sales for the month for these three accounts in the Sales Journal. Pencil foot before inking the totals.
D. Find the balance due from each customer by pencil footing the debit side of each customer's account.

Problem Solving as an Objective

Problem solving in mathematics is the theme for the 1980 yearbook of the National Council for Teachers of Mathematics, and its importance is pointed up by issues and implications for all instructional levels. Themes for special issues of professional journals have been devoted to problem solving. Conferences devoted to learning about learning have devoted a considerable amount of time and energy to learning theory as it relates to problem solving. Recent research about the special functions of the two halves of the human brain has implications about learning, since each half of the brain seems to be specialized for different modes of thought. For these reasons, problem solving is becoming a major thrust of contemporary learning strategies.

Problem solving is a stated or implied objective for lists of general instructional objectives, and it is implied in statements of classroom behavioral objectives, which reflect programs stressing problem solving. Recommendations about how to teach problem solving have been a part of methods courses for teachers in both elementary and secondary schools for many years.

With problem solving receiving this attention in objectives and programs, the problem becomes a necessary item in achievement testing. Problems presented in classroom tests become vehicles to integrate the program, the test, and posttest activities. The connection between problems and objectives is easy for students to recognize. For other item types this connection may not be as clear as it is for the problem-type item.

5 Supply-Type Items

How the test response is to be given can determine the nature of demands made on the test taker. In this chapter those items and tests which require a student to create the response (supply-type) are considered for their contribution to educational measurement. The supply-type item is probably the most widely used and popular of all types of classroom test items.

Varying demands can be made for responses for supply-type items:

1. The student may be presented a sentence in which one or more words have been omitted and replaced by blanks and asked to replace the blank(s) with word(s) which complete the meaning of the sentence. Known as the *completion item,* it requires the student to remember and recall specific information or knowledge in much the same way as it was learned.

2. The student may be asked a direct question which requires a word or phrase as a response. Known as the *short-answer item,* it places a demand that is similar to that of the completion item in that the student can usually respond correctly with a bit of knowledge or a fact which has been learned. Since the response is not limited to a word or a series of related terms, the opportunity to go beyond simple recall is sometimes offered in short-answer items.

3. The student may be presented a task or asked a question which requires a paragraph or more as a complete expression of a fully developed thought. Known as the *essay item,* the item demands recall of knowledge, facts, concepts, and principles plus the organization of interrelated factors that go beyond the use of information in the way that it was first learned.

Supply-type items require the student to supply information in a definite hierarchical order, from least to most, moving from completion, to short answer, to essay. The level of cognitive demand required by supply-item tests is also closely related to the same hierarchical order, and demanded responses follow a sequence, from knowledge to understanding to application to the three highest orders of analysis, synthesis, and evaluation.[1] The amount of freedom in response allowed the student also should increase in the same order, with the essay item allowing the greatest amount of freedom for the student and for the person who scores the response.

The freedom that supply-type items give the student to construct his/her response may be useful when measuring in the upper levels of complex behavior, but at the same time this freedom may harm the accuracy of the measures because it is difficult to score the responses with a high degree of reliability. Too much freedom in responding erodes the common basis needed for making comparisons. The degree of freedom permitted in the response can be controlled by the type of supply item utilized. If the essay item is used, the freedom of response can be limited by the directions and how the item is presented. However, limitation of freedom in responding to supply-type items may place limitation on the level of behavior measured.

Advantages

Taken as a group supply-type items have several advantages over selection type items. In general, the advantages are related to the fact that the response is created by the student rather than by the test maker. Advantages which are associated with all supply-type items are:

1. The student becomes an active participant in the process by creating an answer. Lists of general educational objectives from the national, state, or local level imply or state that students are to develop into independent beings able to function on their own, and this objective is supported when students are required to create responses.

2. Tests made up of supply-type items are relatively easy to construct. Completion and short-answer items mainly test for recall and do not require large amounts of time or effort to construct. Since only a limited number of essay items can be presented in a testing session, essay tests require much less time to construct than do equally effective selection tests.

[1] Benjamin Bloom et al., *Taxonomy of Educational Objectives: The Classification of Educational Goals. Handbook I: Cognitive Domain* (New York: David McKay Co., Inc., 1956).

3. The possibility of getting correct answers by guessing is low for supply-type items. With any supply-type item a correct response by a blind guess is very unlikely. With the essay item guessing is reduced to a minimum and in some instances is eliminated entirely.

Limitations

Supply-type items also have several limitations. In general the limitations are related to scoring student responses. Limitations which are associated with all supply-type items are:

1. Responses are time consuming to score. Since each response must be considered for its tenability, the scorer must consider each response on its own merit. Even in completion items where strict limitations are incorporated, the writer of items can not be assured that in every case that one, and only one, word would encompass the response set. For short-answer and essay items the response will rarely if ever be so restricted that it can be scored objectively to a set phrase or paragraph. The scorer usually has to read for components presented by students in many different ways.

2. Scoring supply-type items is not only time consuming, but also requires that the scorer have knowledge of the subject being tested. Only rarely could aides, machines, or uninformed persons be used to relieve the teacher of the burden of scoring.

3. The student who has highly developed skills in written expression may be favored over students who have difficulty creating or expressing their knowledge and thoughts in words. If two students have the same knowledge and are at the same level on all factors except written expression, the one who rates higher in writing skills is likely to perform better on the test responses.

4. Some supply-type items may be subject to bluffing by a student who does not know the answer but who can write around the task without really coming to grips with it. The scorer can be more objective in reading shorter answers, and bluffing can be controlled by writing items which require limited responses.

5. There may be a considerable delay in returning the results to the student. If the results are needed to guide further instruction, the delay in getting the results may be crucial.

6. The question about how to deal with the problem of misspelled words in a response for an item in a test in a content subject must be resolved. Since the test is for achievement of the subject, a spelling component may confound the purity of the final score. If spelling of certain words is important to the subject, such as in physical geography,

a portion of the table of specifications should be given to spelling. If spelling a certain word or words is not important to the subject being studied, spelling should not be a part of the final score. However, since all teachers deal with the general education of students, the importance of spelling could be reflected by a separate score for spelling. Two scores could be given for the test—one for content and a second for spelling. A third score for the mechanics of handwriting could also be given.

Guides to Writing

In spite of their limitations, supply-type items should be used when they are able to call forth the type of behavior and test the learning of content called for in educational objectives. By paying careful attention to item construction, the writer can overcome the limitations or reduce their effects to a minimum. The following suggestions can direct writing of supply-type items to overcome their limitations:

1. Write each item clearly so that the task is well defined and that an answer is definitive and can be defended as the correct response. Students should not be held accountable for choosing a particular answer when more than one response is, indeed, correct. If a knowledgeable student provides a correct response, s/he should be given credit even though the teacher may have chosen and outlined another response. Careful writing should reduce the probability of multiple answers, but item writers find it difficult to be successful in this regard for every item written.

2. To reduce sampling error (content), the item writer should include as many scorable units in the test as possible. The chance of building a representative sample of content is increased with more items.

Completion Items

The supply-type item most like the objective item is the completion item. The task is presented in a sentence in which a word, a number, or a symbol has been omitted. The student is asked to fill in the sentence by choosing a response which makes a complete thought in the context of the material which has been studied. The completion item is the most structured of all supply-type items and, consequently, offers the least freedom of response. The completion item is considered by some writers as an objective or "semi-objective" type of item because only one answer is expected for a blank or a specific series of answers for a series of blanks. If an item can be defined as objective when someone without knowledge of the subject matter can score the response sheet, then completion items cannot be considered objective since student responses to completion items must be judged for correctness. Scoring completion items involves more than checking for a specific symbol or number given on a key and scoring each item without knowing why it is correct or incorrect.

When the teacher needs a direct way to test a student for recall or factual information, the completion item may be the best way to present the test tasks. Since a completion item is largely limited to testing student recall of learned facts, and if it is used to the exclusion of more appropriate types of items, the student may only learn facts in isolation and neglect cognitive functioning at the more complex levels. However, facts are the basis for the higher levels of behaviors, and their importance should not be discounted. Completion-type items provide an efficient vehicle to measure at the most basic level.

SPECIAL CONSIDERATIONS

When choosing the most appropriate item type to call forth a particular student behavior, the teacher must consider the following advantages and limitations of the completion item.

Advantages

1. Recall of information for response to completion items should not be time consuming for the test taker. Since the task is very direct, many bits of information can be collected in a test period, thus increasing the size of the sample.

2. Well-constructed completion items can be scored more quickly than other supply-type items. Although some time will be needed to judge certain answers, the limited domain of possible answers allows a considerable degree of objectivity in the scoring process.

3. Scorer reliability should be high for completion items. Judgments, if any, made by different scorers should be similar.

4. Because, in order to respond at the knowledge level, the student must recall information, this item type may be superior to one for which the answer is provided. Since this level of cognition merely deals with information in the same form as it was learned, recognition may mean picking up clues from the original presentation. If the student must recall the information rather than identify it, the process may be a better measure of achievement.

Limitations

1. The completion item usually measures the learning of facts at the recall level. Teachers of some subjects, especially language, feel that this generalization does not hold for all topics they cover. If a new test situation can be created, then the levels of understanding and comprehension may be required for the student to respond.

2. Writing the item may be difficult. To present a clearly defined task with only one correct answer may require qualifiers which make a sentence complex. Much rewriting may be required to shorten it to an acceptable level.

GUIDES TO WRITING

1. Place the blank or blanks at or near the end of the incomplete statement. If the blank(s) appear at the beginning, the student must read the sentence first to understand the task. If it is placed at the end, a second reading may not be necessary. (See examples below.)

2. Do not replace so many words with blanks that the meaning cannot be discerned. If more than two blanks are used, they should be of a self-contained series.

Example A

The _____ (capital) _____ of Indiana is
_____ (Indianapolis) _____ . (Poor item)

Example B

The capital of Indiana is _____ (Indianapolis) _____ .

Example C

The capitals of the New England states are
_____ (Boston) _____ , _____ (Providence) _____ ,
_____ (Hartford) _____ , _____ (Concord) _____ ,
_____ (Montpelier) _____ , and
_____ (Augusta) _____ .

[Any order. If a separate answer sheet is to be used, this item could be written with smaller spaces.]

The capital cities of the New England states are _____ , _____ ,
_____ , _____ , _____ , and _____ . [Any order]

3. Make all of the blank spaces the same size. Do not leave short blanks for short words and long blanks for long words because

this will give unintended clues which will limit the possible responses. Since younger students can be permitted to place their responses directly in the sentence, be sure that the size of the blanks is large enough for the longest word. Older students should be expected to use a separate answer sheet to record their responses to facilitate scoring. If an answer sheet is used, space can be saved by making small blanks in the incomplete sentence.

Example

The four states which meet at one point are
(Utah), (Arizona), (Colorado), and (New Mexico). (Poor item)

Improve this item by writing it as follows:

The four states which meet at one point are

_____(Utah)_____	,	_____(Arizona)_____ ,
_____(Colorado)_____	, and	
_____(New Mexico)_____	.	

For use with an answer sheet use short blanks:

The four states which meet at one point are

_____, _____, _____, and _____.

4. Word each item so that all students have the same frame of reference. A wide range of plausible answers may result from a poorly written completion item.

Example

Portland, Oregon is on_____(Poor item)_____.

The scorer would have to accept as correct answers of "a river," "Pacific Standard Time," "the Columbia River," "the Washington border," "the Willamette River," or several other correct responses. To make the task clear the item could be presented as:

Portland, Oregon is located at the junction of the
_____(Columbia)_____ **and**
_____(Willamette)_____ **rivers.**

5. Omit only important words.

Example

A pulley is a type of machine that can lift a heavy
_____(weight)_____ **vertically ten feet. (Poor item)**

To test the student the item could better be presented as:

A type of machine which can lift a heavy load ten feet vertically is the _____(pulley)_____ .

6. Indicate what unit is to be used if the answer requires reporting the answer in units. Also indicate how the answer is to be approximated.

Example

The circumference of a circle which has a diameter of twenty (20) inches is _____(5.24)_____ feet. (nearest hundredth)

7. Check the grammar of the sentence to make sure that the sentence does not include an indication of whether the answer is singular or plural or an adjective which indicates that the word starts with a vowel or consonant.

Example A

What Bill needs to complete the experiment are _____(subjects)_____ . (Poor item)

The item can be improved by writing it as follows:

To complete the experiment Bill needs _____(subjects)_____ .

Example B

If the teacher wants to test a student's ability to synthesize concepts, s/he should use an _____(essay)_____ item. (Poor item)

The item can be improved by writing it as follows:

A student's ability to synthesize concepts can best be measured by _____(essay)_____ items.

8. Do not lift a sentence or part of a sentence directly from any source and leave out a word or two as blanks to be filled. Students may remember a sentence they have read. More important, the sentence out of context of supporting material may need the surrounding sentences to give it full meaning.

9. Check "GUIDES TO CONSTRUCTION" on p. 61.

10. Check "GUIDES TO WRITING" on p. 85.

EXEMPLARY ITEMS

The following items are models which reflect the suggestions about how to construct completion items. No attempt has been made to cover all guides or subject areas.

Elementary School Subjects

1. The last name of the man who invented the telephone is
   _____(Bell)_____ .

2. The combined length of an automobile which is 15 feet 11 inches long and a trailer which is 17 feet 10 inches long is equal to _____(33 $\frac{9}{12}$ or 33 $\frac{3}{4}$)_____ feet. (Change inches to a fraction of a foot.)

3. To locate a position on the earth's surface, a ship's captain would give reference points in regard to the ship's positions of _____(latitude)_____ and _____(longitude)_____ . (Either order is correct.)

4. When there are no sharps and no flats in the key signature, the music is written in the key of
   _____(C)_____ .

5. Fill in the blanks in the sentences below.
   Use these words:

   run   bunt   bat   team   important

   1. The last game was a very _____(important)_____
      game.
   2. Hank was told to _____(bunt)_____ .
   3. Hank planned to swing his
      _____(bat)_____ as hard as he could.
   4. Hank hit a home _____(run)_____ .
   5. Mr. Hawthorn told Hank he was not a
      _____(team)_____ player.

Secondary School Subjects

1. Flats are placed in the key signature in the following order:
   __(b)__ , __(e)__ , __(a)__ , __(d)__ , __(g)__ , __(c)__ .

2. A three-speed standard transmission makes a clicking sound in low and reverse gears only. The fault is a defective __(low-reverse sliding gear)__ .

3. The clutch release bearing is controlled by the _____(release fork)_____ .

4. In the three-step arrangement called the syllogism, steps 1 and 2 are called _____ (premises) _____ **, and the third step is called** _(conclusion) (inference)_ **.**

5. Electrolysis of water creates the two gases _____ (hydrogen) _____ **and** _____ (oxygen) _____ **.**

Short-Answer Items

Short-answer items are very similar to completion items, and in many cases the test maker could change a completion item to a short answer item by phrasing it as a question. (See examples for completion items.) The short answer does allow the test constructor to make a somewhat greater demand on the student than can be made using the completion format. Since the response is not limited to a word, a number, or a symbol, it can be extended to a short phrase. Some short-answer items could be constructed at the level of comprehension or application, but in general the short answer item best measures facts and knowledge.

The short-answer item can offer more freedom for the student's response than the completion format. Although the item is severely limited in the type of response expected, it is a step toward the extensive response of the essay item.

Teachers of young children who are interested in development of expression find that the short-answer item can introduce the child to written expression without requiring a complex answer. The use of short-answer items for tests in the primary grades supports the total instructional program because they provide a vehicle to develop written expression.

SPECIAL CONSIDERATIONS

When choosing the most appropriate item type to call forth the particular student behavior, the teacher must consider the following advantages and limitations of the short-answer item.

Advantages

1. The short-answer item which uses a phrase for an answer can be used with young children to prepare them to express their thoughts in written format and to prepare them to answer essay items at a later time.

2. Since the student must recall the response rather than recognize it, well-written short-answer items may be better than selection-

type items for measuring knowledge of facts. For use in the real world, facts must be recalled by the learner. It has been suggested that application of information is as much a part of learning as the putting it in the mind in the first place. An answer may be apparent in a selection item because the test is of knowledge and the presentation is limited to presenting it in the same way that it appeared in learning. A better test of achievement may be to ask the student to recall it on his own.

3. Tasks are easy to set with a well-written question since directions can be made explicit. The task is easy to clarify, thus avoiding ambiguity.

4. Teachers of mathematics and science courses find extensive use for the short-answer item. The short-answer item is very efficient when testing for formulas and principles which must be learned in a specific form.

Limitations

1. In general, short-answer items measure at the knowledge level and make little demand beyond recall. There are exceptions in some, maybe most, subject areas.

2. Use of short-answer items to the exclusion of other items limits the testing to lower levels of cognitive functioning. This limitation is easily overcome by using items which require other student behaviors.

GUIDES TO WRITING

1. Provide the same amount of space for each response unless you have a particular reason for specifying the length of the response. It is a good idea to arrange the order so that one-word answers are all together and phrases all together. Give the same amount of space for all one-word responses and the same amount of space for all phrases unless the intent is to direct the length of the response.

2. Include rules for responding in the item or directions. Designate units to be used, length of responses, approximation rules, and any other needed guidance.

Example A

How long is the unit formed by attaching a trailer which is 17 feet 10 inches long to an automobile which is 15 feet 11 inches long? ___(33)___ **feet** ___(9)___ **inches**

Example B

In the space provided, tell the primary difference between the folk tale and the literary fairy tale. _____

3. Check "GUIDES TO CONSTRUCTION" on p. 61.
4. Check "GUIDES TO WRITING" on p. 85.

EXEMPLARY ITEMS

The following items are models which reflect the suggestions about how to write short-answer items. No attempt has been made to cover all guides or subject areas.

Elementary School Subjects

1. What are the two prime movers of soil which cause erosion? _____ **and** _____

2. What is the main reason that a human being has always belonged to a group of other human beings? _____

3. To whom does the title "Winners of the West" refer?

4. What is business which is carried on between different countries called? _____

5. What are the openings at the top of dams that let the water through called? _____

Secondary School Subjects

1. Why does a gas-stove flame turn yellow when the contents of a pan spill over? _____

2. What would Newton's spectrum look like if a light source consisted of red and violet light only? _____

3. In a long parade, the marchers far from the band may be out of step with the band members. Account for this difference. _____

4. What is a caste? _____

5. Where is the Plain of Skåne? _____

Essay Items

The essay item is the most complex of supply-type items. The essay-test item demands a fully developed response from the student. The test taker must respond in one or more sentences which constitute a reasonable answer to the question. The accuracy and quality of the response must be judged by someone who is knowledgeable in the subject being tested, usually the person who wrote the item. For classroom testing, the person best able to make the required judgments about responses to essay items is the classroom teacher.

The essay item can serve classroom testing in two ways, depending on how an item is written and how much freedom is given to the writer in composing the response. An essay item can be presented with a broad scope but a limited time allotment. This kind of item tests the writer's skill in choosing what to write and how much to write about each of the several parts. The student's ability to organize and express a logical thesis are also challenged. This type of item, the **extended-response** essay item, is helpful in assessing written expression, especially in the language arts.

Another way to structure an essay item is to put carefully designated limits on the response. The scope may be narrow or broad, but the student should know exactly what the limits are. This type of item, the **limited-response** essay item, is especially useful to the classroom teacher who is testing achievement in a content subject. The skills of expression and organization should not be reflected in the evaluation of a response to an item in a subject-matter achievement test. This can not be avoided entirely because the answer must be created, but in contrast to the extended response, which is intended to measure writing skill, the limited response is used to measure achievement in a content subject. Each has its place in classroom testing, but the test maker must keep this difference in mind when writing the items. For tests in the language arts, specifically for measurement of writing skills, the extended response should be used; otherwise, the test maker should write limited response essay items for all other subjects.

Scoring responses to essay items is, at best, difficult and time consuming. This fact should be considered when deciding what type of item to choose for the test. If it is imperative that scores be available soon after the testing session, the selection-type item is a logical choice. If the behavior to be measured requires the essay item, then the teacher must set aside enough time to read the responses.

As a check on reader reliability the first reading of the responses can be followed by a second reading of the responses by the teacher or by a colleague who can judge the responses independently. A reconciliation of the two judgments is likely to be more reliable than the original reading alone. Special consideration and rules for evaluating student essay responses[2] can do much to overcome the lack of reader reliability, but little can be done to reduce the time needed to score the responses.

One of the greatest assets of the essay item is the freedom

---

[2] Charles D. Hopkins and Richard L. Antes, *Classroom Testing: Administration, Scoring, and Score Interpretation* (Itasca, Ill.: F. E. Peacock Publishers, Inc., 1979).

allowed the student in responding. Such freedom allows tasks which measure complex cognitive functioning that is not possible with selection-type items, which structure a specific and very limited domain of responses. This asset is not without its corresponding liability: scoring objectivity is likely to suffer because of the freedom allowed the scorer in making highly subjective judgments. Since the student is free to take one of many paths, the reader can only form general rules about what the response should contain, not about how it is written in specific terms. Ebel says, "To a considerable degree, freedom is the enemy of precision of measurement."[3] The scores are also subject to unconscious inclusion of such factors as handwriting, grammar, and spelling in the final test score because these characteristics can unintentionally influence a scorer's judgment.

SPECIAL CONSIDERATIONS

When choosing the most appropriate item type to call forth the particular student behavior, the teacher must consider the following advantages and limitations of the essay item.

Advantages

1. The essay item can be written to allow the student maximum freedom of response. The amount of freedom can be leveled by the way the item is written to set the scope of the expected response.

2. Freedom of response can be used to test the student in the higher cognitive behaviors of analysis, synthesis, and evaluation. The student can be asked to apply, compare, explain, describe, and contrast knowledge and principles.

3. The essay item allows the test maker to ask a student his/her opinion without making a judgment about the response. Unlike the objective item, which must be scored as right or wrong, the major factor of the response to the essay opinion item can be the student's ability to defend that opinion, not whether the student's opinion agrees with a keyed opinion.

4. A good essay test requires less time to construct than a well-prepared selection test. Although each essay item may take more time to prepare than, for example, a true-false or multiple-choice item, only a few items need to be written. This means that it takes less time to construct an essay test than a selection-type test.

[3] Robert L. Ebel, *Essentials of Educational Measurement* (Englewood Cliffs, N.J.: Prentice-Hall, 1972), p. 132.

5. Opportunities to organize and express ideas allow the testing session to also serve as a learning experience. Although the primary purpose of the classroom test is to measure achievement, the second purpose of supporting learning should be taken advantage of whenever possible.

6. By providing maximum freedom of response, the extended-response item can be analyzed and/or evaluated for written expression and organization of material.

Limitations

1. Judgment of student responses requires much time. Since each response must be scrutinized by analytic or global scoring, the time saved in preparation of the essay test is more than used up in the time needed to score the responses of the students reliably.

2. Essay responses are difficult to score with high reliability. Without special precautions in scoring, the scores on essay tests are likely to lack the objectivity needed to make the scores useful and valid measures of student achievement.

3. Essay responses are apt to provide a sample of subject matter that is less than desired because each item requires considerable time to answer. The limited sampling provided by relatively few items may cause the content validity to be reduced.

4. If a student has difficulty in expressing ideas and thoughts in writing, s/he may not be able to offer a good representation of achievement. Two students who have the same level of achievement in absolute terms, but different levels of skill in expression may receive very different scores on an essay test.

GUIDES TO WRITING

1. Use essay items when one or more of the following student behaviors is/are expected: explanation, comparison, contrast, description, analysis, synthesis, and evaluation. The essay item also allows a student the freedom to give an opinion and defend it without having the opinion itself judged. The extended response essay item may be employed to measure student skill in language expression, communication, and organization of material.

2. Do NOT use an essay item to measure simple recall of facts and information. Other supply-type and some selection-type items are more efficient for measuring at the knowledge level.

3. Prepare the item so that the question presented or implied is explicit, concise, and clear to the student. Ambiguous words

and phrases leave doubt in the mind of the student about what s/he should respond to. If necessary, definitions of words can be given to clarify the task being presented to the student.

4. Only present tasks which are new and unfamiliar to the student. If a task incorporates a familiar situation, the student may be required only to recall what was learned and incorporate it in a response in the same way that it was learned.

5. Establish within each item the scope expected in the response and the detail to be included by defining and "fencing in" the expected response. The limits of the response should be established within the content studied. In addition, the length of the expected response can be indicated by the amount of time to be spent on it or by the number of points for an entirely correct answer. The answer can be further limited by the amount of space to be used in responding. Relative weights of the several items on an essay test can be indicated in these ways.

6. Tell the student how to handle terms which have special meaning in the area being tested or which are technical in nature. The student should know whether to define and/or explain these in the answer.

7. Each item should be written so that students spend their time on, and are given credit for, those aspects of the study which differentiate levels of achievement in the topics studied. The task should not be presented so that the response must include general information.

8. When setting the task, use descriptive words which are clear in their meaning. Unless the test is intended to measure the student's understanding of technical words, technical words should be defined. Directions which include words like *compare, defend, trace, contrast,* and *explain differences* give specific directions for the response. Words or phrases like *review, tell all that you know,* and *report your knowledge* are nondirective and should not be used in directions for essay items. Terms such as *discuss, outline,* and *evaluate* should be used sparingly, and, if used, the precise meaning must be clear.

9. All students should write on the same set of items without a choice from a list of possible (optional) items. Comparisons of differences in the set of scores can be made only when each score is based on the same set of items. If six items are proposed but only four are to be answered, differences in test scores have little meaning since the combinations of six items taken four at a time is sizable (fifteen different ways of choosing the four items to write on). Educational measurement, whether norm referenced or criterion referenced, needs the common base for interpretation.

However, there is an exception: individually prescribed instruction or a class organized such that students have studied in different areas by choice may cause a teacher to modify the above guide. If students have studied different content, then measures on the test should reflect achievement in appropriate content. Selection from a wide list of topics may be acceptable testing procedure under these conditions; however, the teacher should consider making a special test for each student. The teacher could have a common set of items and build the tests individually for each student from these items according to how each student had studied in the material. Nevertheless, the scores must be judged for their absolute value when selection is made rather than judged in comparison with other student scores.

10. Choose the extended-response essay item only as a vehicle to measure writing expression, communication, or organization of material. Use of this item type for content other than language arts should be limited to an in-class or take-home assignment. It should not serve as a measurement· procedure, and students should view it as a learning assignment *not* as a test.

11. Check "GUIDES TO CONSTRUCTION" on p. 61.
12. Check "GUIDES TO WRITING" on p. 85.

EXEMPLARY ITEMS

The following items are models which reflect the suggestions about how to construct essay items. No attempt has been made to cover all guides or subject areas.

Elementary School Subjects

1. **Trace the circulation of the blood through the parts of the human body, naming the organs and their contribution to the blood.**
2. **Draw a diagram of the heart showing the different parts and the direction of circulation through each part. Show entry points, and tell where the blood comes from. Show exit points and where the blood goes.**
3. **Name the organs of the human digestive system and their functions, placing them in the order in which food passes through them.**
4. **Here is a list of statements that are usually true. They are *not* true in the case of early Egypt. *For each one explain why it is not true for Egypt.* Collectively, how did these help the Egyptians to develop a fine early civilization?**
    1. **When rivers overflow in a populated area, they usually cause nothing but damage.**
    2. **Almost nothing grows on a desert, but the soil is often rich in plant food.**
    3. **Very few people live in desert regions.**
    4. **Travel is difficult in a hot, dry desert land.**

5. Describe conditions which made travel difficult in the United States before the middle nineteenth century. Include in your answer two reasons why people traveled by water whenever possible.

Secondary School Subjects

1. Describe how the introduction of railroads in a typical underdeveloped country could be expected to change the *political* climate of that country.
2. The War of 1812 has been called "The War Nobody Won." What is meant by this reference? In your opinion, how did that war change our country? Support and defend your opinion with specific examples.
3. In what ways is a diode detector like a half-wave rectifier for use on a 60-Hz power line? In what ways are the two different? Include in your discussion of the above questions filter circuits to illustrate.
4. During the last six weeks you have had an opportunity to grow a *Mimosa* plant and observe it under various conditions. It is fair to assume that the response behavior of *Mimosa* is of benefit to its survival. Formulate some hypotheses about the advantages of this behavior to the plant's survival. Document support for each hypothesis with one or more examples of response behavior to various stimuli noted during your experiments.
5. Explain with a narrative and a set of three or four sketches how to make a blood smear to be viewed through a microscope. Include in your discussion any particular things to avoid doing as well as those which you should do.
6. When reading music, what effect does a natural have on sharps and flats? Consider all possible uses.
7. Torts are private wrongs such as fraud, libel, slander, and negligence. A tort is an actionable wrong other than a breach of contract. Crimes are public wrongs. Crimes are considered to be an offense against society. Some wrongs are both a tort and a crime.

   DIRECTIONS: Read the following descriptions of wrongful acts. Classify each act as either a crime, a tort, or both. Explain what crime and/or tort was committed.

   A. While playing touch football, Howard fell into a prize camellia bush in the neighbor's garden, completely destroying it.
   B. Mr. Eks was a witness in a court trial. He promised under oath to tell only the truth. At the trial he violated his oath and lied to protect a friend.

Expression as an Objective

Basic to learning at all levels of the process of education is the usefulness of what is learned. Students must be able to draw on what has been learned to serve them in daily living and to integrate learned facts to meet new and novel situations. English composition, for instance, is a vehicle which is intended to allow organization of what a student knows and to develop within the student skill in expression.

Educational objectives from the earliest school years, even preschool age, are directed to development of a child socially. To perform in society, each individual must be able to communicate through words, either oral or written, to other human beings. Supply-type items on tests, although not the only way of developing these skills, do allow the testing sessions to support the instructional objectives directed to written expression.

Whenever possible data-collection procedures should include items which allow students to create responses. The essay item requires the student to think reflectively and in creating an answer the student gains experience in organizing knowledge into a well-formulated composition. In this way the measurement in the classroom becomes an integral part of the instructional activities devoted to developing the skill in written expression.

6 Selection-Type Items

Selection-type items present the task to the student through various situations which require a student to choose from the alternatives provided. They are popular for classroom achievement tests because they are flexible and can be used to collect valid data about how well students met objectives. The items are self-contained and do not permit the student to go beyond what is actually stated in the item for a response. In general, the student is asked to select the correct or best response from the alternatives provided, hence the term *selection*. Selection-type items are also referred to as "objective items" since they can be scored independently by one or more scorers from a key or by machine. The same results are obtained in all cases because judgment of correctness only extends to comparison of a response with the keyed answer.

The learning outcomes which can be measured by selection-type items range from simple through complex behaviors, depending upon the skill of the item writer. The quality of an item is determined by the skill with which it is written and its ability to measure the desired learning outcomes. The quality of a test made up of selection-type items, therefore, depends upon the item writer. In choosing the type of items to measure, the teacher must consider the desired learning outcomes, the nature of the subject matter, the specific objectives for the student, the amount of time available for testing, the age and developmental level of students, and other pertinent considerations.

This chapter provides guidelines and useful information for writing selection-type items as well as evaluating those items that appear on standardized tests and in other materials. Advantages, limitations, and guides to writing all kinds of selection-type items are given attention. True-false, multiple-choice, matching, and classification items are discussed separately for special considerations, advantages, and limitations for each of those item types. Exemplary items for each kind of item are presented for both elementary and secondary school levels.

Advantages

The selection-type items have some common advantages. In general, these are related to the objectivity in scoring and to the large number of items which can be answered in a relatively short period of time. Advantages associated with all selection-type items are:

1. Selection-type items can be scored objectively. Once the scoring key is developed, each student's set of responses is compared to it by hand or machine, and knowledge of the subject matter is not needed for judging whether the response is correct or not.
2. The act of scoring items is easy and can be accomplished quickly. In the event a teacher wishes to give a test to a large number of students and return the scored papers quickly, selection-type items should be utilized.
3. Selection-type items have high scorer reliability. All results of scoring from a key arrive at the same score for each paper unless there is a clerical error in the hand-scoring process.
4. Comprehensive coverage of subject matter content can be obtained in a relatively short period of testing time. A more comprehensive sample of student achievement in each content area is possible.
5. The student can be presented a clearly defined task and a definite response can be keyed for scoring. Well-written items reduce ambiguity in tests to a minimum.
6. The alternative responses are provided by the test writer, and the quality of handwriting and expression are not factors which can affect scoring and are not reflected in measures of demonstrated achievement. In essay and short-answer items, scoring may be affected by student's handwriting, and the ability to express ideas and organize material may enter into judgment of responses without the reader being aware of it.
7. Selection-type items are adaptable to most content areas as well as a wide range of behaviors. For these reasons selection-type items are popular in classroom tests.

Limitations

The limitations are based on the fact that the responses are provided for the test taker and there is no opportunity to interact or communicate beyond the provided alternatives. Limitations associated with all selection-type items are:

1. A student who does not know a response may guess. When guessing is involved in selection of responses, the reliability of the test is lowered. A large amount of guessing in a testing situation could reduce the reliability coefficient below acceptable levels.

2. Good selection-type items and, therefore, tests are time consuming and difficult to construct. Items at the higher levels of the cognitive domain are more difficult to write while items for the lower levels are easier to construct.

3. The test writer must judge the difficulty level of each item before students react to them. Selection-type items for norm-referenced tests are written to be of medium difficulty, but the difficulty level of an item for a class is not known until students have reacted to that item on a test.

4. Opportunity for originality in the response or expression of opinion is not available. When these factors are important, a supply-type test should be utilized.

5. Selection-type items have been criticized because students who are test-wise can pick up clues from the item and identify a correct alternative without understanding the concept being measured. A properly constructed item on a test will not open the door to identification of the keyed response without understanding of the concept, thus overcoming this criticism.

True-False Items

A true-false item consists of a declarative statement and the student responds "True," if it conforms to accepted truth, or "False," if it is essentially incorrect. True-false items are also referred to as alternative-response items, and variations of the item ask the student to react with yes-no, right-wrong, correct-incorrect, or some other dichotomous way of responding. Regardless of the response style, the item provides the student with a choice of two alternatives.

True-false items are particularly helpful in determining how well students remember facts and definitions but may also be written to measure at higher levels. Although true-false items are generally used to measure recall, the item writer can extend their use to measurement of understanding, interpretation and other behaviors from the higher levels of the cognitive domain. The criticism that true-false items are inherently limited to measurement of facts and definitions is unfounded since the item writer determines the quality of the item, coverage, and the learning outcome which the item measures.

SPECIAL CONSIDERATIONS

When choosing the most appropriate item type to call forth particular student behavior, the teacher must consider the following advantages and limitations of the true-false item.

Advantages

1. Students are able to respond to more true-false items in a given time period than any other selection-type item. Generally, students can respond to about two true-false items per minute. When a specified period of time is set for a test, quicker response allows for more extensive coverage of learning outcomes than other selection-type items provide.
2. When responding to a true-false item, the student is reacting in much the same way that s/he does when answering a question in class or in a real-world situation. Many students feel comfortable with true-false items because of the alternative response propositions directed to them by parents, peers, teachers, and other people they come in contact with.
3. True-false items can be used in special situations, such as tests for young children, poor readers, and slow students since this type of item may be written in relatively few words. This makes it easier for students to read the item and understand the task to which they are to respond.
4. True-false items provide a simple and direct means of measuring learning outcomes in the knowledge category of the taxonomy of the cognitive domain. A skillful writer can develop items which call for identification of cause

and effect as well as items requiring distinction between fact and opinion.

5. True-false items are amenable to item analysis which enables the teacher to determine how the items functioned with the students tested.

Limitations

1. Guessing on true-false items may artificially increase student scores. There is a 50 percent chance of guessing the correct response, which provides a high probability of chance success.

2. True-false items presume a dichotomous relationship of being absolutely true or false. In reality, there exist degrees of correctness, and a statement may not always be totally true or totally false, which may make response to some items difficult for a student even when the material is familiar.

3. True-false items are susceptible to ambiguity and misinterpretation if careful consideration is not given to the principles of good item writing. If sufficient time is devoted to writing items and principles of construction are considered, then true-false items become a valuable means of assessing student achievement.

4. In general, true-false items are less discriminating of levels of achievement than other selection-type items. The element of chance responses reduces the effective range of student scores, and this limits the discrimination power of true-false items.

5. Writing items which measure behaviors beyond recall of facts may be more time consuming than writing simpler recall items. However, it is probably no more time consuming than writing another type of item to measure the same concept.

GUIDES TO WRITING

1. Base the true-false item on one important main idea which is essentially true or essentially false. More than one idea within an item tends to be ambiguous since the student may not know how to mark an item which is partly true and partly false. If an item includes two ideas, the student who knows one part but not the

other may not receive credit for the part that s/he knows. A better way is to separate the one item and write two items to test the two ideas separately.

Example A

T F The Mackley credit card is a general purpose credit card in which an interest rate equal to 18 percent per year is charged if a bill is not paid by the due date. (poor item)

The student may know that the Mackley credit card is a general purpose credit card, but s/he may not know the interest rate charged and therefore not know how to respond to that part of the item without guessing. The item could be broken into two items, one concerning the general purpose of the credit card and the other concerning the interest rate per year, as the following example illustrates.

Example B

Ⓣ F The Mackley credit card is a general purpose credit card.
Ⓣ F The interest rate on a Mackley credit card is equal to 18 percent per year on the unpaid balance.

2. When a clue word (specific determiner) is used in a true-false statement, the test taker may have a word which qualifies the response as true or as false. Statements containing words such as *always, never, all,* and *none,* are associated with false items, while *usually, often, may, most,* and *should* are associated with true statements.

Example

**T F Climate and weather always have the same meaning.
(poor item)**

An alert student could get a clue that the statement is false from the word *always* and receive credit for the item without understanding the difference between "climate" and "weather."

3. Avoid the use of negative word(s) in true-false statements as much as possible.

(a) If a negative word must be used, it should be underlined so that the student's attention is directed to it. When words like *no* and *not* are not underlined, they tend to be overlooked by students.

Example

Ⓣ F **Specific determiners are <u>not</u> acceptable in true-false statements.**

(b) Double negatives are confusing to students and unacceptable grammatically.

Example

T F **Undesirable family budget management means that a family should <u>not</u> use credit.** (poor item)

Double negatives are confusing to the student, and they make it difficult for the student to decide what task is presented. A straightforward positive statement creates a situation in which a knowing student will respond correctly to the item.

(c) Adding the word "not" to a true statement to make it false is inappropriate.

Example A

Ⓣ F **The capital of Ohio is Columbus.**
T F **The capital of Ohio is <u>not</u> Columbus.** (poor item)

The first statement is straightforward and knowing students would mark it true.

Example B

T F **The legislative branch of government is <u>not</u> called the Congress.** (poor item)

This item could have been stated without using the word *not* as follows:

Ⓣ F **The legislative branch of the government is called the Congress.**
Ⓣ F **Congress is the legislative branch of the government.**

4. Avoid long, complex, and involved statements. When statements are not relatively simple and direct, the students' reading ability, rather than achievement in subject matter, is tested.

Example

T F **The French zoologist Dujardin, in 1835, recognized protoplasm which occurs in living organisms.**
(poor item)

This item includes information not necessary to test whether a student knows that all living things contain protoplasm. False responses could result from the student thinking (1) that France is the wrong country, (2) that Dujardin was not a zoologist, (3) that someone else recognized protoplasm, or (4) that this is the wrong date.

5. Statements should be written in the teacher's own words. Statements taken verbatim from textbooks encourage rote memorization. In other cases an item can be answered by remembering a phrase or sentence from the book without having understanding of the content if the sentence sounds familiar.

6. A false statement should be written so that the statement sounds plausible to someone who has not studied the subject-matter content being tested. When false statements are written in this way, a measure of how much has been learned in the course can be obtained since knowledgeable students should get the itém correct. This supports the principle basic to all item writing: those students who know or understand a concept should get an item based on that concept correct, and all others should get it incorrect.

7. True statements should be about the same length as false statements. True statements tend to be longer than false statements, and a test-wise student may connect the length of an item and a correct response. This difficulty can be avoided by varying the lengths of both true and false statements.

8. The number of true and false statements should be approximately the same for each test. False statements tend to be more discriminating than true items, but if more false statements appear on all tests, the test-wise student will probably mark items s/he does not know false, thus receiving above chance level for those guesses.

9. Check "GUIDES TO CONSTRUCTION" on page 61.

EXEMPLARY ITEMS

The following items are intended to provide models which reflect the suggestions about how to construct true-false items. No attempt has been made to cover all guides or subject areas.

Elementary School Subjects

Ⓣ F 1. **The first national park established was Yellowstone.**
Ⓣ F 2. **North America is west of the Atlantic Ocean.**
T Ⓕ 3. **When the weather is humid, it is very pleasant.**
Ⓣ F 4. **Sheep eat grass.**
Ⓣ F 5. **A turtle is a reptile.**

Secondary School Subjects

Ⓣ F 1. **The Dred Scott decision stated that Negroes were citizens of the United States.**
Ⓣ F 2. **Sales credit is offered by a bank or finance company.**
Ⓣ F 3. **Miss Helen Keller compares herself before her education began to a ship adrift in a dense fog.**
Ⓣ F 4. **The surface of the earth's moon has mountain ranges, broad plains, and vast craters.**
T Ⓕ 5. **The range is the set of all first coordinates of the ordered pairs that comprise the function.**

Multiple-Choice Items

The multiple-choice item consists of a premise and a set of alternatives. The premise, known as the stem, is presented as a question or incomplete statement which the student answers or completes by selecting one of several alternatives. Usually either four or five alternatives are available. One is the correct or best response, and the others are referred to as distracters. Alternatives may consist of numbers, single words, letters, phrases, sentences, or formulas.

The multiple-choice item is generally recognized as the most versatile and widely used of all item types, since items can be written to assess a wide range of subject-matter content and cognitive behaviors. The ability and skill of the item writer will determine the range and content levels of the cognitive domain that are measured. This type of item is especially useful to measure at the cognitive levels of comprehension and application. Although the multiple-choice item can be written to measure one of several levels of cognitive behavior, it should not be used exclusively of other types of items. Variations of the question and incomplete statement multiple-choice items exist, but they are not recommended for classroom achievement testing. When multiple-choice items do not follow the conventional forms, students may find the items difficult to understand and respond to.

SPECIAL CONSIDERATIONS

When choosing the most appropriate item type to call forth particular student behavior, the teacher must consider the following advantages and limitations of the multiple-choice item.

Advantages

1. The multiple-choice item is adaptable to subject-matter content areas as well as different levels of behavior. It can be used in assessing ability to reason, discriminate, interpret, analyze, make inferences, and solve problems.
2. The structure of a premise and four or five alternatives provides less chance for guessing the correct response than the true-false item does. A well-constructed item at the appropriate level of difficulty reduces correct answers from blind guessing; therefore, the higher-achieving students should get the item correct. Since more lower-achieving students should select one of the plausible distracters as compared to a true-false item, there is less chance of guessing the correct response.
3. In general, the multiple-choice test is expected to provide greater test reliability than the true-false test. The basis for this is related to less score variation due to guessing in a multiple-choice test as compared to a true-false test.
4. Four or five options provide more incorrect choices for selection of responses by the student who does not know the best or correct answer.
5. The difficulty of each multiple-choice item can be controlled by changing the alternatives. The more homogeneous the alternatives, the more difficult it is to select the correct response from the given alternatives.
6. The number of alternatives in a multiple-choice item helps provide information which may be utilized for diagnostic purposes. The teacher is able to pursue the reasons for understanding or lack of understanding content in specific topics based on the alternatives chosen.
7. Multiple-choice items are amenable to item analysis

which enables the teacher to determine how well the items functioned with the students tested. The improvement of alternatives and the item stem can be undertaken according to the difficulty level, discrimination index, and how well each alternative functioned in discriminating between the higher achieving and lower achieving students.

Limitations

1. Quality multiple-choice items are time consuming and difficult to write. Locating four or five plausible alternatives for an item is arduous, and without adequate distracters the item is of limited value.
2. More skill is needed in writing multiple-choice items than other selection-type items. The ability and skill of the teacher in writing this type of item are factors influencing the quality of the item and test.
3. More time is required to respond to a multiple-choice item than a true-false item. The time required for responding also varies based on the complexity of the task.

GUIDES TO WRITING

1. Set a definite task in the stem of a multiple-choice item. The directions and clarity of the task may be checked by covering the alternatives and reading the stem. A good stem presents a task which can be responded to without seeing the distracters.

Example

__(C)__   **Who was the first president of the United States?**

     A. John Adams
     B. Thomas Jefferson
     C. George Washington
     D. James Madison

This example provides a definite task by the question presented. Suppose the stem read, "The first president was" or "Who was the first president?" The reader immediately wonders, president of what, and the task will not stand alone without the alternatives. The stem could refer to the president of the local bank, civic organization, or one of several other possibilities. On the other hand, there is no doubt concerning the presidency referred to in the example above. Based on the age and intellectual level of students, the question presented in the stem should be answerable without seeing the alternatives. In other words, students should be able to respond without having alternatives available if the item stem is appropriately presented. When a student can respond without seeing the alternatives, the item would be similar to either a completion item (incomplete stem) or a short-answer item (stem as a question).

2. When the item is presented in statement form, the alternatives should finish an incomplete sentence. Time is lost if the student must read the stem again and again.

Example A

_____ **The _____ is a device to measure specific gravity of liquids.** **(poor item)**

    A. dosimeter
    B. barometer
    C. hydrometer
    D. manometer

A student reading example A does not find the task presented directly, and there is a tendency to reread each alternative into the item until the best response is located. In many cases the four alternatives are read into the statement before the response is selected. Presenting the task as in example B eliminates this situation.

Example B

_(C)_ **A device used to measure specific gravity of liquids is called a**

    A. dosimeter.
    B. barometer.
    C. hydrometer.
    D. manometer.

3. Avoid repeating words in the alternatives. Words repeated in the alternatives should be included in the stem of the item.

Example A

_____ Which of the following best summarizes "I Hear America Singing?" (poor item)

A. The greatness of America is in its industrial strength combined with an adequate labor force.
B. The greatness of America is in the recognition of the individual's abilities.
C. The greatness of America is the individual's working independently and yet harmoniously.
D. The greatness of America is in each individual's appropriate work choice.

Example B

(C) In Walt Whitman's "I Hear America Singing," the greatness of America is summarized by

A. its industrial strength combined with an adequate labor force.
B. the recognition of the individual's abilities.
C. individuals working independently and yet harmoniously.
D. each individual's choice of work.

A comparison of examples A and B illustrates that attention is clearly directed to the alternatives by reducing the wording in each alternative. The readability of the alternatives is also improved.

4. The use of negative words and wording is to be avoided in the stem and alternatives. If a negative word is necessary, it should be emphasized by underlining or capitalizing all letters of the word.

Example A

_____ Which of the following is not always compatible with automobile safety? (poor item)

A. four-wheel brakes
B. safety glass
C. power
D. dual brake system

The item could better be presented as follows:

Example B

(C) All of the following are compatible with automobile safety EXCEPT

A. four-wheel drive.
B. safety glass.
C. power.
D. dual brake system.

Students can easily overlook words such as *no* and *not* in the stem of an item. The use of a negative word usually does not reinforce what students are to learn.

5. Alternatives in each item should be about the same length. When qualifying a correct alternative, it may become longer than the distracters, which may be a signal to the alert student that the long alternative is likely to be the correct response.

Example A

_____ **In the poem Hardy seems to be saying that men**
                                              (poor item)

    A. in death are the same as men in life.
    B. display courage in war.
    C. still wage senseless wars as they did in prehistoric times, early history, and modern times.
    D. wage war in Christ's name.

Example B

_____ **The line "if death is the loser and life is the winner"**
suggests that   **(poor item)**

    A. beggars are poor in every respect.
    B. love is dead for the speaker.
    C. life is a continual process that is always renewed.
    D. lazy creatures have no wisdom.

In each example, A and B, the longest alternative is the best response. Students tend to select more detailed responses which are longer alternatives if they do not readily know the answer.

6. All alternatives should be parallel with the stem.

Example A

_____ **An automobile coil can be used**   **(poor item)**

    A. to charge the battery.
    B. to increase the voltage of electric current.
    C. it cools the ignition system.
    D. delivering the current to spark plugs.

Both alternatives C and D are eliminated from being the correct response because they are not parallel with the stem. This can be corrected by rewriting the item with all alternatives parallel as shown in Example B.

Example B

__(B)__ **What is the purpose of the automobile coil?**

    A. charge the battery
    B. increase the voltage of electric current
    C. cool the ignition system
    D. deliver the current to the spark plugs

7. Include only one clearly best or correct response. Authorities on the subject content should agree on the keyed response.

Example A

_____ **What borders Ohio on the north?**   (poor item)

    A. Michigan
    B. The Ohio River
    C. Indiana
    D. Lake Erie

In example A it is impossible to identify a best response or to fully understand the task, let alone obtain agreement on a response. If the item were written as follows, agreement could be reached concerning the best response.

Example B

__(A)__ **The northern border of Ohio is also the southern border of what state?**

    A. Michigan
    B. Indiana
    C. Kentucky
    D. Pennsylvania

8. Eliminate verbal clues to the correct alternative or a clue which could eliminate one or more alternatives. Students not knowing the correct response may be able to respond correctly to the item by finding a clue in the stem or alternatives.

Example

_____ **If a trucking firm wants to increase its cross-country shipping rates, which of the following commissions has the job of approving or disapproving the rate increase?**   (poor item)

    A. Federal Communications Commission
    B. Securities and Exchange Commission
    C. Federal Aviation Administration
    D. Interstate Commerce Commission

The step specifies that the response is a "commission" and alternative C, "Federal Aviation Administration," is eliminated as a plausible response since it is not a commission. In addition, the words *securities and exchange* in alternative B in relationship to the stem are verbal clues which eliminate them as plausible. The word *commerce* in alternative D may be a clue that D is the correct response.

9. All alternatives should be plausible. Unknowing students should select each distracter an equal number of times. The example in number 8, above, illustrates an item in which some alternatives are not plausible. Another example follows:

Example

_____ **A person's health is influenced by all of the following EXCEPT** (poor item)

    A. environment.
    B. lack of organized sports.
    C. heredity.
    D. emotional reactions.

Option B is not homogeneous with the other alternatives provided and may give an unknowing student a clue to the correct response. The more homogeneous the alternatives the better the distracters serve to discriminate between knowing and unknowing students.

10. When possible, avoid using "all of the above" as an alternative. When "all of the above" is the correct response, students feel that they have been penalized for choosing any of the other correct alternatives without being given credit for a correct response. If this type of item is used, it would be better to have the first alternative presented as "all of the below" or "all of the following," which focuses attention on the possibility of more than one response being correct.

Example A

_____ **Which would be another name for 7?** (poor item)

    A. 5 + 2
    B. 15 − 8
    C. (4 + 5) − 2
    D. all of the above

For this item the student may recognize that alternative A is correct and make that response without continuing.

If the keyed response is D, then the student would be marked incorrect for what was indeed a correct response. The student can be alerted to the possibility of more than one correct answer in the alternatives by presentation as in example B. If "all of the below" is used, it should be used when it is not a correct choice as well as when it is a correct choice so as not to give a clue to it always being correct.

Example B

(A)   **Which would be another name for 7?**

     A. all of the below
     B. $5 + 2$
     C. $15 - 8$
     D. $(4 + 5) - 2$

Example C

(C)   **Which would be another name for 7?**

     A. all of the below
     B. $(4 + 5) - 3$
     C. $(5 + 6) - 4$
     D. $(6 + 6) - 3$

11. Place alternatives in a vertical list to allow students to clearly compare and study the options. The following example has the alternatives arranged to follow the stem in a continuous line (tandem).

Example A

_____ **Ranchers sometimes supply food to their cattle during the winter by (A) carrying hay to them by airplane, (B) feeding them in the barn, (C) shipping them to farms in the North Central Plains, (D) driving them southward to warmer regions.**   **(poor item)**

Example B demonstrates the difference in readability between the tandem and vertical arrangement of alternatives.

Example B

(A)   **How do ranchers sometimes supply food to their cattle during the winter?**

     A. carrying hay to them by airplane
     B. feeding them in the barn
     C. shipping them to farms in the North Central Plains
     D. driving them southward to warmer regions

12. If possible, write the stem as a question which helps to clearly set the task. The question is usually advantageous, although it may be necessary to write a stem in statement form when it can be presented more simply, directly, and briefly.

13. Randomly position the correct response so that each alternative is utilized approximately the same number of times. In utilizing each position, care should be given to a random assignment avoiding a pattern which the alert student could detect.

14. Four or five alternatives theoretically help reliability. As the number of alternatives is reduced, the chance of guessing the correct response increases. Practical considerations, such as the age of students, the content, and the time available for testing, may determine the number of alternatives feasible for a particular test. Three alternatives are commonly used with students in the first, second, and third grades.

15. Use "none of the above" as an alternative sparingly. When the directions specify that a correct response should be chosen, "none of the above" can be used if there is not a correct answer given in the other alternatives. "None of the above" can be used for answers to mathematics problems so that a student who gets an answer other than those given has a place to mark without being given a clue about the correctness of his/her solution. "None of the above" is also used in spelling tests that use the multiple-choice format.

16. Avoid trickery in items. Words with multiple meanings, misspelled words, or phrases foreign to students are not consistently interpreted and should be avoided. Anything extraneous which causes a knowing student to miss the item is not only unfair to the student but also affects the reliability and validity of the test.

17. Check "GUIDES TO CONSTRUCTION" on page 61.

EXEMPLARY ITEMS

The following items are intended to provide models which reflect the suggestions about how to construct items. No attempt has been made to cover all grades or subject areas.

Elementary School Subjects

1. (B)   What is the name of the grassland on which animals graze in the West?
           A. the prairies   C. the dust bowl
           B. the range   D. a farm

2. (C)   Where was the first permanent English settlement in the New World?
           A. Plymouth   C. Jamestown
           B. Boston   D. Annapolis

3. (A)   What is a man who plays a guitar called?
           A. musician   C. gambler
           B. dancer   D. magician

4. (A)   In what year did the first successful flight of an airplane occur?
           A. 1901   C. 1913
           B. 1903   D. 1928

5. (D)   What does an astronomer study?
           A. plants   C. history
           B. music   D. stars

Secondary School Subjects

1. (D)   In a gasoline engine where is the air mixed with gasoline?
           A. distributor   C. intake manifold
           B. cylinder   D. carburetor

2. (B)   What principle demonstrates that the work done in rubbing your hands together is equivalent to the amount of heat produced?
           A. inertia   C. conservation of energy
           B. kinetic energy   D. relativity

3. (D)   What is a lead storage battery made up of?
           A. lead and lead dioxide
           B. sulfuric acid and lead
           C. graphite, lead, and sulfuric acid
           D. lead dioxide, lead, and sulfuric acid

4. (C)   What is the critic's most important element in an objective critical review?
           A. personal opinions
           B. style in writing
           C. standards for judging the work
           D. education and professional experience

5. (C)   The violin, viola, cello, double bass, and harp are members of what musical family?
           A. percussion   C. string
           B. woodwind   D. brass

Matching Items

The matching item consists of a list of premises in one column and a list of possible responses in another column. The two lists of terms and/or phrases are arranged in parallel columns with the premise on the left and the responses on the right. The directions instruct the student to make an association or connection between pairs of elements, such as countries with capitals, events with dates, names of individuals with accomplishments, and so on. The nature of the matching item adapts itself to testing knowledge of names, events, conditions, places, structures, and such when recall of facts is important.

Matching items are useful in measuring students' ability to make associations, discern relationships, make interpretations, or measure knowledge of a series of facts. Many varieties of homogeneous classes are ideally suited for measurement by this type of item. Adaptations of two lists allow the principle of matching a set of responses to a set of premises to be used widely in many subject areas. For example, in geography or history, places can be marked on a map to serve as premises and students asked to associate a name from a given list for each place marked.

SPECIAL CONSIDERATIONS

When choosing the most appropriate item-type to call forth particular student behavior, the teacher must consider the following advantages and limitations of the matching item.

Advantages

1. Matching items allow for a large quantity of associated factual material to be measured in a small amount of space while student time needed to respond is relatively short. For example, a matching item of eight related terms or phrases may be utilized to measure the same things that eight multiple-choice items could measure. The amount of space necessary for the eight multiple-choice items is at least double that required of the matching item to measure the same learning.

2. The effects of guessing are reduced since the student will have one chance out of the number of responses available of guessing correctly. If all responses represent plausible options for each premise, then blind guessing should be reduced to a minimum.

Limitations

1. There may be a tendency to use materials of little importance just to be able to construct a matching item. The item writer should use this type of item only when significant pairs of elements can be identified.
2. The item mainly measures factual information which is based on memorization. The item writer's careful attention to item writing can avoid the pitfall of overemphasizing factual memory.

GUIDES TO WRITING

1. The premises and responses should be as homogeneous as possible. When a matching item deals with one area, each response acts as a plausible option for each item. Heterogeneous premises and responses provide an opportunity to arrive at responses based upon association. Superficial knowledge of a subject area may also provide sufficient background to arrive at the correct response if differences limit the possible responses for each premise.

Example A

Directions: For each name in column I, find the achievement in column II and place the letter on the line provided. Each achievement in column II is used one time or not at all. (poor item)

Column I Name	Column II Achievement
_____ 1. Thomas Edison	A. Chief Justice
_____ 2. John Marshall	B. novels
_____ 3. Eugene O'Neill	C. cotton gin
_____ 4. Carl Sandburg	D. aviation
_____ 5. Eli Whitney	E. electric light bulb
_____ 6. Orville Wright	F. poems
	G. plays
	H. paintings

Example A does not have homogeneous content in the strict sense, since the names include inventors, a government official, and men of the arts. The achievement column is heterogeneous, and some students can easily identify the achievements by areas which limits the name(s) that would fit the grouping by specialty. A matching item could be constructed for each of the categories or fields of endeavor if the subject content would lend itself to such an arrangement. One matching item could be as follows:

Example B

Directions: For each inventor listed in column I, find his invention in column II and place the letter on the line provided. Each invention in column II is used one time or not at all.

	Column I Inventor	Column II Invention
(D)	1. Thomas Edison	A. cotton gin
(E)	2. Robert Fulton	B. telegraph
(F)	3. Cyrus McCormick	C. air flight
(B)	4. Samuel Morse	D. electric light bulb
(A)	5. Eli Whitney	E. steamboat
(C)	6. Orville Wright	F. mechanical reaper
		G. air brake
		H. telephone

In Example B, each list is homogeneous, which meets the specification that premises and responses be homogeneous. Alphabetize for further improvement.

2. Arrange the lists of premises and responses logically.

Example

Directions: On the line to the left of each state listed in column I, write the letter of the capital city in column II. Each capital city will be used once or not at all.

	Column I States	Column II Capital Cities
(A)	7. Georgia	A. Atlanta
(G)	8. Illinois	B. Annapolis
(D)	9. Indiana	C. Columbus
(B)	10. Maryland	D. Indianapolis
(E)	11. Michigan	E. Lansing
(C)	12. Ohio	F. Richmond
		G. Springfield

This example exhibits the convenience in locating a response when, in this situation, the premises and responses are listed in alphabetical order. Other arrangements may be by order of dates on numerical sequence.

3. Keep the list of premises and responses to a maximum of twelve items. Five to eight premises provide the most efficient item since looking for an answer in a long list of responses is time consuming. A long item can be broken into two or more separate items to be more efficient.

Example A
(Poor Item)

Directions: For each of the definitions in column I place a letter for a sailing term from column II. A sailing term will be used only once or not at all.

Column I Definitions	Column II Sailing Terms
_____ 1. away from the wind	A. bowsprit
_____ 2. boat carrying mail and passengers on regular schedule	B. brig
_____ 3. crane used to lower lifeboats	C. crow's nest
_____ 4. fibers of flax or hemp	D. davit
_____ 5. handle used to turn the rudder	E. forecastle
_____ 6. heavy spar projecting ahead of ship	F. galley
_____ 7. left side	G. gunwale
_____ 8. lookout's platform	H. larboard
_____ 9. right side	I. lee
_____ 10. rear of a ship's upper deck	J. male
_____ 11. sailboat having one mast	K. masthead
_____ 12. shallows	L. packet
_____ 13. sailor's quarters forward of the foremast	M. quarterdeck
_____ 14. ship's kitchen	N. rigging
_____ 15. top of a ship's mast	O. shoals
_____ 16. tackle for working masts, yards, and sails	P. sloop
_____ 17. track left by a moving ship	Q. starboard
_____ 18. upper edge of a boat's side	R. tiller
	S. tow
	T. wake

The following examples illustrate how the longer item may be divided into three separate items with a logical grouping.

Example B

Directions: For each of the definitions in column I place a letter for a sailing term from column II. A sailing term will be used only once or not at all.

Column I Definitions	Column II Sailing Terms
(E) 1. boat carrying mail and passengers on regular schedule	A. bowsprit
	B. brig
(C) 2. crane used to lower lifeboats	C. davit
	D. masthead
(I) 3. fiber of flax or hemp	E. packet
(H) 4. handle used to turn the rudder	F. rigging
(A) 5. heavy spar projecting ahead of the ship	G. sloop
(G) 6. sailboat having one mast	H. tiller
(D) 7. top of ship's mast	I. tow

Column I Definitions	Column II Sailing Terms
(A) 1. lookout's platform	A. crow's nest
(E) 2. rear of a ship's upper deck	B. gunwale
(C) 3. sailor's quarters forward of the foremast	C. forecastle
(D) 4. ship's kitchen	D. galley
(F) 5. tackle for working masts, yards, and sails	E. quarterdeck
(B) 6. upper edge of a boat's side	F. rigging
	G. tow

Column I Definitions	Column II Sailing Terms
(B) 1. away from the wind	A. larboard
(A) 2. left side	B. lee
(D) 3. shallows	C. male
(E) 4. right turn	D. shoal
(F) 5. track left by a moving ship	E. starboard
	F. wake

4. Place the list with the longer words or phrases in the left hand premise column since this column is read first, then shorter responses can be surveyed for the correct match.

Example

Directions: On the line to the left of each historical event listed in column I, write the letter of the time period in column II. Any time period can be used as often as you want or not at all.

		Column I Historical Event	Column II Time Period
(C)	21.	Constitutional Convention at Philadelphia	A. 1775–1779
			B. 1780–1784
(D)	22.	Washington's Proclamation of Neutrality	C. 1785–1789
(E)	23.	Kentucky and Virginia Resolutions	D. 1790–1794
			E. 1795–1799
(A)	24.	The Second Continental Congress	
(E)	25.	Ratification of Jay's Treaty	
(C)	26.	Northwest Ordinance	
(A)	27.	Declaration of Independence	

5. When a series of multiple-choice items is being utilized to measure a homogeneous area of concern, it may be possible to avoid a series of multiple-choice items by developing a matching item.

Example A

(C) 1. What is the name of the device used to measure specific gravity of liquids?
A. dosimeter   C. hydrometer
B. barometer   D. manometer

(D) 2. What is the name of the device used to measure atmospheric pressure?
A. hydrometer   C. dosimeter
B. manometer   D. barometer

(A) 3. What is the name of the instrument used to determine the amount of heat in a substance?
A. calorimeter C. barometer
B. galvanometer D. manometer

__(D)__   4. What is the name of the instrument used to measure electric currents?
    A. calorimeter   C. radiometer
    B. photometer   D. galvanometer

__(B)__   5. What is the name of the device used to measure fluid pressure?
    A. hydrometer   C. dosimeter
    B. manometer   D. barometer

__(B)__   6. What is the name of the instrument used to study the particle nature of light energy?
    A. galvanometer   C. calorimeter
    B. radiometer   D. photometer

__(A)__   7. What is the name of the device used to measure radiation exposure of the body?
    A. dosimeter   C. barometer
    B. hydrometer   D. manometer

Example B

Directions: On the line to the left of each characteristic measured and listed in column I, write the letter of the instrument utilized in the measurement and listed in column II. Each instrument will be used once or not at all.

	Column I Characteristic Measured	Column II Instrument
__(B)__	1. amount of heat in a substance	A. barometer
__(A)__	2. atmospheric pressure	B. calorimeter
__(E)__	3. electric currents	C. closimeter
__(G)__	4. fluid pressure	D. dosimeter
__(I)__	5. particle nature of light energy	E. galvanometer
__(D)__	6. radiation exposure of the body	F. hydrometer
__(F)__	7. specific gravity of liquids	G. manometer
		H. photometer
		I. radiometer

The seven multiple-choice items included in Example A have been condensed into one matching item with seven premises and nine responses as demonstrated in Example B. Advantages of the matching item over a series of multiple-choice items in measuring homogeneous content are: (1) less space is needed to present the item, (2) less time is required in responding, and (3) the same knowledge is measured in a more efficient way.

6. Students must know the basis for establishing the rela-

tionship in a matching item. For example, when one list is inventions and the other list inventors, the directions should state this basis for responding and also indicate if responses can be used more than one time.

7. Avoid an equal number of premises and responses, which permits a one-to-one matching, since the process of elimination can lead to all correct responses if the student knows all but one response. An exception is made for primary grade students, where the premises and responses usually match one-to-one. For best discrimination there should be more plausible responses than premises. It is possible that some responses can be used twice, others not at all, or a combination of these. The directions for each item must specify that responses may be used more than once, not at all, or any other circumstances.

8. Present the entire item on one page, thus avoiding a situation where the student would have to turn the page back and forth from one part of the item to the other.

9. Label the premise column and the response column to help clarify the task. The basis for matching is emphasized and the label guides the item writer in developing homogeneity for information in each column.

10. Check "GUIDES TO CONSTRUCTION" on page 61.

EXEMPLARY ITEMS

The following items are intended to provide models which reflect the suggestions about how to construct items. No attempt has been made to cover all guides or subject areas.

Elementary School Subjects

1. Directions: Find the word in column II that matches each definition in column I. Write the letter of the vocabulary word before the definition. Each word will be used one time or not at all.

[Editor's note: Items appearing on a test should not be divided. This rule is violated here to conform to book format.]

	Column I Definition	Column II Vocabulary Word
(H)	1. an assigned job or duty	A. antic
(A)	2. a silly trick or prank	B. collide
(C)	3. join together, unite	C. combine
(B)	4. to come together with force	D. envy
(G)	5. to clean or polish by rubbing	E. fluke
(F)	6. to move slowly; fall behind	F. lag
(E)	7. a stroke of luck	G. scour
		H. task

2. Directions: Write the letter of the word from column II that has the opposite meaning of each word listed in column I. Each word in column II will be used one time or not at all.

	Column I Word	Column II Opposite
(F)	1. attract	A. insult
(D)	2. chronic	B. joyous
(E)	3. fatigued	C. plain
(A)	4. flatter	D. rare
(G)	5. lenient	E. refreshed
(C)	6. ornate	F. repel
(H)	7. rapid	G. severe
		H. slow

3. Directions: Match each health profession with its description of the duties and write the letter that corresponds to the description on duties on the line provided. Each health profession will be used one time or not at all.

	Column I Duties	Column II Health Profession
(A)	1. advises diabetic patients about menu planning	A. dietician
		B. hospital administrator
(E)	2. diagnoses and prescribes medicines	C. medical technologist
		D. pharmacist
(B)	3. directs the work of the hospital staff	E. physician
		F. psychologist
(G)	4. operates equipment that helps a doctor decide if a bone is broken	G. X-ray technologist

[See editor's note page 127.]

_(C)_ 5. performs laboratory tests used in diagnosis

_(D)_ 6. prepares medicines according to a doctor's prescription

4. **Directions:** Match each phrase in column I with the term in column II which best describes it. Each term is used one time or not at all.

Column I Phrase	Column II Term
_(G)_ 1. atoms closest together	A. compound
	B. electron
_(D)_ 2. atoms farthest apart	C. element
_(A)_ 3. different kinds of atoms	D. gas
_(B)_ 4. negative particle	E. neutron
_(E)_ 5. neutral particle	F. proton
_(C)_ 6. one kind of atom	G. solid

5. **Directions:** Read each statement carefully. Find the official of the county government listed in column I which matches each statement of duties in column II and write the letter of the official in front of the statment. Each official may be used once, twice, or not at all.

Column I Statement of Duties	Column II Official
_(D)_ 1. arrests lawbreakers	A. assessor
_(F)_ 2. collects taxes	B. auditor
_(E)_ 3. determines the boundaries of lands	C. clerk
	D. sheriff
_(B)_ 4. examines financial accounts	E. surveyor
_(C)_ 5. issues licenses and supervises elections	F. treasurer
_(D)_ 6. keeps the jail	

Secondary School Subjects

1. **Directions:** For each event listed in column I, find the name of the explorer listed in column II and place the letter on the line provided. Each name is used one time or not at all.

[See editor's note page 127.]

Column I Event	Column II Explorer
(A) 1. discovered the Pacific Ocean	A. Vasco Balboa
(H) 2. explorer for Spain whose fleet sailed around the world	B. John Cabot
(F) 3. first Englishman to sail around the world	C. Jacques Cartier
(B) 4. first sailor to plant the English flag in the New World	D. Hernando Cortez
(E) 5. first to sail around the tip of Africa	E. Bartholomeu Diaz
(G) 6. first to sail around Africa to India	F. Francis Drake
	G. Vasco da Gama
	H. Ferdinand Magellan

2. **Directions:** In the blank to the left of each painter listed in column I, write the letter of the painting listed in column II. You may use a letter in column II once or not at all.

Column I Painter	Column II Painting
(B) 1. Leonardo DaVinci	A. Central Park in Winter
(D) 2. Albrecht Durer	B. Mona Lisa
(A) 3. William James Glackens	C. Night Watch
(H) 4. Pablo Picasso	D. Praying Hands
(I) 5. Odilon Redon	E. The Apache
(C) 6. Rembrandt	F. The Gleaners
(G) 7. Johannes Vermeer	G. The Letter
	H. The Lovers
	I. Vase of Flowers

3. **Directions:** In the blank before each life insurance phrase in column I, write the letter of the word or phrase in column II that is most closely associated with it. Each term in column II may be used once or not at all.

Column I Concepts	Column II Key Terms
(G) 1. the chance of something happening	A. annuity contract
	B. beneficiary
(E) 2. a major reason for the family wage earner to have insurance	C. cash surrender value
	D. endowment
	E. premature death
	F. premium

[See editor's note page 127.]

(H)   3. provides protec-
           tion for a specific   G. probability
           period of time
                                      H. term insurance
(I)   4. also called "per-
           manent insur-   I. whole life
           ance"

(F)   5. a dollar amount
           based upon mor-
           tality tables

(C)   6. the money the in-
           sured can get for
           the policy when
           cashed in

4. Directions: In the blank before each definition listed in
   column I, write the letter of the term used in
   recipes listed in column II. You may use a letter
   from column II once or not at all.

	Column I Definition	Column II Term
(C)	1. cut food in small cubes of uni- form size and shape	A. baste
(E)	2. work and press dough with the palm of the hands	B. caramelize C. dice
(H)	3. precook until partially done	D. dredge
(A)	4. moisten foods during cooking	E. knead
(I)	5. cook in small amount of hot fat	F. marinate
(B)	6. melt sugar slowly over low heat until it becomes brown	G. mince H. parboil
(D)	7. sprinkle or coat with flour or other fine substance	I. saute J. steep

Classification Items

The classification item consists of a list of statements or
words and a key list of categories. The two lists may be arranged in
parallel columns with the statements on the right and the categories on
the left. When set up in this manner, the classification item resembles
the matching exercise. Another type of arrangement is to place the key
list of categories above the list of statements or words. The directions
instruct the student to classify each entry of the list by recording the
letter of the category for classification. The key list of categories consists
of exhaustive classes to which the student assigns each premise.

Classification items may be more useful than matching-type
items in specific situations even though they both use a single set of
responses. In classification items a larger number of stimulus situations

can be used. Specific things to be classified consist of names, descriptive phrases, pictures, or statements, and each premise is keyed to the appropriate class to which it belongs. Classification items measure student ability to use a classification system with facility since the categories represent the larger classes and the student identifies the class to which each premise belongs. Part of almost every body of knowledge fits into some sort of classification system which must be understood in order to organize all or part of the knowledge.

SPECIAL CONSIDERATIONS

When choosing the most appropriate item-type to call forth particular student behavior, the teacher must consider the following advantages and limitations of the classification item.

Advantages

1. Classification items require a small amount of space and provide a relatively large number of scoreable units. The single set of responses (key list) is applied to a number of situations.
2. This item type requires a relatively short period of time for students to respond to each situation presented. The small number of alternatives allows for responses to be made without a time delay caused by searching through a large set of possible responses.
3. The classification item can be used to test the ability to compare and contrast through discriminative thinking. This type of item requires the student to make decisions concerning differences among similar things as well as to recognize similarities.
4. The effects of guessing are reduced since the student will have one chance out of the number of classes (alternatives) available of guessing correctly. For example, when five classes are available, the student has one chance out of five of guessing the correct response.

Limitations

1. The item mainly measures factual information, and in some instances superficial outcomes may be measured. If the material does not lend itself to a classification system, the classification item should not be used.
2. There must be enough relationship and yet differences between key words or phrases before an item can be

developed. This makes it difficult to develop classification items.

GUIDES TO WRITING

1. Each of the words or statements must definitely belong to only one class or category. For each item there can be only one correct response or class to which it belongs.

Example

Directions: Below is a list of animals doing something. Place the letter before each one that identifies the setting in which each animal is carrying out the activity. (poor item)

F—in the forest	**U—under an old log**
O—high in an oak tree	**W—in the wild grass**

      1. mouse running
      2. rabbit keeping very still
      3. bear crashing through branches
      4. bear crawling on a branch
      5. chipmunk eating acorns
      6. rabbits looking for supper
      7. snake crawling

This item does not meet the requirement of having only one correct response class for each item. For example, a mouse may be running in the forest, under a log, or in the wild grass. The class in an item should be related to all other classes but mutually exclusive. Overlapping of classes should not occur as in the example above.

2. A clear explanation of the task and classification system must be provided. Without knowledge of the relationship between the key responses students may not be able to proceed in responding to the items.
3. The number of classes should be limited to the number which can be appropriately utilized. A maximum of five classes usually makes the task and judgments needed clear in classifying each item.
4. The categories in the key list of alternatives are to be exhaustive, mutually exclusive, and yet related.
5. Check "GUIDES TO CONSTRUCTION" on page 61.

EXEMPLARY ITEMS

The following items are intended to provide models which reflect the suggestions about how to construct items. No attempt has been made to cover all guides or subject areas.

Elementary School Subjects

1. **Directions:** Below is a list of words which you are to read. If *ea* sounds like *ea* in *eat*, place an *A* before the word.
   If *ea* sounds like *ea* in gr*ea*t, place a *B* before the word.
   If *ea* sounds like *ea* in h*ea*d, place a *C* before the word.
   Use A, B, or C as many times as necessary.

	A—*eat*			B—gr*eat*			C—h*ea*d	
(A)	1.	beat	(A)	4.	cream	(A)	7.	mean
(B)	2.	break	(C)	5.	instead	(C)	8.	ready
(C)	3.	breadth	(A)	6.	leaves	(A)	9.	stream

2. **Directions:** Read each name below and place an *F* before it if it is a fruit, a *V* before it if it is a vegetable, or *FL* before it if it is a flower.

	F—Fruit			V—Vegetable			FL—Flower	
(V)	1.	celery	(FL)	4.	marigold	(F)	7.	tangerine
(F)	2.	peach	(V)	5.	turnip	(V)	8.	beet
(FL)	3.	daisy	(F)	6.	banana	(FL)	9.	petunia

3. **Directions:** The titles of the five stories in the unit are listed. Read each sentence and put in the blank the letter of the story which it tells about. Each letter may be used one time or more.

A. *Down the Mississippi*
B. *Chipmunk Goes Hunting*
C. *No, No, Rosina*
D. *Andy's Hide-Out*
E. *Grand Canyon National Park*

- (D) 1. A whole family helps a boy find a place to sleep.
- (A) 2. A boy wakes up because of a storm.
- (C) 3. Someone does what she is told she may not do.
- (E) 4. A boy decides that he will visit a big park again.
- (B) 5. A boy must wait until he is older to learn to hunt.
- (C) 6. Two brothers and a sister go crab fishing.
- (A) 7. Two brothers and a sister hear a loud sound at the door.
- (D) 8. Two sisters who are the same age know about a secret room.
- (E) 9. Mules go down into a steep, rocky place.

[See editor's note page 127.]

4. Directions: Write *N* in the blank if the word names something. Write *D* if the word tells about doing something.

Example: ____D____ running   ____N____ ball

N—names something		*D*—does something	
(N)	1. cloth	(N)	5. paper
(N)	2. glue	(D)	6. play
(D)	3. listen	(D)	7. read
(D)	4. look	(D)	8. sing

5. Directions: In the blank space write *M* before the unit of measure that is used in the metric system. Write *E* if it is used in the English system.

M—Metric		*E*—English	
(M)	1. centimeter	(M)	7. liter
(M)	2. gram	(E)	8. mile
(E)	3. foot	(M)	9. millimeter
(E)	4. inch	(E)	10. pint
(M)	5. kilogram	(E)	11. pound
(M)	6. kilometer	(E)	12. yard

Secondary School Subjects

1. Directions: Each of the following scientific laws or principles is attributed to particular scientists. Write the letter that represents the scientist and the law or principle connected with him in the provided space. Use each name as many times as necessary.

A—Newton's law of gravity
B—Dalton's atomic theory
C—Boyle's law
D—Beroulli's principle

(A)	1. The force of attraction increases as the mass of the objects increases.
(A)	2. The force of attraction decreases as the center of the mass of the object is approached.
(B)	3. Each different kind of atom represents a different element.
(B)	4. The atoms of different elements differ in mass.
(C)	5. The volume of a dry gas varies inversely with the pressure on it, provided the temperature remains constant.
(D)	6. Air pressure decreases as the velocity of the gas increases.

[See editor's note page 127.]

2. **Directions:** Below is a list of kinds of musical instruments. Read each one and write the *B, P, S,* or *W* according to the following classification:

B—Brass		*S*—Strings	
P—Percussion		*W*—Woodwinds	
(B)	1. trumpet	(S)	6. bass
(P)	2. tambourine	(B)	7. tuba
(S)	3. cello	(P)	8. bells
(W)	4. clarinet	(P)	9. snare
(S)	5. guitar		drums
		(W)	10. saxo-phone

3. **Directions:** For each of the phrases listed below, write the letter for the property which is described in each phrase.

    A—Acids   *B*—Bases   *S*—Salts

(B)	1. change red litmus to blue
(A)	2. have a sour taste
(S)	3. are compounds containing a metal and a negative ion
(A)	4. change blue litmus to red
(B)	5. feel slippery or soapy to the touch
(B)	6. have a bitter taste
(A)	7. have a corrosive action on metal
(S)	8. gives a tang or piquancy to anything

4. **Directions:** The listed crops are produced in one or more of the three regions listed. On the line before each crop place the letter where each crop is produced. You may use a letter more than one time.

    A—The Choa Phraya Valley
    B—The Northern *Central* Plains
    C—The Northern *Great* Plains

(B)	1. corn
(C)	2. flax
(A)	3. rice
(C)	4. sorghum
(C)	5. spring wheat

5. **Directions:** Indicate the correct method of spelling the plural form of each of the following words. Use the following code system and record *A, B,* or *C* on the line provided.

[See editor's note page 127.]

A—add *s* **B—add** *es* **C—change** *y* **to** *i* **and add** *es*

(A)	1. epic	(A)	6. siren
(B)	2. bus	(B)	7. birch
(A)	3. alley	(B)	8. thrush
(A)	4. highway	(C)	9. comedy
(C)	5. enemy	(C)	10. beauty

Other Types of Items

The discussion of problem-, supply-, and selection-type items has dealt with what are considered to be standard and traditional approaches to writing items for paper-and-pencil tests. There are several other forms and variations of test items which in most instances consist of combinations or variations of the items previously presented in this book. Many of the variations and combinations of the basic types of test items have come about through the efforts of writers and publishers of textbooks for the elementary grades to create appropriate tasks for instructional materials.

Special attention at the elementary school level reveals a multiplicity of skill handbooks, workbooks, worksheets and similar materials being utilized daily in the classroom. Although these achievement-oriented materials may not be specifically labeled as tests, they are used extensively in guiding student learning and the instructional program. Most teachers realize that the materials are used differently by different teachers, but in final analysis the tasks included in workbooks are the same or similar to the types of items used in any testing carried out by the classroom teacher. *In reality many students feel that they are being tested daily.* Daily worksheets are used by teachers, who score and return them to students, as indicators of student progress in learning and, hence, achievement. Teachers summarize student achievement and progress for parents during parent-teacher conferences and through pages from workbooks and similar materials carried home by students. A teacher may require each child to return a response sheet weekly from the parent indicating that the worksheets arrived home safely and were reviewed. Additional information and comments may be supplied by either or both teacher or parent.

Looking at the worksheets and related materials used in the school classroom, one becomes aware of the diversity of kinds of instructional materials being introduced to students. Since these materials contain the traditional types of test items discussed in this text as well as the numerous variations of these items, they are worthy of mention and concern in regard to their use and quality. Some teachers use these worksheets as part of the evaluation process including assignment of marks.

Whether teachers write their own worksheets or use professionally prepared materials, they must be cognizant of the impact of these materials upon teaching, learning, and student achievement. Therefore, these materials should be evaluated as carefully as the classroom teacher's achievement tests which are to be administered to students. Planning worksheets and similar materials is as important as test planning, particularly in those situations where the materials are heavily relied upon in the teaching-learning process and evaluation.

Worksheets and workbooks are also used in junior and senior high schools, but on a much smaller scale. Some students may never see another workbook after the elementary years. Although students may not be required to purchase workbooks, they are available in most subject areas. Many of these are marketed as self-help approaches or programmed approaches to learning, and each focuses attention to a particular subject area.

The elementary-level skill booklets are claimed to be an important and integral part of the instructional program. Each page of the booklet is designed to strengthen and extend the skills important in instruction and learning. Evaluation pages are strategically located to help the teacher assess strengths and weaknesses in the skill areas taught at specific points in the program. The entire booklet is usually meant to be used diagnostically. One skills handbook selected at random for a third-grade reading book contained color-coded pages to indicate types of lessons being stressed. For example, page numbers outlined in blue dealt with comprehension, red for creativity, gray for evaluation, and so on. On each work page the skill and activities involved with that page are specified; for example, for a page devoted to organizational skill, classifying words into categories, inferential comprehension, and understanding related concepts would be listed. As the following examples are reviewed, the reader should reflect on earlier discussions about problem-, supply-, and selection-type items in this chapter and in chapters 4 and 5.

Example A

Directions: Put an *X* before the word or group of words that best completes each of the following sentences.

A "doctor's right hand" is the
	homemaker health aid.
X	registered nurse (R.N.).
	dental hygienist.

[See editor's note page 127.]

Example B

Directions: **Underline the word or phrase that best fits the missing part in each of the sentences below.**

Far-sighted people see close objects _____
poorly   not at all   clearly

Example C

Directions: **Underline the correct response.**

The largest United States agency is
FDA   HEW   WHO

Example D

Directions: **Select the word or phrase needed to make the statement true. Underline the word or words selected and write the letter which comes before it in the blank.**

__(B)__   Grouping certain tones of a song together is called?
A. the melody
B. phrasing
C. the pitch

Example E

Directions: **Underline the word that fits in each sentence.**

Did the bear _____ for the missing acorn?
search   earth   earn

Examples A through E illustrate only a few of the ways in which the basic multiple-choice type item may be altered to break the monotony that would occur in the elementary grades when students are responding to workbook items daily. Opportunities are provided when other item types are used to expose students to reading and understanding varied directions. Junior and senior high school students probably will not use workbooks and the types of items they are exposed to in testing follow standard item formats.

The alternate response item provides the student with the opportunity to respond one way or the other. The true-false item is an alternate response item. Example A, below, allows students to respond to whether or not the phrase sounds right or strange. Example B combines the "yes" and "no" response with another type of task.

Example A

Directions: **Put an *X* in the blank if the phrase sounds right. Write *O* if it seems strange.**

[See editor's note page 127.]

X	1. dinner at dinnertime
O	2. lunch at breakfast
X	3. put dinner on the table
O	4. put lunch on your shirt

Example B

Directions: Read the question and underline any words that have the letter *g* standing for the same sound as *g* in *gem*. Then answer the question by writing *X* for yes, and *O* for no.

1. Does a giant live in your house?	O
2. Does a cow eat grass?	X
3. Can basketball be played in a gym?	X
4. Are most dogs gentle?	X

ARRANGEMENT ITEMS

Arrangement items ask the student to put the words, phrases, or sentences in a prescribed order. The arrangement may be alphabetical, chronological, or sequential in nature. Examples A and B illustrate the use of this type of item in study of the dictionary with young students. The arrangement type of item is also useful in mathematics and related areas in sequencing of numbers as illustrated in Example C.

Example A

Directions: Put the list of words below in alphabetical order.

toy   cat   house   milk   apple

Example B

Directions: Put the list of words below in alphabetical order by their second letter.

fish   fun   flower   feed

Example C

Directions: Arrange the following fractions in order according to size from the smallest to the largest.

$\frac{2}{3}$ $\frac{5}{6}$ $\frac{1}{2}$ $\frac{1}{4}$ $\frac{3}{8}$ $\frac{5}{16}$

The next example, D, may be used to study the calendar, particularly the order of the months of the year.

Example D

Directions: Number the following list of months of the year in chronological order beginning with the month of January.

[See editor's note page 127.]

_____	April	_____	December	_____	August
_____	July	_____	November	1	January
_____	March	_____	June	_____	February
_____	October	_____	September	_____	May

Example E relates the sequential process in cell division or reproduction in the subject of biology, health, or a related subject.

Example E

Directions: **The sequence of events in the continuous process of mitosis is separated into five distinct phases. On the line before each phase place the number which indicates its place in the process.**

_____	anaphase	_____	interphase	_____	metaphase
_____	prophase	_____	telephase		

Example F

Directions: **Rearrange the following planets according to their distances from the earth, starting with the one that is nearest to the earth.**

Mars	**Venus**	**Saturn**	**Jupiter**
Mercury	**Uranus**	**Pluto**	**Neptune**

Examples A through F illustrate the use which can be made of arrangement-type items. Examples A and B are useful in determining students' understanding of alphabetical ordering which is a skill necessary for use of the dictionary and textbooks. Example C illustrates the use of this type of item in understanding the concept of fraction size. Examples D, E, and F show other possible uses. These examples show how the arrangement item may be used to measure understanding of sequence, relationship, or order.

PUZZLES

The puzzle type of item requires the student to read a word, phrase, number, or sentence and then supply the appropriate word, which is usually in the form of a term that fits into the number of spaces allocated. One type of puzzle lists definitions for each number of spaces across the page and definitions for each number of spaces down the page, as in Example A.

Example A

Directions: **Write the definition that matches each phrase for the number of squares across and down.**

[See editor's note page 127.]

Down 1—part of a rocket in which men ride
2—a person who travels in a spaceship
3—a machine which lifts up and down

Across 4—a ship with a large flat deck
5—the action of a rocket as it rises into the air
6—an airtight suit that protects the astronaut
7—a short name for liquid oxygen

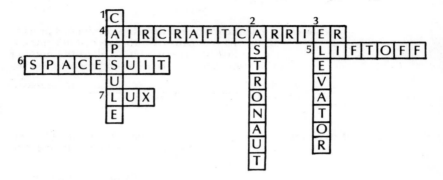

Example B

Directions: Write the letter *dr* or *gl* in the spaces in the puzzle. The sentences will help you decide which letters are correct. Write the correct words in the sentences too.

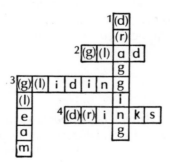

Across

2. Miss Jones was _____ (glad) _____ to hear that Jeff would be coming back to her school.
3. Everyone watched Jack as he went _____ (gliding) _____ across the ice.
4. Kim _____ (drinks) _____ four glasses of milk each day.

[See editor's note page 127.]

Down
1. The dog next door was _____ (dragging) _____
   a branch across the back yard.
3. There was a _____ (gleam) _____ in Tom's eyes.

Example C

Directions: Use the letters at the left and right of the symbols *or* to make as many English words as possible. Write the words below.

w	– or –	ch
th	– or –	k
f	– or –	d
p	– or –	t
h	– or –	n
st	– or –	m
t	– or –	
c	– or –	
b	– or –	

Example: **porch**

Example D

Directions: Use the weekly spelling list to see how many words you can find. Mark the words going across in blue and those going up and down in red. Two words have been done for you.

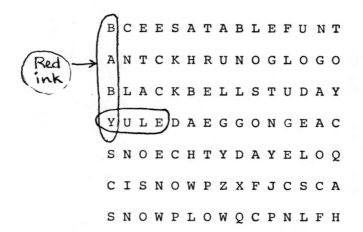

Words to be found:

ant	baby	black	bells	day
egg	fun	gong	log	plow
snow	table	toy	tree	yule

Examples C and D are adaptations of the crossword puzzle. Many variations of this type of exercise are possible, and the type of variation depends on the ingenuity of the teacher. This type of item would be used sparingly in a test situation since it is difficult to construct the item to relate closely to the unit of instruction as well as provide meaningful information for measurement.

INTERPRETATION

Interpretation items use visuals such as maps, laboratory equipment, transparencies, slides, and drawings as the basis for the items to be presented on a test. For example, a teacher may pass around the room leaves with identification numbers or letters and ask each student to identify each leaf by writing its name on the appropriate line with the corresponding letter or number. A teacher may have pictures of the same leaves and project them on a screen and have students write down the correct names. Either of these approaches uses an interpretation item.

Example A

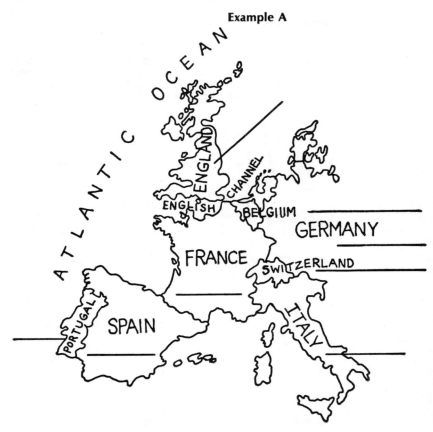

1. Draw a circle around the name of all countries shown on the map.
2. Write the capital of each country on the map in the space provided.
3. Print the directions on the map (north, south, west, and east).
   [Students could be asked to write the names of the countries and the capitals of each or many other alternatives, such as the identification of cities, natural resources, etc.]

Example B

In a physical science class the teacher dissolves a sample of sodium chloride in about 10 ml of water and asks the class to describe the solution. A sample of silver nitrate is dissolved in 10 ml of water, and the class is asked to describe the solution. The two solutions are then mixed together and the students observe and describe the changes that occur.

Example C

In an English class a group of students acts out part of a story or play, and the class is asked to interpret what they have viewed and describe the plot.

Technically the interpretation item is usually a hands-off type of experience where the student sees something and responds as directed, but with maps, globes, and other teaching instruments they may be able to touch the item as well as write down the information requested.

ANALOGY

Analogy items require students to recognize the relationship between two words. A third word is supplied, and the student must provide the fourth word which establishes the same analogy as between the first and second words.

Example A

Directions: Each of the following items consists of a pair of words having a certain relationship to each other. The third word provided relates to a word which you are to provide in the same relationship as in the first pair. Place your word on the line provided.

1. jail: crime as cemetery: _____

An alternative form of this item may be set up as follows, which provides a multiple-choice response.

Jail is to crime as

A. judge is to criminal.
B. cemetery is to death.
C. prison is to thief.
D. freedom is to bird.

Example B

Directions: In the following items the first three words are provided, and you are to supply the fourth word, which is in the same relationship as the first pair of words.

1. **Cherry is to radish as apricot is to**
   _____(carrot)_____ .
2. **Inch is to foot as rod is to**
   _____(mile)_____ .
3. **Inventory is to merchandise as house is to**
   _____(furniture)_____ .
4. **Father is to brother as mother is to**
   _____(sister)_____ .
5. **4 is to 16 as 8 is to**
   _____(64)_____ .

In this discussion of other types of items a few examples of the combinations and variations of traditional test items have been given, and four additional item types—arrangement, puzzles, interpretations, and analogies—are illustrated. Which item is used depends on what information is to be collected and the characteristics of the item to do particular things. Decide what kind of information is needed and then choose the proper item type.

Selection as an Objective

Instructional activities are designed to prepare students to function in the modern world. At all ages we must make choices from two or more alternatives—situations, persons, ways of proceeding, and such. In today's media-intensive world we are increasingly being called on to make rational choices from sets of alternatives. For example, the medium of TV bombards the listener with advertising which requires him/her to bring to bear all skills of choice making to sift through the ad makers' pitches.

The game of chess could be viewed as a series of multiple-choice selections. Each time it becomes a player's turn to move, s/he must select from a finite number of possibilities. Some moves are better than other moves. The winner is conceivably the better alternative selector. Many people consider selection-type test items as apt metaphors for the "game of life."

The component of intelligent choice making is implied or stated in most lists of broad educational goals. If students are to be prepared to make intelligent choices, then the school program should have a component devoted to developing this skill.

With intelligent selection of choices receiving this attention in goal statements and programs, use of selection-type items in tests can support the instructional program. The selection-type item as used in tests provides a direct opportunity for a teacher to integrate the school program and testing activities. As the student becomes more skillful in making choices in the testing situation, teachers (as well as other concerned individuals) can assume that the student's ability to use this skill in the real world has improved. Skill in choosing developed in the school program should prepare students better to make rational choices presently and in later life.

7 Test Appraisal

Analysis of test results is an important part of a classroom testing program. Test appraisal aids the teacher in improving skill in testing by identifying where s/he has been successful or unsuccessful in fulfilling the requirements of good testing. By analyzing the difficulty, discrimination, balance, specificity, and objectivity of the tests s/he writes, a teacher can improve his/her test-writing skill. Since each of these test characteristics contributes to the degree of validity assigned to the test results, the higher each characteristic rates with ideal standards, the higher the validity and, thus, the more successful the test. The usefulness of a classroom test in measuring student achievement rests in how successful it was in carrying out its intended purpose. Test appraisal assesses how well the test was built and how well it did what it was supposed to do.

Test appraisal is intended to answer two questions about test construction:

1. How effective was each item in supporting the purpose of this testing?
2. How well did the test do what it was supposed to do?

An answer to the first question requires statistical analysis of each test item, and an answer to the second question requires appraisal of the test as a whole. Effective appraisal of student progress requires at least minimal statistical data about the quality of test items as well as other information about how well the test met other criteria established for good tests.

Different kinds of tests have different emphases and, thus, require different standards. Application of guidelines and procedures for assessing test quality can provide information which allows the teacher to determine instructional success and levels of student learning. Balance, specificity, and objectivity are important characteristics for both criterion-referenced tests and norm-referenced tests. Difficulty and discrimination levels are more important for norm-referenced tests than they are for criterion-referenced tests.

The thrust to make testing a part of learning activities is common to both criterion-referenced and norm-referenced tests. It is doubtful that much learning takes place during a test session itself; however, a review of test items after the test administration allows students to clarify important points and to learn those concepts they failed to understand at the time of testing. The post-test session can be especially productive if the teacher analyzes the student responses before the discussion period and directs the session as an instructional activity.

A teacher's formal appraisal of a test should lead to better future tests as s/he uses appraisal information to refine items for future tests. Student comments about items help identify items which are, by their nature, ambiguous. In addition, comments from students may point up other weaknesses of items and help the teacher to improve them for future tests. When a teacher maintains a file of test items and item analysis results for each item, the time and effort required to build future tests can be reduced considerably. For these reasons test appraisal becomes an important component of testing and classroom procedure.

Item Analysis

After a test has been administered and scored, two important questions are in the mind of a teacher who is appraising a test to assess its ability to function as a useful measuring instrument. These questions are:

1. **What is the frequency of correct responses (and incorrect responses) associated with each multiple-choice and true-false item?**
2. **Which students responded correctly and which students responded incorrectly?**

The teacher who asks these questions seeks answers about the test's generation of acceptable difficulty and discrimination levels. The difficulty of an item can be determined by comparing the percentage of students who missed the item to the number of students who tried the item. Discrimination can be measured by establishing a coefficient which can be determined by comparing correct responses for a high-scoring group of students with correct responses for a low-scoring group of students.

In both cases the results for difficulty and discrimination are compared to ideal standards set for multiple choice and true-false items.

Since item analysis is used largely with norm-referenced tests, the items must support the ability of the test to scale differences in what is being measured. In other words, the test must be able to measure differences in achievement among the students being tested. The scores should be **isomorphic** to the true achievement differences found among the students. An item which nearly all of the students answer correctly can not support the scaling of the scores. On the other hand, an item which nearly all students miss can not support the scaling. In general, correct responses to an item should be about halfway between the frequency expected from **blind guessing** and the frequency of a total correct response set.

To further support the scaling feature of the test, the better students should be making correct responses while the less-able students should be missing the items. Any other combination of correct and incorrect responses will not support the scaling and can conceivably be a negative factor to the scaling if more of the less-able students get the item correct than the better students do.

Used with selection-type items, the process of item analysis provides:

1. **a measure of how difficult each item was for the students (difficulty level).**
2. **a measure of how well each item distinguished between the high- and low-scoring students (discrimination power).**
3. **for multiple-choice items, information about how effectively the alternatives in each item functioned.**

This information is important for test appraisal and test improvement since it indicates which items were: (1) too easy, (2) too difficult, (3) nondiscriminating between high- and low-scoring students, (4) in need of improvement through revision, or (5) so poor that they should be discarded. This information can also be useful in making judgments of instructional effectiveness, identification of an individual student's weaknesses, and needed remediation for a student or for the class as a whole.

ANALYSIS FOR NORM-REFERENCED TESTS

The item-analysis process allows the teacher to study how students collectively responded to each test item. First, a level of difficulty, the difficulty index P, is determined by a formula that gives a proportion of students missing an item. Second, the power of an item to separate student achievement levels, the discrimination index D, is determined by comparing the responses of high-scoring students to those of low-scoring students. If two or more classes have taken the same true-false or multiple-choice examination, then the papers for all classes can be combined for item analysis.

In order to carry out the second part of the analysis, two differing groups of papers must be selected according to total test scores. One set is selected from the papers of high-scoring students, and one set is selected from the papers of the low-scoring students. When choosing these criterion groups, the teacher should have as many papers as possible in the two groups but also have two groups that represent the opposite extremes of the attribute being measured. To maximize the combination of these two desired circumstances certain procedures are followed.

The two criterion groups are selected as follows:

1. Order the papers from lowest to highest.
2. Select the ten highest papers for the upper criterion group.
3. Select the ten lowest papers for the lower criterion group.[1]

These two groups of papers will be used to perform the item analysis. For example, if a total of forty papers were available for the item analysis, the number of papers in the high-achieving criterion group would be ten, the lower criterion group would be ten, and the middle group would be twenty. In general, the larger the middle group of omitted papers, the greater the probability that the upper and lower groups are different on the attribute being measured.

At the start of the actual process of item analysis, the middle set of papers, which will not be used, should be set aside. Next, the papers from the two criterion groups should be scanned and the numbers for student responses recorded according to the following instructions. For multiple-choice items the number of papers in the upper group which have the alternative "A" marked for the first item should be counted first. This should be done for each alternative in the first item. (In the following example: A—9, B—3, C—2, D—1). This procedure should be continued for each item for the upper group. Unanswered items (omits) are recorded separately and disregarded for analysis. The same procedure

---

[1] If there is less than a total of twenty papers, the papers may be divided into halves for item analysis. If there is an odd number of papers, omit the middle paper. For more than forty papers, select about one-fourth to one-third of the papers from the extreme ends of the ordering.

is then followed for all papers in the lower group. These data are combined on a master sheet for each multiple-choice item. For example, an item with four alternatives and fifteen papers in each of the upper and lower groups could generate the following values for item 32:

32.	option	upper group	lower group
	*A	9	3
	B	3	4
	C	2	5
	D	1	3
	Total	15	15

* Indicates the correct response

For true-false items simply count the number of papers with the correct answer in each group. The number of correct responses subtracted from the total number in both criterion groups gives the number of incorrect responses. Record as follows:

Item	Correct Response Upper	Lower	Incorrect Response Both
1	14	12	4
2	13	10	7

The count for multiple-choice items is recorded according to responses to each alternative and right and wrong responses for true-false. The collected data can be conveniently recorded on a copy of the original test as shown for multiple-choice item number 32 and true-false items 1 and 2 below:

32. **What arithmetic process should be used when deciding how many cookies each child should get when distributing twelve cookies equally among three children?**

9 3 *A. division
3 4 B. addition
2 5 C. subtraction
1 3 D. multiplication

The correct response is marked, and the number of students in the upper and lower groups who responded to each option is written in the left margin of a test copy.

14 12 4 1. **If a girl had eleven feet of fencing material, she would have enough fence to make a puppy area 6 feet long and 4 feet wide. (F)**
13 10 7 2. **A building shaped as a pentagon will have five sides. (T)**

For true-false items the numbers for correct responses of the upper and lower groups are recorded separately. The numbers for incorrect responses are recorded in a third column. Next, the percentage of students getting the item incorrect is computed.

$$P_D = \frac{N_w}{N_t}(100), \text{ where,}$$

P_D is the difficulty index
N_w is the number who got a wrong answer, and
N_t is the number who tried the item.

For item number 32 the arithmetic looks like this:

$$P_D = \frac{6+12}{30}(100) = \frac{18}{30}(100) \quad = .60(100) = 60 \text{ (or 60\%)}$$

Some procedures for item analysis use the number correct, rather than the number wrong, for the numerator of the formula. If you have occasion to use someone else's values for difficulty, check to see which formula was used. Either way can be interpreted to determine the item's difficulty, though we have chosen to use the index which is a direct measure of difficulty (P_D) rather than the other method which is really more a measure of easiness than it is of difficulty (P_E).

Finally, the discrimination index for each item is computed. The formula for determining the discriminating power of an item is:

$$D = \frac{U-L}{N}, \text{ where,}$$

D is the discrimination index
U is the number in the upper group who answered correctly
L is the number in the lower group who answered correctly
N is the number in one of the criterion groups

Using the figures in item 32, the arithmetic looks like this:

$$D = \frac{U-L}{N} = \frac{9-3}{15} = \frac{+6}{15} = +.40$$

Watch the sign of the numerator. You can have a negative value when more students in the lower group than in the upper group answered correctly. Items with negative values should receive special attention in analysis, and either should be discarded from the test-item file and further tests or be revised to accommodate for deficiencies of the items.

The formula for the discrimination index can be used in

calculating an index for distracters, which indicates how effectively each distracter is operating. For item 32 the procedure is as follows:

Option	Criterion group		D
	Upper	**Lower**	
*A	9	3	+.40
B	3	4	−.07
C	2	5	−.20
D	1	3	−.13

$$D = \frac{U - L}{N}$$

Distracter B

$$D_B = \frac{3 - 4}{15}$$

$$D_B = \frac{-1}{15}$$

$$D_B = -.07$$

Distracter C

$$D_C = \frac{2 - 5}{15}$$

$$D_C = \frac{-3}{15}$$

$$D_C = -.20$$

Distracter D

$$D_D = \frac{1 - 3}{15}$$

$$D_D = \frac{-2}{15}$$

$$D_D = -.13$$

The negative values for distracters B, C, D indicate that more low-achieving students chose each of these distracters than did the higher achieving students and that each is performing as expected. Notice also that the D-value for alternative A (the correct response) is the discriminating power of the item.

Using the values in true-false items 1 and 2, item analysis follows. For item 1 the procedure is as follows:

$$P_D = \frac{N_w}{N_t}(100) = \frac{4}{30} = 13 \qquad D = \frac{14 - 12}{15} = \frac{2}{15} = +.13$$

For item number 2 the procedure is as follows:

$$P_D = \frac{7}{30}(100) = 23 \qquad D = \frac{13 - 10}{15} = \frac{3}{15} = +.20$$

The procedure for item analysis can be summarized as follows:

1. **Order the scored papers from high to low by total scores.**
2. **Choose the number of papers for criterion groups.**
3. **Count the number of responses marked for each alternative.**
4. **Record the data from the student responses.**
5. **Determine: a difficulty index for each item.**
6. **Determine: a discrimination index for each item.**
7. **Measure the effectiveness of the distracters of multiple-choice items.**

Difficulty

The difficulty of a test item is measured by the number of students in the two criterion groups who missed the item compared to the number who tried the item. The greater the percentage of students who missed the item, the more difficult that item was for that administration of the test. If the item were presented to another class or some other group of students, the difficulty level would be expected to change since the difficulty depends on the proportion of students who missed the item. When a test item is answered correctly by nearly all students, the difficulty index is close to zero. When a test item is answered correctly by only the number expected to get the item correct by blind guessing, the difficulty index is close to a chance value.

In most testing situations the teacher has the option of choosing how difficult the items will be. To avoid either of the extreme conditions, test makers write items for a norm-referenced test so that items have a medium difficulty level. An item is classified as being of medium difficulty if the proportion of students answering incorrectly is about halfway between a chance value and the point where no student misses the item.

The difficulty index can range from zero (0) to one hundred (100). For item number 32 the data gave a difficulty index of 60 (60 percent of the students missed the item). The ideal difficulty index for all four-alternative multiple-choice items is 37 to 38, a value halfway between 0 and 75 (expected from chance selection). An item with a difficulty index less than 37 is easier than desired, while an item with a difficulty index greater than 38 is more difficult than desired. An item which has another number of alternatives has a different ideal difficulty level.

No teacher expects to get an ideal value for difficulty for each item, but values are expected to fall within a range of desirable values. For four-alternative multiple-choice items the teacher would set the desirable range of about 25 to 50 as target values and would attempt to write four-choice items to generate difficulty indexes within that range.

How should the difficulty index of 60 for item 32 be interpreted? Since 60 percent of the students answered incorrectly, the item is somewhat more difficult than the maximum of 50 percent that the teacher set as the limit for maximum difficulty. Perhaps the item should be written so it would be somewhat easier next time it is used. The fact that the item is somewhat more difficult than expected does not cause us to interpret the item as a poor item since the discrimination index must also be considered. If the discrimination index is satisfactory, then the teacher may not want to change the item. Administration to other groups may give a better idea about how the item will function in general. Use on other tests may result in more favorable outcomes in regard to difficulty and discrimination.

Medium difficulty level for true-false items is 25, the point halfway between a perfect response rate of 0 and chance level of 50. The range of desirable P values for true-false items is from about 20 to 35. The percentage of incorrect responses to true-false items is, in general, smaller than the percentage of incorrect responses to multiple-choice items.

Discrimination

The discrimination index measures how well a test item identifies differences in achievement levels of students. Since the purpose of testing with a norm-referenced test is to place a student's achievement on a scale, the discrimination index provides important information for test appraisal. A test of highly discriminating items is able to distinguish levels of achievement and will rate high in reliability.

The discrimination index can take values from −1.00 to +1.00. The higher the D value, the better the item separated high-achieving from low-achieving students. The difficulty level of an item can limit the value of the discrimination index. The highest possible D value can occur only when exactly half of the students in the criterion groups miss the item, and that 50 percent must be the low criterion group. As P values move away from 50, the maximum possible D value is no longer +1.00. Since a P value of 50 for a true-false item is chance level, items with desirable P values (20 to 35) will limit D values considerably. Multiple-choice items also place a limit, but the possible maximum D values are greater for multiple-choice than for true-false items, assuming appropriate P values for both types.

The higher the D value for an item, the better that item discriminated. Any item which has a D value of +.40 or above is considered to be very effective in discriminating student differences. D values between +.20 and +.39 are usually considered to be satisfactory, but items with lower values in this range should be reviewed and revised to make them more effective discriminators. Effective and ineffective distracters can be identified from analysis, and those which are not working as planned can be rewritten or replaced. A change in alternatives for a multiple-choice item can increase discrimination. A more favorable discrimination index can be obtained by making a very difficult item easier or a very easy item somewhat more difficult by rewriting the stem or the alternatives before the item is used again.

Items with D values of 0.00 through +.19 have done little

to differentiate levels of student achievement. Each item in this range should be revised to increase discrimination before it is used in another test. There are two exceptions to the need for revision, however. First, some easy items may be included in the first part of the test to help relieve students' anxiety of the test session. Second, an item may be included on the test to determine how well students have grasped a certain important concept. In both cases a low D value would result if nearly all in each group got the item correct, since the numerator of the D formula would be at or near zero.

Items which discriminate negatively must receive special attention, and rewriting is in order for items which have values below 0.00. If it appears that revision will not increase the effectiveness of the item, it should be discarded by removing it from the test-item file. When a test is being built to be used again and again, the content validity of the test must be preserved by replacing any discarded item with another item which fits the same cell in the table of specifications. For tests built with a different set of items from the test item file or new items, the latter consideration does not pertain. Since most classroom tests are and should be built to new tables of specifications, the teacher need not write a new item solely because one was discarded from the test file.

Ideally the distracters of a multiple-choice item should have negative indexes of discrimination indicating that more low-achieving students selected each distracter than high-achieving students. A distracter which is not selected by any of the lower-achieving students is not functioning and should be rewritten or replaced.

Consideration

Special attention should be given to the difficulty level (P) for items which have D values near zero. Very small and very large P values do not allow for large differences in the numerator of the D formula, and, therefore, D values can only be very low. Low D values can be investigated by checking the corresponding P values. Items can be adjusted to allow for larger D values by writing items of medium difficulty.

If the level of difficulty seems about right but the discrimination index remains low, then the rewriting must be done on other factors than difficulty. Interpretation of difficulty and discrimination indexes and examination of how alternatives for multiple-choice items functioned allow the teacher to pick up cues on how to improve items and tests. Item analysis can indicate trouble spots in poorly functioning items, but the cause of the inferior quality must be identified by the teacher as s/he develops his/her expertise in test construction and appraisal that should produce better tests in the future.

ANALYSIS FOR CRITERION-REFERENCED TESTS

The teacher expects nearly all students to respond correctly to each item on a criterion-referenced test, especially mastery tests. For this reason, item analysis for criterion-referenced tests has limited use. P values can show the teacher the proportion of students who answered incorrectly, but since most will get a correct response, the original use of the D formula has little meaning. However, a form of a discrimination measure for a criterion-referenced test can be obtained from student performance by comparing responses of those who met the criterion to those who did not meet the criterion. The measure of difficulty indicates how the class as a whole met the criterion.

Criterion-referenced item analysis could be valuable as a guide for planning future class activities which are intended to raise class members to criterion. The difficulty index indicates how many missed an item and can be used to compare to some predetermined criterion level for class performance.

$$P_D = \frac{N_w}{N_t} (100)$$

Discrimination could be viewed as the difference between the proportions of the two groups (those who met the criterion and those who did not) who got the item correct. Thus:

$$D = \frac{U}{N_u} - \frac{L}{N_l} \text{ , where,}$$

D   is the discrimination index
N_u is the number in the group which met criterion
N_l is the number in the group not meeting criterion
U   is the number in the group meeting criterion who answered correctly
L   is the number in the group not meeting criterion who answered correctly.

Item analysis for three items on a criterion-referenced test administered to twenty-seven students will be computed for examples. Of the students who took the test, twenty-one passed criterion and six did not. The difficulty index for item 5 in figure 7.1 is computed.

$$P_D = \frac{3+3}{21+6} = \frac{6}{27} = .22$$

Computation of D value for item 5:

$$D = \frac{18}{21} - \frac{3}{6} = .86 - .5 = .36$$

P and D values for items 6 and 7 appear in Figure 7.1. These values can be used to compute the difficulty and discrimination values for items 6 and 7. Computations can be checked by looking at the tabled values.

| Item Number | Number answering correctly | | P | D |
	Above Criterion	Below Criterion		
5.	18	3	.22	+ .36
6.	21	0	.22	+1.00
7.	18	6	.11	− .14

Figure 7.1. Analysis for three criterion-referenced items.

To investigate how well the concept was understood by the class as a whole, the difficulty level of each item should be studied to see if it is within the expected limits. Items with high P values may indicate poor items. More importantly, a high P value for the difficulty index may point out an idea which has not been conceptualized by the class as a whole and, thus, give direction to further study of the content.

The values in the D column point up how the two groups performed in relation to each other. High values indicate that those passing did proportionately better than those who fell below criterion performance. The lower the values, the closer the performance of the groups compared by proportions. Of course, negative values indicate better performance for those who did not meet the criterion. For example, item 7 has a negative value for D. Inspection of the data about the performance of each group shows that only three persons in the class missed the item and that they were in the upper group. Such a result could happen because of the instructional program and its effect on the students or because of a poorly prepared item. Review of both instruction and the item itself should be undertaken to make proper changes in classroom activities or the test item.

Other Factors

Many factors contribute to the quality of a test. In addition to previously discussed characteristics of difficulty and discrimination of

test items, test balance, specificity, and objectivity deserve special attention when appraising the ability of a test to measure student achievement.

In the final sense, all characteristics are judged by the ability
of each to increase the validity of the test scores. Balance and specificity
are related directly to validity. Objectivity contributes directly to reliability
and indirectly to validity through the relationship of reliability to validity.
Balance, specificity, and objectivity can be investigated for supply-type
tests as well as selection-type tests.

BALANCE

When appraising whether or not a test has been successful
in doing what it is supposed to do, the individual should ask two questions
about the items which make up the test.

1. **Are the items selected for the test representative of the
   achievement (content and behaviors) which is to be
   assessed?**
2. **Are there enough items on the test to adequately sample
   the content which has been covered and the behaviors
   as spelled out by the objectives?**

Balance is satisfactory if the test includes enough items to adequately
sample the content and behaviors and if the items on the test can be
considered to be a representative sample of the important outcomes desired from the instruction.

The best way to assess the adequacy of balance of a test
is through the table of specifications, since a direct check can be made
of topics and behaviors. Proper use of the table as a blueprint for test
construction is the best way to structure choice of items to assume test
balance for either selection or supply tests.

SPECIFICITY

Tests are also appraised for specificity: how closely the
items are to content studied.

1. **Do the test items require knowledge in the content or
   subject area covered by the test?**
2. **Can general knowledge be used to answer the test items?**

To rate high in specificity the first question should be answered "yes"
and the second answered "no" for each test item.

When writing or choosing items for a test the writer should
be careful to include only items about the specific study to avoid giving

credit to an astute student for outside knowledge, test-taking skills, or general problem-solving ability. Although a teacher has no control of what a student learns before instruction or outside of school, effort should be made to control for this factor when constructing the test by writing items within the parameters of the offerings of the course. Specificity is high when a novice to the subject field scores at chance level.

OBJECTIVITY

Further appraisal of a test investigates how well the tasks are presented.

1. Is it clear to the test taker what is expected?
2. Is the correct response definite?

To rate high in objectivity both questions should be answered "yes."

Skill in item writing supports objectivity of test items. A check for objectivity can be made by asking knowledgeable colleagues to respond to the test items and by assessing the amount of agreement among the responses. The more the agreement, the higher the level of objectivity.

Using Appraisal Information to Improve Test Quality

Information gathered about item difficulty, discrimination power of items, balance, specificity, and objectivity can be used to improve future tests. Effective items can be developed and good testing practices determined from what has been successful in the past. Since individual test items determine the nature of the test and the extent to which the test measures what the teacher intends it to measure, successful testing begins with a set of effective items. Test quality can be improved by using appraisal information to make appropriate revisions. This involves rewriting distracters, rewording statements, and modifying items, all of which improve technical defects and the factors causing them.

Certain steps to increase test quality should be taken before the test is constructed and administered. The table of specifications can be used to provide a representative sample of items on the test. Since content validity is of primary importance for achievement tests, the use of the table allows for appraisal of the balance of the test. Further investigation of the degree of content validity can be made by determining the degree of specificity. If a test is to be valid for a particular body of content, then the parameters of topics covered in study should include all items on the test. If the items are not directed to that body of knowledge and go beyond the parameters, then the content validity of the test is reduced because of low specificity. Concern about balance and specificity should direct the test constructor to those points most directly related to validity.

The validity of a test is indirectly related to its reliability. For a test to do what it is intended to do, it must function consistently. A human temperature thermometer which gives different readings for the same absolute temperature has little use for the medical profession, which relies heavily on changes in the body temperature of human beings for information about patients. Educators also need highly reliable readings from their measuring instruments, since they rely heavily on test scores for information about their students.

When the test constructor is concerned about the objectivity of a test instrument, s/he is directing attention to building reliability into the test. Examinee performance—although not the only contributing factor to reliability—must be consistent if the measures are to be reliable. The test constructor is limited when trying to control student-centered variations (error), such as state of health, anxiety, emotional state, tiredness, or alertness; however, the test constructor can take definite steps to reduce variations (error) created by the test itself. The task (direct or implied) must be clear, so that each respondee reacts to the same thing. There should be no **intrinsic ambiguity** attached to the item in terms of the proposed task or in alternatives provided with selection items.

After the test has been administered, analysis of the responses to selection-type items can be made to indicate to the test maker where s/he was successful and where weaknesses in the test items reduced the value of the results. Item analysis provides a structured procedure designed to point up items which functioned as predicted and to identify inferior items which are weak or defective on some points. These can be revised for use later or, if not salvageable, can be discarded.

Item analysis provides a difficulty level for each item and points out (1) items that are too easy and possibly in need of revision to make them more difficult, (2) items that are too difficult and in need of revision to make them easier, and (3) those which were in the range of acceptable difficulty level. The discrimination coefficient allows the test constructor to see which items are contributing to identification of levels of achievement. Those which are not making a contribution are in need of revision if they can be saved and those which cannot be saved should be discarded.

Nonfunctioning distracters can be located and investigated for lack of plausibility or other defects. Rewriting of one or more nonfunctioning distracters may be all the item needs to turn it into a useful item.

Future tests are almost certain to be of higher quality if they are made up of items which have generated acceptable levels of data from item analysis and/or items improved by revision. Although most classroom tests should be rebuilt each time units are taught from year to year, some teachers have found that if the content taught and the way that it is presented do not vary too much, a test can be used again and again. If a test is used in this way, any items which are revised must be checked carefully to see that they still relate to the same cell in the table of specifications after revision. To preserve content validity, any discarded item must be replaced with an item which is associated with the same table cell as the one being replaced if the same table of specifications is used.

Using Test Appraisal to Help Students and Teachers

Ultimately the appraisal of test items benefits the student as well as the teacher since the teacher obtains a more valid appraisal of achievement. Furthermore, the classroom discussion of test results and individual test items with students can be used as a learning experience. The teacher at the same time receives feedback concerning learning and effectiveness of instruction as well as information from students as they point out their interpretation of tasks presented on the test.

The teacher's appraisal of test items prior to classroom discussion assists in making the class experience more meaningful since the teacher is aware of the technical defects of each test item before discussing it with the students. Any item which the teacher deems from item analysis to be ambiguous should be presented to the class before long periods of discussion lead to negative feelings by students. It is more appropriate to next discuss the items answered correctly by only a few students. The reason(s) for missing the items may be determined as being (1) the lack of adequate classroom coverage of material, (2) ambiguity in the item itself or (3) lack of understanding of the information by the student.

The teacher may discover that students' poor performances on some items may be due to inadequate instruction of the content involved in particular items, and more class time can be assigned to those topics in further classroom instruction. Test appraisal may provide information to point up strong areas of learning as well as weak areas of learning. For example, students may be adept in vocabulary and understanding of principles in a content area but weak in ability to interpret data for practical application. Learning by particular students below that which is expected or necessary for further progress in the subject or content can be further identified and appropriate remedial action taken.

Students will be left with a much more positive feeling about the entire test experience and the part they themselves play in assisting in the improvement of test items for current and future use if they are allowed to actively participate in test appraisal. At the same time the teacher is improving the quality of a test through test appraisal and item revision, s/he is improving skill in item and test development. Practice in writing and revising items is very beneficial to the development of measurement skill, and it supplements and refines formal cognitive development of good test appraisal. The teacher's capability in teaching in the subject area is hopefully increased through careful attention to, and consideration of, good test practices because test building relates test tasks to the objectives and course content and causes teachers to interrelate the elements of the process of education.

Specifically, test information and test appraisal help the teacher and students in the following ways:

1. **Provide a basis for discussing test results.**
2. **Provide a learning experience for students.**
3. **Determine why a test item is or is not discriminating between the better and poorer students.**
4. **Identify alternative responses which are or are not functioning appropriately.**
5. **Provide a basis for item improvement.**
6. **Determine where additional instruction or remedial work with individual students or the class is necessary.**
7. **Determine if the teacher has met his/her instructional objectives in specific content areas.**
8. **Help develop and improve the teacher's skills in test construction.**
9. **Help develop more valid and reliable measures of classroom achievement.**
10. **Provide a check against the table of specifications for balance.**
11. **Provide a check for objectivity and specificity of the test.**
12. **Help students discover errors and misunderstandings.**

Only through careful test appraisal can acceptable levels of reliability and validity be developed. The quality of good future tests is based upon adequate test appraisal of past tests, which is the responsibility of the classroom teacher.

8 Performance Tests

The classroom paper-and-pencil test which measures student achievement in a content subject requires a student to perform or react to certain prescribed tasks. In this sense the test measures performance; however, that performance is not the main interest of the tester. The primary function of a paper-and-pencil test is the measurement of student achievement in the cognitive domain: the measurement of verbal and mathematical aspects of classroom objectives. Some classroom instructional objectives are directed to development of skills which are difficult to measure with paper-and-pencil tests. These skills vary widely and range from cognitive skills, such as silent and oral reading, to motor skills, such as welding, playing a musical instrument, or the mechanics of handwriting.

The discussion of performance testing in this chapter is directed to measurement of skill development. Ways to collect data as students actually perform the skill and to judge the results and the process used are presented. Some classroom objectives require that classroom tests measure, in part, the application of principles and practical use of knowledge. Principles of performance testing are also suitable for measuring how well students can apply principles and use knowledge in practical situations, and what is presented here also applies to those circumstances.

For measurement and evaluation purposes, performance can be broken down into two parts:

1. a series of actions (process or procedure)
2. the outcome of those actions (result or product)

To judge the level of skill development, the teacher must determine how a student can perform rather than measure what s/he knows. Skill development in all domains, but especially in the psychomotor domain, must be assessed in terms of what the student can do rather than what the student knows. To collect information about what students can do usually requires that students be observed as they perform and that the products of the performance be judged.

Assessment in preschool and kindergarten classes and in classes for severely handicapped students may require the teacher to rely on direct observation supplemented by performance testing because these students have not developed verbal and writing skills needed to take paper-and pencil-tests. Physical education, vocational education, industrial arts, business, speech, drama, journalism, art, music, and primary grade class assessment procedures are also likely to use performance testing extensively. In addition, laboratory skills in physical and biological sciences and in psychology can best be measured by performance tests. Objectives for these classes should be directed to development of skills, good work habits, social acceptance, and physical facility, and serve as reminders that evaluation of performance is an integral part of classroom activities.

Natural Situation

General objectives direct teacher attention to the preparation of students for the real world; however, the classroom setting is the only place where a student will be asked to perform many paper-and-pencil test tasks. The usual classroom test offers students tasks which are artificial when compared to tasks performed in a real-world environment. The classroom may be the only place where a student is asked to perform many test tasks, but this is not true for performance tests. Hopefully, the student can and will be placed in a natural or near-natural situation for collection of information to be used in evaluation of the level of skill development. If a teacher uses data about performance collected under natural conditions, the prediction about performance outside the classroom should be maximized.

Increasing realistic conditions for all tests is a desirable goal. Possession of certain knowledge rarely guarantees that the student will use it to his or her advantage beyond the classroom. Ability to implement knowledge in real-world situations remains questionable unless specific steps are taken to increase the realism of the test. Certain subject matter resists any attempt to create natural or near-natural conditions. In such cases teachers must assume that the student would perform the same way in a natural situation as s/he did in the artificial classroom environment; however, that assumption may or may not be borne out. For example, a student who exhibits knowledge of the system of electing public officials may not use good judgment when voting in a local, state, or national election several years later.

Cognitive knowledge about a noncognitive skill is not a good measure of the level of skill development. A student may be able to pass a written test on driving or on how to weld silver to make jewelry but perform unsatisfactorily when asked to drive a car or make a set of earrings. There seems to be a close relationship between knowing about how to do something and actually doing it, but cognitive knowledge about a noncognitive skill only supports the skill and does not guarantee high skill performance. To measure how well students perform the teacher must give students opportunities to exhibit their skill levels.

Better measures of students' levels of goal attainment are made under the most realistic conditions possible. If the true natural situation can not be used to collect the data, then the closest conditions possible should be used as a criterion. By creating conditions much like the real world, requiring the student to act in that context, and collecting data about the process and the results, the teacher can extend data-collection procedures beyond the paper-and-pencil test. Teachers can overcome the common tendency in education to make the paper-and-pencil test the only device used to collect data for judgments of students' levels of accomplishments.

Procedure and Product

When instruction deals with performance, a student is asked to produce, create, construct, fabricate, build, or in some way to bring forth something as evidence that s/he has met a specific objective. The degree of accomplishment is evaluated by using information about (1) the process used and (2) the result of the process.

PROCESS

In part, performance is concerned with *process,* the actions used to bring forth a result. To a large extent the quality of the product is determined by the use of proper procedures. It is difficult to imagine high-level performance without acceptable procedures. Proper use of carpentry tools is needed to fabricate furniture that has utility and at the same time is aesthetically pleasing. Certain techniques of running are expected to result in faster times for the sprinter while other procedures may be better for the distance runner. Observation of procedures is the first step in the measurement of performance. When a series of actions is particularly important to performance, teachers look at the way the student proceeds to assess the student. Since there is no tangible aspect of process, special techniques must be set up to collect data about procedures to aid in judgment of performance. Structured direct observation, use of devices to record information during action, uses of mechanical devices to record the procedures, and inspection of a physical product (if one exists) aid the judgment of process.

Procedural actions are, on the whole, judged by predetermined standards external to the class or group. The judgment of the correctness of process involves the same basic elements of criterion-based evaluation made about other student achievement; however, certain principles need to be applied differently because the nature of that which is being evaluated is different.

Certain school subjects deal more with procedure than other subjects do. Classes in art, music, shorthand, typing, speech, home economics, and physical education are especially involved with procedural aspects of performance. For each subject and in each classroom certain procedures are preferred over others; in other words, acceptable procedures for one class may be less than acceptable for other classes. What is preferred should be defended on its merits, and students should know on what basis process is to be judged. The relative importance of process and result in performance assessment should be made clear to the student.

Procedures are usually second in importance to the product, but they must be considered when assessing performance. Poor procedures are associated with poor products, good procedures with good products. Procedures are concerned with the formal structure of those actions that create the product. Separation of procedure and product can be very difficult if the product is intangible, yet it is important to the evaluation of performance. Since the intangible product is intermingled with the procedures, the procedures may be confused with the product itself.

Assessment of process involves information about procedures. For example, judgment of performance for a piano solo would include an evaluation of process. *Procedural evaluation* of piano playing would consider such factors as sitting position, positioning of the feet and hands, arrangement of the printed music, relationship of piano and player to the audience, the striking of the keys, and any other action which contributes to the result. *Product evaluation* of piano playing would consider the sounds which reach the listener's ear. Unless a record or tape is made of the product, the teacher may find it difficult trying to separate the procedure from the product. A record or physical object allows certain judgments about procedures, since they can be discerned from the product itself. Other information must be collected by means of structured direct observation of the student's performance.

RESULT

To a great extent, performance is concerned with the *result* of actions. Judgment of a product is especially crucial since the result of the procedures is, in most cases, the most important aspect of performance. Performance testing, therefore, relies heavily on assessment of the product, either tangible or intangible. Since a tangible product exists in physical form, it is easier to judge than an intangible product, which is created and then lost. A tangible product could be a cake, a blueprint, an essay, an oil painting, a printed handbill, or one of hundreds of objects which could be created in a school setting. An intangible product could be a speech, a piano solo, a 100-yard sprint, or one of hundreds of different actions.

Evaluative methods for intangible products take much the same form as evaluation of procedures. Structured direct observation using specially designed devices to record information during action and use of mechanical devices to record the performance aid the judgment of intangible products.

Assessment of tangible products takes advantage of the physical aspects of the product. They may be scored by weighting of important aspects, by rating on a scale, or comparison to preconstructed objects.

Judgment of products must be as objective as possible. Some products, such as repair of a puncture in an automobile tire, can be judged very objectively: if the seal holds and the tire does not lose pressure, then the performance should be considered satisfactory. The height of a jump is the primary criterion to consider when evaluating an attempted high jump. In competition, the athlete is judged first for rank in the final standings. Beyond this, a coach may attempt to determine the extent to which procedures increased or decreased the height of the jump. An English theme or speech would be more difficult to assess objectively.

Judgments of products should have appropriately chosen standards for assessment. Junior high school athletes would not be judged by Olympic standards. The products of a student in cooking class should not be judged in comparison to those of an experienced cook. In the same way student products should not be compared to products produced by professionals unless the students are expected to perform at that level, such as students in advanced vocational classes.

Evaluating Performance

When evaluating performance, the teacher should collect the needed data from a natural situation, if possible, or by simulation which approaches real-world conditions. The final assessment can be made by comparing these data to established standards.

SIMULATION

The teacher has a wide range of simulation features to select from that will help to create natural conditions for performance evaluation. Since the simulation can range from near-artificial environment to virtually real-world conditions, certain factors must be taken into consideration when designing a testing situation. The following steps seem appropriate general guidelines for setting up a simulation.

Any simulation involves choices and compromises. Four steps may be identified in making those choices and compromises:

1. Determine through careful analysis the critical aspects of the criterion situation it is desired to simulate in view of the purpose of the simulation.

2. Determine the minimum fidelity [degree of realism] needed for each aspect and estimate the worth of increasing fidelity beyond the minimum.

3. Develop a scheme for representing a reasonably comprehensive set of aspects, within the limits of available resources.

4. Adjust comprehensiveness and fidelity, compromising as necessary to achieve a balancing of considerations but with primary attention to the aspects shown by analysis to be most critical for purpose at hand.[1]

When the teacher is interested in using simulation for performance testing, the relative importance of environmental factors will direct the creation of the testing situation. Judgments about what is important may differ from teacher to teacher, depending on how the total situation is conceptualized. Performance testing is used because it can

---

[1] Robert Fitzpatrick and Edward J. Morrison, "Performance and Product Evaluation," in *Educational Measurement,* ed. by Robert L. Thorndike (Washington, D.C.: American Council on Education, 1971), p. 241.

conceivably provide better information than the usual paper-and-pencil test. The principles of good testing do not change, so the thrust is to create an environment where more reliable and more valid data can be generated.

The principles of setting objectives for the student and then evaluating the students' performance in accordance with those objectives are the same for performance tests as for other types of tests. The manner of collecting the data is the major difference in evaluative procedures for performance tests.

DATA COLLECTION

Information about performance must be collected with the same considerations that are associated with collection of data from other types of tests. All of these concerns relate to generation of valid data. The following devices and techniques can be used to structure collection of data about procedures and products to permit valid evaluation of student performance.

Mechanical Devices

Any devices (cameras and recorders) which make a permanent record of the performance can enhance the likelihood that reliable data are generated. Since the action is frozen on film or tape, the teacher or judges can repeat the performance as many times as needed to assess the parts (procedure and product) of the performance as well as the total performance.

Intangible products and procedures lack the physical features which allow repeated viewing of a performance. With a film or tape, the teacher can scrutinize certain important aspects of a performance for comparison with established standards. In addition, diagnosis of the procedure allows for instruction to overcome weak or incorrect procedures.

The coverage of a tape recording, a movie or film, or video recording is limited. Advanced planning is important to assure that the needed data are recorded. If certain camera positions are needed to record particular aspects of the performance, the person operating the camera must be programmed for proper camera manipulation. Similarly, the right kind of equipment and sensitive recording tape are important to reproduce a musical performance accurately. Every mechanical device must be selected to assure that (1) the data are of the highest quality and (2) the needed data are available for evaluative procedures.

Direct Observation

A valuable technique for collecting data for student performance is to view the students' actions. At first thought this may seem to be an easy way to assess levels of performance, but a more careful look at direct observation suggests that it reveals little unless the observer knows what to look for and how to record the data. This is why the observation must be structured for the observer. Checklists and rating scales, which are discussed later, are helpful in assuring that the needed data are collected and that the recording process facilitates the performance evaluation.

Checklist

The checklist is the simplest device used to structure direct observation. It is made up of details to be considered in evaluation of a procedure of an intangible product. The checklist allows for a record to be made while the action is taking place. The teacher can mark with a quick check desirable or undesirable actions of the student and points in the product, thus avoiding the dependence on reflection to the actions after they have been completed.

The checklist (see Figure 8.1) can be organized to indicate if something happened that should have happened, if something that should have happened did not happen, if something that should not happen did not happen, and if something that should not happen did happen. In addition, with good organization the frequency of these occurrences can be built into the checklist. Each device is designed so that each important characteristic is observed and recorded. If the sequence of the separate actions is crucial to the process, then the sequence must be recorded.

The checklist can be used as a learning device during instruction if it is made available early in the instructional period because it allows the student to know what is important. Organizing the points sequentially in the order that they appear should also guide learning and facilitate marking during the performance.

Consideration should be given to each of the following points when constructing a checklist:

1. **Specific points to be observed are listed.**
2. **The order of the list should be in the expected sequence of actual occurrence.**
3. **The reaction can be made by a tally mark or a check.**
4. **Space should be provided for compilation of the data on the checklist itself.**

DIRECTIONS: Below are definable aspects that are important to successful volley return. Check each one for each volley for one set. Determine the percentage of attainment for the set.		PERCENTAGE
Number of volleys	1̶ 2̶ 3̶ 4̶ 5̶ 6̶ 7̶ 8̶ 9̶ 10̶ 11 12 13 14 15 16 17 18 19 20 21 22 23 24 25 26 27 28 29 30 31 32 33 34 35 36 37 38 39 40 41 42	
Racket in FRONT	~~NH~~ ///	80
Racket head HIGH	~~NH~~	50
Knees BENT, but head UP	~~NH~~ /	60
LEAN or STEP into shot	~~NH~~ ////	90
Keep racket head moving FORWARD	~~NH~~ //	70
Watch the ball CONTACT the racket face	///	30
NO FOLLOW-THROUGH	~~NH~~ ~~NH~~	100
BE AGGRESSIVE	~~NH~~ ///	80

Figure 8.1. Checklist for volley returns in tennis.

Rating Scale

The use of a scale as a form of measurement has widespread utility. Scales can be used informally as in the case of the statement, "Rate that brunette on a scale from 1 to 10," or they can be used more formally as a measure of attitude or motivation. Since our interest is focused on assessment of performance, the scaling techniques will be discussed primarily for judgment of procedures and intangible products.

A rating scale (see Figure 8.2) allows the teacher or judge to measure the worth of a performance in relation to predetermined important aspects. When performance is measured by a rating scale, numerals are assigned to those important aspects such that an isomorphism is created between the assigned number (point on the scale) and each person's level of performance. A rating scale could be considered to be a sophisticated checklist that can supply everything from a report of frequency of occurrence to a measurement of critical attributes of the performance.

Date: _____

Name: _____   Composition: _____

Score each item by circling numbers at left. 5 = outstanding; 4 = excellent; 3 = acceptable, could be improved; 2 = somewhat weak, needs considerable improvement; 1 = very weak, needs much improvement

A. 5 4 3 2 1 *General Manner* (confident, authoritative, energetic, positive)
B. 5 4 3 2 1 *Posture* (erect, relaxed, confident, commanding)
C. 5 4 3 2 1 *Starting Position* (commanding, easily visible, positive); maintained distinctive movement
D. 5 4 3 2 1 *Visual Contact* (not score-bound, especially at opening)
E. 5 4 3 2 1 *Beginning* (together, in tempo, good dynamic level, spirit)
F. 5 4 3 2 1 *Baton Technique* (correct pattern, character, size, position)
G. 5 4 3 2 1 *Clarity* (pulsation clear, definite, regular, commanding)
H. 5 4 3 2 1 *Cues* (adequate number, effectiveness, clarity, accuracy)
I. 5 4 3 2 1 *Balance* (attention shifts among prominent sections, supportive)
J. 5 4 3 2 1 *Left Hand* (reserved for special effects, cueing, dynamics)
K. 5 4 3 2 1 *Phrasing* (shape not ignored, nuance, variability of beat size, speed)
L. 5 4 3 2 1 *Facility* (graceful, well-coordinated, accurate)
M. 5 4 3 2 1 *Efficiency* (size and energy of beat appropriate, no excess)
N. 5 4 3 2 1 *Dynamics* (markings observed, good taste indicated)
O. 5 4 3 2 1 *Accuracy* (general freedom from conducting errors)
P. 5 4 3 2 1 *Expressiveness* (interpretation, feeling, freedom, musicianship)
Q. 5 4 3 2 1 *Tempo* (appropriate for expressive character, marking observed)
R. 5 4 3 2 1 *Ensemble* (rhythmic unity, articulative unity, neatness)
S. 5 4 3 2 1 *Quality* (intonation, tone quality, balance, unity)
T. 5 4 3 2 1 *How well did the group follow your conducting?*
U. 5 4 3 2 1 *Score Study* (detailed, thorough, well fixed in mind)
                        (Be as honest as possible with yourself on this point.)
V. 5 4 3 2 1 *Individual Practice* (with tape, other recording, conducting own singing of parts of the score, anticipating difficulties)
                        (Again, be honest with yourself.)
W. 5 4 3 2 1 *Overall Conducting Effectiveness*

Figure 8.2. Rating scale for conducting an orchestra.

SOURCE: Richard Colwell, *The Evaluation of Music Teaching and Learning* (Englewood Cliffs, N.J.: Prentice-Hall, Inc., 1970), pp. 108–9.

Since procedures and intangible products are not physical in form, the measurement consists of assessment of the actions or intangible product by the person judging the performance. The scale is important for building reliability into the measurement and generating valid scores. The same principles of construction used for good paper-and-pencil tests apply to scaling devices.

Scales built for measuring performance are, in general, built in a positive direction; i.e. there is no problem of positive and negative positions such as might be the case with a study of attitudes or other characteristics. The scale is usually built from zero, although the zero point may or may not appear on the scale. There should be five to ten points on the scale, depending on the performance being measured. Too few points (say two or three) may not allow fine enough discrimination. Too many points (say fifty or one hundred) may be too fine in discrimination and require too much time to mark. Since rating scales will be used as the performance is going on, they must be made functional for collecting the data. When developing the scale the intervals between points on the scale should be as equal as possible to make it easier to establish relationships among scores. If scores are to be averaged, the assumption of equal intervals is made when the mean is determined. Descriptions for each number are helpful for the judge and allow for increased reliability within an evaluation and between/among different evaluations.

Suggestions for construction of rating scales follow:

1. Avoid the use of too few or too many points on the scale. Too few points result in a crude measure. Too many points make discrimination of differences difficult, and the procedure becomes time consuming for the observer.

2. Allow reactions at only designated points on the scale. Marks between points require interpretation and may be ambiguous to the interpreter.

3. Select meaningful descriptions for points on the scale if the added directions are helpful to the rater. Careful selection of adjectives and modifying adverbs gives direction to the observer.

Product Scale

A product scale is a special type of rating scale. A set of tangible products which vary in level of quality is used to describe the points on the scale in relative terms. Four or more products are constructed or selected from student products so that they are evenly spaced in difference to support the assumption of equal intervals.

Product scales are relatively easy for the teacher to develop and can serve as long as the objectives remain the same. Pupil products (see Figure 8.3) are probably best to use for a product scale, but the teacher can construct products of varying quality if student products are not available.

The use of the scale for assessment of performance is straightforward. Each student product is compared to those in the scale and matched as closely as possible to one of them. The position on that scale is then given as a measurement of the student product.

The product scale does not give specific detail to important aspects, and it may be difficult for the student to be aware of how the product is deficient unless s/he has an opportunity to make a visual

176

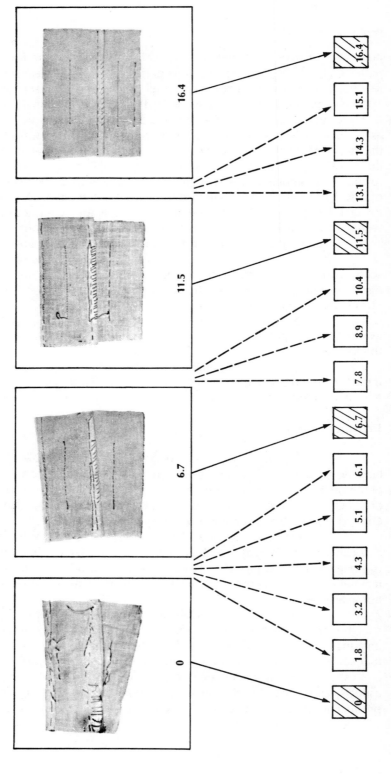

Figure 8.3. Product scale for certain selected elements of sewing. Four of the fifteen levels exhibit the principle of hierarchy.

SOURCE: Katharine Murdoch, *The Measurement of Certain Elements of Hand Sewing* (New York: Teachers College, Columbia University, 1919), p. 120.

comparison. The product scale should be presented to the student early in the learning stages so that s/he will know what is needed to build quality into the object. If the student sees what represents quality, then s/he can work toward that end during instruction. In this way the desired learning outcome can be presented in physical form before and during learning.

Ranking

When a ranking is made, order is assigned to a set of something using some particular basis for the ordering. A set of students could be ordered by their height—shortest to tallest. A set of products produced by students could be ordered according to the degree to which they meet accepted or predetermined standards. The rank of each element is determined by its position relative to all other elements, but measurement is not made in absolute terms. This may or may not be meaningful. In most cases for procedures and products, certain standards are available, and to know that a student's product ranked sixth out of eight products says little about how those standards are met. In other words, performance testing is primarily criterion referenced rather than norm referenced, and the value of ranking students' products is reduced when evaluation of procedures and products is being conducted.

In most cases teachers can find a better way of measuring performance than reporting the relative position of the student. If a ranking is used, the basis for ordering should be made available to the students during the learning process. Relative importance of certain actions or characteristics should be understood by both teacher and student. If a rank is reported, the total number of elements ranked must also be reported. There is probably a great difference between a rank of two when two are being ranked and a rank of two when sixty-four are being ranked, but this is not necessarily so.

COMPARISON TO STANDARDS

Standards for performance must be based on professional knowledge—the teacher's and colleagues'—taking into consideration the age of the student, level of student maturity, and student experiential background. The criteria for judging the performance should be clearly stated and communicated to the students. As mentioned earlier, checklists, rating scales, and product scales serve to communicate to students what is important for judging the performance. If none of these devices is used, then the objectives and standards to be used should be explained to the students.

The teacher must decide the relative importance of procedure and product. Since the product is considered to be of primary concern, it will usually receive most, if not total, weight for the performance standards. Most evaluators of performance will find it difficult to lower the ratings of performance if the product meets criteria even though the procedures may not be according to the established standards. Since students are different in many ways, their procedures may vary from established forms but still result in acceptable products. For this reason certain variance in standards for procedure is expected in acceptable methods for evaluating performance.

Established procedures may be used to direct learning because, in general, those procedures have stood the test of time. In developmental stages and in new learning situations, teachers are likely to emphasize evaluation of procedure and discount the product itself. The assumption is made that the quality of the product is expected to improve as procedures improve. A guideline which is widely used in performance evaluation suggests that evaluation of performance during instruction and the learning period should focus on process (procedure) and that terminal evaluation of performance should look to the result (product) of the performance.

The complex nature of performance does not allow measurement of all the aspects of procedure or product. Regardless of all of the objective data which can be gathered, the final judgment about the quality of the performance must be made subjectively. The purpose of structuring the evaluation as a comparison of data to standards is to make that final assessment as valid as possible. Careful attention to setting reasonable standards and then comparing the student's performance to them can result in more valid and reliable evaluation than a method which does not include the formal approach to performance evaluation. Such structuring also directs attention to the same aspects for all students and assures that all students are judged on the same standards.

Using Performance Tests

Performance tests should be used when the teacher feels that paper-and-pencil tests can not provide the information needed to assess student attainment of goals. They should not be used exclusively in any classroom, but nearly all classrooms should use them sometimes. If an adequate and relevant paper-and-pencil test is available, it should be used because performance tests are more costly in time and money.

The value of the use of performance tests rests in the creation of real-world conditions for the collection of information about students' ability to execute prescribed skills. Performance tests should be used to measure skill development and to assess how well students can utilize knowledge in the real world. The ability to choose between paper-and-pencil tests and performance tests develops as measurement and evaluation techniques become an integral part of the ongoing activities of the classroom and as teachers try new ways to evaluate and assess their success in doing so.

The degree of reliability is always a question with classroom tests, but the performance test is especially susceptible to low reliability. For this reason close attention should be given to all aspects of performance testing to raise the reliability to the highest possible levels. Classroom testing of performance should consider points made throughout this chapter and the following suggestions:

1. **Be sure that the sample of performance which is considered is adequate to provide a representative sample.**

2. **Techniques for collecting the data must be selected so that the right kinds of data are available in maximum quantity.**

3. **Structure the observation of the performance so that observation per se does not affect the performance. Be reasonably sure that the data are not significantly different from performance without observation.**

4. **Take precautions to avoid the possibility that the interdependence of procedure and product might affect the evaluation of performance. The two parts of performance must be separated for evaluative purposes and each given its proper weight.**

5. **Consider use of mechanical devices to record performance for repeated viewing. If an objective is in terms of what a student can do, then measurement of what a student does is necessary to evaluate how well s/he has met that objective. The above guides should direct effective performance testing.**

Glossary

Since this book on construction of classroom tests is somewhat technical in nature, certain words may be new to the reader. Other commonly used words may take on a different meaning in this book. These words are denoted in the list below. Words which are explained within the narrative of the book are not listed. For a more complete explanation of other terms in measurement and evaluation, refer to the *Dictionary of Education*[1] and *Classroom Measurement and Evaluation*.[2]

Accountability: A system of holding the school administration and teachers responsible for student attainment of educational objectives.

Algorithm: A method of computation. Usually set up so that calculation can be made routinely without mathematical understanding from the computational scheme.

Anecdotal record: An objectively written description of a student's behavior. What s/he said or did in a specific situation recorded as being either typical or unusual behavior.

Blind guessing: The selection of an alternative for a selection-type item without using any knowledge or rational approach to the choice. The probability of choosing the correct response is at chance level. If there are two choices, a blind guess

[1] Carter V. Good, ed., *Dictionary of Education,* 3rd ed. (New York: McGraw-Hill Book Company, 1973.)
[2] Charles D. Hopkins and Richard L. Antes, *Classroom Measurement and Evaluation* (Itasca, Ill.: F. E. Peacock Publishers, Inc., 1978), pp. 414–33.

should result in the correct selection about 50 percent of the time, for four choices, 25 percent of the time, and so on.

Construct: An idea or concept invented to explain an aspect of human behavior or some other idea. It primarily exists to name a certain nonphysical characteristic. Example: hostility.

Correction for guessing: An alteration of test scores used to increase the reliability of the scores by removing the chance factors involved with guessing blindly for responses to multiple-choice and true-false items.

Criterion-referenced: A way of interpreting a test score which compares an individual's performance to an established standard of performance.

Direct observation: Noticing of phenomena without any intervening factor between the observer and that which is being observed. A record of the situation is made.

Domain: A sphere of human activity. The three major categories are cognitive, affective, and psychomotor.

Error: Variation produced by the inaccuracies of **measurement.** The source of the variation may be within the test instrument, within the subjects of measurement, or in the way the **test** was administered.

Evaluation: The continuous inspection of all available information concerning the student, teacher, educational program, and the teaching-learning process to ascertain the degree of change in students and to form valid judgments about the students and the effectiveness of the school program.

Extended response: The answer to an essay item which asks or implies a question which has no definite limits to restrict the student response. The response set is open ended. (See **limited response.**)

Formative evaluation: A judgment of an ongoing program used to provide information for product or program review, identification of the effectiveness of the instructional process, and the assessment of the teaching process.

Intrinsic ambiguity: Uncertainty about the task on a test item which results from the way the item is worded or otherwise presented.

Isomorphic: Something similar or identical in structure or appearance to something else.

Item analysis: An examination of student performance for each item on a **test.** It consists of reexamination of the responses to items of a test by applying mathematical techniques to assess two characteristics—difficulty and discrimination—of each objective item on the test.

Item sampling: A technique used in schoolwide, state, or national testing that administers only a part of a **test** to each student. This allows a longer test to be administered but does not require a long test session for each student involved. If each student is administered only one-fourth of the test, a four-hour test could be administered with no student giving more than one hour of his/her time.

Limited response: Essay item which asks a question or gives instructions for restricting the area to be covered in responding to the stated tasks. The coverage expected is well fenced in for the student. (See **extended response.**)

Measurement: A process that assigns by rule a numerical description to **observation** of some attribute of an object, person, or event.

Needs assessment: A process whereby the educational requirements of students collectively or individually are determined. Usually thought of as a formal structured approach, but may be done informally by the teacher.

Norm group: The set of subjects used to establish the averages to be used to interpret student scores on a **standardized** test.

Norm-referenced: A form of interpreting test scores that employs the practice of comparing a student's performance to the class performance or to some exterior average performance, such as local, state, or national averages.

Observation: Any fact which is used as a basis for evaluation procedures. The output of the process of observing. In education the results of observing (the observations) are used to make **evaluations.**

Problem-solving: Settlement of a perplexing question or situation. In education, problem solving is usually thought of as the solution of a puzzling situation which has been posed by the teacher.

Raw score: The first score given to a test paper. It may include weighting and a **correction for guessing** but no other transformation.

Representative sample: Any subset of persons or items selected to represent a larger group or population which has the same inclinations as the total group or population with reference to some characteristic or characteristics. In testing, the test instrument is composed of tasks which are intended to reflect the characteristics of the larger population of possible test tasks which could be asked.

Standardized: A process of preparing a test instrument for use in widely separated locations. The **test** is **standardized** so that administration and scoring procedures are the same for all test takers. Score interpretation is made to averages of performances of groups of test takers whose scores are then used for making comparison to interpret scores obtained from other students.

Summative evaluation: A terminal **evaluation** employed in the general assessment of the degree to which the larger outcomes have been obtained over a substantial part of or all of a course. It is used in determining whether or not the learner has achieved the ultimate objectives for instruction which were set up in advance of the instruction.

Taxonomy: A system of classification and the concepts of identification, naming, and categorization underlying the coordination.

Technical problem: A complex situation from a specialized field of study which is presented to a student for solution within the structure of that field. Usually used for assessment of general understandings of a wide set of principles and ideas rather than for special skills and talents.

Test: An instrument, device, or procedure which proposes a sequence of tasks to which a student is to respond. The results are then used as measures to define relative value of the trait to which the test relates.

Test-item file: A collection of individual items on cards which are arranged by content areas for future use in **test** assembly.

Unobtrusive observation: Instances of noticing made in such a way that the person being observed does not know that s/he is being observed.

Validity: The degree to which **observation** accurately describes what is being observed.

Bibliography

Anderson, Scarvia B., et al. *Encyclopedia of Educational Evaluation.* San Francisco: Jossey-Bass Publishers, 1975.

Bloom, Benjamin S., ed. *Taxonomy of Educational Objectives: The Classification of Educational Goals, Handbook I: Cognitive Domain.* New York: David McKay Co., Inc., 1956.

Buros, Oscar K., ed. *Mental Measurements Yearbook*s. Highland Park, N.J.: Gryphon Press, 1938, 1940, 1949, 1953, 1959, 1965, 1972.

Buros, Oscar K., ed. *Tests in Print II.* Highland Park, N.J.: Gryphon Press, 1974.

Ebel, Robert L. *Essentials of Educational Measurement.* Englewood Cliffs, N.J.: Prentice-Hall, Inc., 1972.

Fitzpatrick, Robert and Edward J. Morrison, "Performance and Product Evaluation," in *Educational Measurement,* Robert L. Thorndike, ed. Washington, D.C.: American Council on Education, 1971, 237–270.

Good, Carter V., ed. *Dictionary of Education.* 3rd ed. New York: McGraw-Hill Book Co., 1973.

Gronlund, Norman E. *Preparing Criterion-Referenced Tests for Classroom Instruction.* New York: The Macmillan Company, 1973.

Harrow, Anita J. *A Taxonomy of the Psychomotor Domain.* New York: David McKay Company, Inc., 1972.

Hills, John R. *Measurement and Evaluation in the Classroom.* Columbus, Ohio: Charles E. Merrill Publishing Co., 1976.

Hopkins, Charles D. *Describing Data Statistically.* Columbus, Ohio: Charles E. Merrill Publishing Co., 1974.

Hopkins, Charles D. and Richard L. Antes. *Classroom Measurement and Evaluation.* Itasca, Ill.: F. E. Peacock Publishers, Inc., 1978.

Hopkins, Charles D. and Richard L. Antes. *Classroom Testing: Administration, Scoring, and Score Interpretation.* F. E. Peacock Publishers, Inc., 1979.

Kearney, Nolan C. *Elementary School Objectives.* New York: Russell Sage Foundation, 1953.

Krothwohl, David R., et al. *Taxonomy of Educational Objectives: The Classification of Educational Goals, Handbook II: Affective Domain.* New York: David McKay Co., Inc., 1964.

Lindquist, E. F., ed. *Educational Measurement.* Washington, D.C.: American Council on Education, 1951.

National Educational Association, Commission on Reorganizing Secondary Education. *Cardinal Principles of Secondary Education.* Bulletin No. 35. Washington, D.C.: U.S. Office of Education, 1918.

Noll, Victor H. and Dale P. Scannell. *Introduction to Educational Measurement,* 3rd ed. Boston: Houghton-Mifflin Co., 1972.

Popham, W. James. *Criterion-Referenced Measurement.* Englewood Cliffs, N.J.: Prentice-Hall, Inc., 1978.

Staib, John H. "The Cardiologist's Theorem." *The Mathematics Teacher* 70(2) (January 1977): 36–39.

Standards of Educational and Psychological Tests and Manuals. Washington, D.C.: American Psychological Association, 1974.

Thorndike, Robert L., ed. *Educational Measurement.* 2nd ed. Washington, D.C.: American Council on Education, 1971.

Index

Accountability, 180
Algorithm, 180
Anderson, Scarvia B., 184
Anecdotal record, 180
Antes, Richard L., vii, 3, 7, 48, 94, 180, 185
Arrangement of items on a test, 54–55; hierarchical by item type, 55; by level of difficulty, 55–56; by subject matter content, 55

Balance in a test, 160
Blind guessing, 180
Bloom, Benjamin S., 20, 22, 83, 184
Buros, Oscar K., 184

Checklist, 172–73; defined, 172; to evaluate performance, 172–73; example, 173
Classification items on tests, 131–36; advantages, 132; exemplary items elementary school subjects, 133–35; exemplary items secondary school subjects, 135–36; guides to writing, 132–33; limitations, 132; nature of, 131; special considerations, 132
Classroom Measurement and Evaluation, 180
Cognitive domain, 20–22; subcategories of, 20–21, 36
Communication, 11–12; classroom and school, 12; students and parents, 11–12
Comparison of standards, 177–78
Completion items on tests, 85–91; advantages, 86; exemplary items elementary school subjects, 90; exemplary items secondary school

subjects, 90–91; guides to writing, 87–89; limitations, 87; nature of, 85; special considerations, 86–87
Construct, 181
Correction for guessing on tests, 48, 181
Correlation, 41–44; calculation, 41–43; coefficient, 43; interpretation of the coefficient, 43–44
Criterion-referenced, 7, 181
Criterion referenced vs. norm referenced, 22–26
Criterion-referenced tests: reference point, 13–14

Decision making, 8–9; classroom level, 8; school level, 8–9
Dictionary of Education, 180
Difficulty, 155–56; desired level, 155–56; index, 153; multiple-choice items, 155; true-false items, 156; level of tasks on tests, 31–32
Direct observation, 172, 181; to evaluate performance, 172
Discrimination, 156–57; desired level, 156–57; index, 153–54
Distracters: in multiple-choice items, 111; plausible, 116
Domain, 181
Domains of educational objectives, 20–22

Ebel, Robert L., 95, 184
Editing test items, 56–57
Educational process: elements of, 5
Error, 181; in measurement, 41
Essay items on tests, 93–99; advantages, 95–96; exemplary items

187

THE BOOK MANUFACTURE

Composition: Kingsport Press
Printing and Binding: Kingsport Press
Kingsport, Tennessee
Cover design: Charles Kling & Associates
Type: Roma with
Roma Semi-Bold
display

THE ART OF THE SAINT JOHN'S BIBLE

Susan Sink offers her books as a starting place for a deeper experience of the images and text of The Saint John's Bible. *I believe she has eminently succeeded. She helps us to ask questions of ourselves and gives us some tools to find our own way without dictating ready-made answers. Finally she bids us God speed on our journey through the Scriptures.*

DONALD JACKSON
Artistic Director of The Saint John's Bible

Sink has outdone herself! If you want to probe the richness of The Saint John's Bible, *you will find this book a real treasure.*

IRENE NOWELL, OSB
Old Testament Editor, The Little Rock Catholic Study Bible

THE ART OF
THE SAINT JOHN'S
BIBLE

A Reader's Guide to Historical Books,

Letters and Revelation

BY SUSAN SINK

DONALD JACKSON – ARTISTIC DIRECTOR

THE SAINT JOHN'S BIBLE

Collegeville, Minnesota

A Saint John's Bible Book
published by
Liturgical Press   www.saintjohnsbible.org

Design by Jerry Kelly
Cover images by Donald Jackson (details from *Joshua Anthology* and *Vision of the New Jerusalem*) and Aidan Hart (detail from *Elisha and the Six Miracles*)

ISBN 978-0-8146-9098-7

LIBRARY OF CONGRESS CATALOGING-IN-PUBLICATION DATA

Sink, Susan.
    The art of the Saint John's Bible / Susan Sink.
        p. cm.
    Includes bibliographical references and indexes.
    ISBN 978-0-8146-9062-8
    1. Saint John's Bible—Illustrations. 2. Illumination of books and manuscripts—Wales. 3. St. John's University (Collegeville, Minn.) I. Title.
    ND3355.5.S29S56 2007
    745.6'721--dc22   2007003564

The author gratefully acknowledges the contributions to this volume by members of *The Saint John's Bible* team. Donald Jackson's presentations on his work to the Committee on Illumination and Text (CIT) were invaluable in understanding his approach and how *Historical Books* and *Letters and Revelation* came together as works of art. Donald Jackson and Sarah Harris in Wales also read the manuscript and offered additional information and clarification. Tim Ternes and Linda Orzechowski provided me with additional information and helped facilitate the research and drafting process. The chair of the CIT, Father Michael Patella, OSB, again generously shared his time and knowledge to help me understand the theological underpinnings of these books and the choices made as to what to illuminate and emphasize. He read drafts of the manuscript and offered suggestions that clarified both the ideas and the prose. My hope for this volume is that it offers a starting place to a deeper experience of the images and texts. I hope that the reader's journey through the Scripture texts will be as rewarding as the *visio divina* that resulted in this book.

CONTENTS

INTRODUCTION

WELCOME TO the third and final installment of *The Art of The Saint John's Bible*. The volumes of *The Saint John's Bible* explored in this book are the final two completed by Donald Jackson and his team at the scriptorium in Wales. *The Saint John's Bible* is organized in seven volumes, and the two covered here are far apart: *Historical Books* is volume 2 and *Letters and Revelation* is volume 7. However, they are part of a single story, the story of God's relationship with humanity and with the natural world that begins with an account of creation in Genesis and moves through the fulfillment of creation in Revelation.

The story of God told in these volumes of *The Saint John's Bible* is of a God who is present in history. This God is engaged with the people and dwells with the people in the ark, in the temple, and finally in the new Jerusalem depicted in the book of Revelation. In these two volumes we enter the story at two significant points—first as the twelve tribes of Israel cross the Jordan into the Promised Land, and then as Paul and other evangelists begin recording the beliefs and practices of the early Christian church. In both cases, we can ask the question, "What is God asking of the people?" In so doing, we ask, "What is God asking of us?"

These volumes, as the final two in the series, are also able to make full use of the rich visual imagery that has been created for *The Saint John's Bible*. Jackson and his team of scribes and calligraphers are able to draw on previous pieces they've done for imagery and motifs, as well as develop more images. *Historical Books* and *Letters* contain a number of insects and plants by naturalist illustrator Chris Tomlin and other elements, such as decorated capital letters, book headings, carpet pages, and even a few corrections. *Historical Books* introduces a number of images that point to the Egyptian heritage of the tribes of Israel. *Revelation* uses many stamps and images found in *Prophets*, as well as stunning representations of the figures in John's vision of the Apocalypse.

On June 18, 2011, Donald Jackson presented the final folios for the volume *Letters and Revelation* to Saint John's Abbey and University. He and his wife Mabel, along with a few other members of the team in

Wales, traveled to Minnesota to deliver the pages and participate in a closing celebration. Jackson began by presenting the pages to the Committee on Illumination and Text, who had worked with him during the decade over which the project took place and who provided the schema that guided the choice of illuminations and text treatments, their context and significance.

The pages were seen by the public for the first time during Evening Prayer in the Abbey Church, when Jackson formally presented the illumination *Vision of the New Jerusalem* to the abbot of Saint John's Abbey, John Klassen, OSB, and the president of Saint John's University, Robert Koopmann, OSB. At a dinner following the liturgy, Donald and Mabel Jackson were presented with the Colman Barry Award for Distinguished Contribution to Religion and Society by Saint John's Abbey and University. This event drew to a close the creation phase of *The Saint John's Bible*.

However, it did not bring to a close *The Saint John's Bible* project. The plan is ultimately to bind the pages into seven volumes, though a date has not been set for binding. For now, framed pages are able to circulate in museum exhibitions. People can view multiple pages from a single volume in a gallery or collections of pages from more than one volume. It is the hope of Saint John's Abbey and University that the collection will continue to inspire and delight people the world over for years to come. High quality reproductions of the pages are also available, and will always be available, for a variety of groups to present in their spaces. For more information on *The Saint John's Bible* project and opportunities for individuals and groups to engage further, visit the website www.saintjohnsbible.org.

HISTORICAL BOOKS

FOR THOSE who love adventure, the Historical Books of the Bible are a great read. Those who are put off by violence might have a harder time. Anyone reading these books straight through might want to take a break and return to the Wisdom books or flip frequently to the Psalms for a respite. In fact, many of the psalms take on a new intensity in light of the historical context that accompanies them.

These books chronicle the history of a conquering people. There are good kings and judges, but there are also many bad kings. Even good kings take terrible falls. These pages are filled with violence and bloodshed—not promising material for an illuminated volume. How do we make sense of all this bloodshed, much of it sanctioned or required by a God we describe as loving and merciful?

First, it is best not to take this "history" literally, although there are some scholars who do. At the very least, we must consider who is telling the story. Libraries are full of books of history told from the perspective of the conquerors, whose veracity, especially when it comes to heroics, doesn't hold up. It is best to read these books with an eye toward conventions in ancient literature. There is much here to compare to the Greek histories, where anthropomorphic, fickle gods guided, obstructed, tricked, rewarded, and punished warriors and kings. And again our primary purpose in reading this history is to learn more about what it says about us and our relationship with God. What is the nature of the covenant and God's commands? What is the trajectory of the Israelites? What does it mean to claim this as our story? There is much to consider —in the opening of Joshua, two spies are sent to scope out Jericho, and they are protected by the prostitute Rahab. If nothing else, this should tell us we are in for an interesting story!

These accounts, like all the genres of the Bible, tell us first and foremost about the relationship between God and humankind. Our God is not absent from history but present and engaged. However, there is no sudden transformation of the people's character from the days of wandering in the desert at the end of the Pentateuch to the conquering days of the Historical Books. God has a plan for the kingdom, but the people are not on board. It is true that in Joshua and Judges we see the Israelites called to conquer the inhabitants of the Promised Land in the worst way—leaving no one standing. But very soon, the books shift to reflect punishment of the chosen people for forsaking the covenant. As Michael Patella, OSB, chair of the Committee on Illumination and Text, points out, "In these later accounts, the people are chastised and punished for neglecting the well-being of the widow, orphan, and foreigner in their midst."

Our clue to how *The Saint John's Bible* approaches these books comes in the marginal text treatment running throughout the first book, Joshua. God lists all that he has done for his people in the closing chapter, Joshua 24, captured in these excerpts:

> They fought with you, and I handed them over to you, and you took possession of their land. . . . I sent the hornet ahead of you, which drove out before you the two kings of the Amorites; it was not by your sword or by your bow. I gave you a land on which you had not labored, and towns that you had not built, and you live in them; you eat the fruit of vineyards and oliveyards that you did not plant. "Now therefore revere the Lord, and serve him in sincerity and faithfulness."

And what did the people do? Look at the text treatment in the first page of Judges:

> Then the Israelites did what was evil in the sight of the Lord. (Judg 2:11)

As people, as nations, we continue to struggle to do what is right. As Fr. Michael Patella has written,

> If we can glean anything from the Historical Books, let it be this: The history of God dealing with his people is not neat and tidy. Humankind, left to its own devices, can spiral downward into a moral abyss, even as we proclaim fidelity to the Lord. Because God has never wavered in his love for the people he has created, we have been spared the worst we could possibly do to ourselves and others. Furthermore, the grace of God's justice and peace can rise from the most unlikely of places, and our redemption is always close at hand.

There is also delight to be found in these books as we encounter key figures of the Bible. The prophets Samuel, Elijah, and Elisha are in these pages, and so is the magnificent story of King Saul and King David and the touching and inspiring account of Ruth, the Moabite from whom David and eventually Jesus are descended; for Christians, there are the rich stories behind the genealogy in Matthew's Gospel that show, again, the motley bunch from which God raised up a savior, God's faithfulness to his people, and the importance of the widow and foreigner.

Donald Jackson's treatment of this volume traces the disintegration of the society for failing to keep to the Lord's commands. The constant comment by the writer of Judges, "In those days there was no king in Israel; all the people did what was right in their own eyes" (Judg 17:6), reaches its logical conclusion with the Babylonian conquest of Judah and the exile of its people to Babylon. The army ants, grasshoppers, and scorpions running through the pages carry this motif, and they are juxtaposed against the bright colors of the promise.

Donald Jackson has packed this volume with color, from the initial capitals of each chapter to the full-page illuminations bursting with energy. The task of writing this volume, with 271 pages of illumination and text, engaged the team for years.

There are 25,812 lines of text in *Historical Books*. In addition, there are 306 initial capital letters in this volume, no two alike. There are seventy-nine different *T*s alone, fifty-six *N*s, and thirty-seven *W*s! And on every page, of course, you will find the gorgeous calligraphy. If you have followed the volumes, you may be able to recognize the different hands of calligraphers. Note the slight changes in the descenders and occasional flourishes as the scribes wrote their way through these foundational stories.

For those who love illuminations, this volume is a treat. Only *Gospels and Acts* has as many illuminations as this volume, which has twenty-six illuminations of biblical passages, in addition to text treatments and marginalia insects by Chris Tomlin.

JOSHUA ANTHOLOGY

THE ART OF THE SAINT JOHN'S BIBLE

What catches your eye in this illumination? How do the images representing nature and culture work together to tell the story of the Israelites' move into the Promised Land?

The book of Joshua opens with these words, "After the death of Moses . . ." We are reminded of the end of the Pentateuch and the illumination of Deuteronomy 34:1-12, *The Death of Moses*. Moses did not reach the Promised Land, and so it falls to Joshua to take the Israelites across the Jordan, out of the wilderness, and into the land that God has given them. But of course, the land is inhabited, and they do not take possession of it without wars and bloodshed.

All of this is packed into the *Joshua Anthology*. Broken and fragmented along the far shore of the Jordan are pieces of Thomas Ingmire's illumination of the Ten Commandments. In fact, the block of text at the bottom right is the exact fragment held by Moses as a symbolic tablet in *The Death of Moses*. Joshua will bring over the ark of the covenant containing the commandments and the Law, but the people will have difficulty following it. The ark of the covenant is depicted here by the stamp of the gold archway. This stamp will be used throughout *Historical Books,* most dramatically in the *David Anthology* when David brings the ark of the covenant into Jerusalem.

On the right side of the Jordan are also ghostly cities, punctuated with flames, the cities that will not stand. This is the bloodshed of conquest, an ongoing theme in coming pages.

On the left side of the Jordan are images from the wilderness, including two pensive lions that watch over the scene. There is also, very prominently, the golden calf of the wilderness disobedience, a menacing scarab beetle that seems prepared to lead the Israelites in the wrong direction, and an image of an Egyptian eye, another sign of the false gods of Egypt.

The Jordan itself is filled with drowned bodies, the cost of this conquering history. It reminds us of Pharaoh's army drowned during the crossing of the Red Sea in Exodus, but

Joshua Anthology

JOSHUA 1–24

Every place that the sole of your foot will tread upon I have given to you, as I promised to Moses. (1:3)

it also points toward the conquering of peoples that is to come. The images of headless bodies in the river come from reliefs in the British Museum from Syrian temples chronicling their own conquests.

In this, the first illumination, Donald Jackson introduces two visual elements he will continue throughout the volume. The first is a three-tiered color scheme. In addition to gold, which depicts the heavenly kingdom and God's presence, Jackson used green to emphasize the presence of the prophets and priesthood. Like the beauty and fertility of nature, green suggests right relationship and order, the natural world reflecting its true purpose and being in harmony with God. Finally, you will notice Jackson's strong use of purple throughout the volume, which he used to represent the earthly kingdom, the people striving to put earthly leaders and kings in place. As you will see, they have very mixed results.

Note all the purple in this first illumination. It is as a conquering people, under the leadership of Joshua (and with drowning and flames), that the Israelites arrive.

The second visual element is found in the striped border. As in other volumes dealing with this period in history, Donald Jackson turned to ancient Egyptian elements for inspiration. The design in this border, which will be repeated again and again, is from a frieze on an Egyptian burial tomb. It is, of course, a reminder of where the Israelites came from and where they may have picked up their tendency to turn again and again to foreign gods.

◖ *If you have the first volume in this series or the reproduction volume* Pentateuch, *put the image of* The Death of Moses *in* Deuteronomy *next to this illumination. What similarities and differences do you see in the focus of these two illuminations?*

What other "gods" call your attention?

This brief illumination draws attention right from the beginning to the mandate given by God. The verse is Joshua 24:15, from the very end of the book, when Joshua addresses the people. Yet it is this verse, this choice by the people, that looms over everything. The full verse reads, "Now if you are unwilling to serve the Lord, choose this day whom

JOSHUA 24:15

Choose this day whom you will serve. (24:15a)

you will serve, whether the gods your ancestors served in the region beyond the River or the gods of the Amorites in whose land you are living; but as for me and my household, we will serve the Lord."

These people arrive in the Promised Land trailing gods. In the illumination we see the Egyptian eye and the bands of color that resemble the rich robes and ornamentation of pharaohs or kings. Much more lightly inscribed is the menorah, that symbol of God's covenant. In *The Saint John's Bible* we first saw an image of the menorah in the illumination *Abraham and Sarah*, when God made his covenant with them. It carries through Psalms and is the image at the heart of Matthew's *Genealogy of Christ*. The question here to the Israelites is twofold: Who will you follow as your earthly ruler, and who will you follow as your God? It is clear that God, who provided the Law, is sufficient for both, but God has competition.

The terms of this relationship are spelled out in the text treatments in this book—God has given the Israelites the land in which they live and everything in it. They are given the choice of whom to serve; God does not control them any more than he controlled Adam in the Garden of Eden. There is no reason for the Israelites to turn to other gods or other rulers, and yet, in the very next book, that is exactly what they do.

◖ *In what way do you demonstrate that you have chosen to follow the Lord God?*

THE ART OF THE SAINT JOHN'S BIBLE

Read Judges 4 and 5. What do you think the song adds to the story of Deborah and Barak and the defeat of Sisera?

The story of the judge Deborah and the rout of the warrior Sisera is a twice-told story. Judges 4 tells the story in narrative form, and then chapter 5 sings it. The story follows an arc we see over and over in these books. Chapter 4 begins, as so many, "The Israelites again did what was evil in the sight of the Lord" (4:1). The Lord gives them to their enemy, King Jabin of Canaan, whose army commander is Sisera. The Israelites cry out for help, and the Lord raises up a judge, this time the prophetess Deborah.

The story of the death of Sisera is highlighted in *The Saint John's Bible* for several reasons; among them is to draw attention to a woman who was a great judge. As the Lord will later raise up a savior in Queen Esther, so the Lord raises up Deborah in this early history to deliver the people from the Philistines. In fact, the warrior Barak will not go out against Sisera's troops unless Deborah rides with him. So it is that a woman is not just the chosen one of the Lord and the wise counselor who commands the troops; she also rides into battle with the other warriors.

There is also a double humiliation for Sisera. Not only is he killed by his enemy, but he is killed by a woman, a great humiliation for a warrior in this region at this time. In the very next illuminated story, the death of Abimelech, the self-appointed king will beg his armor bearer to kill him so that he can escape the fate of being killed by a woman (9:54).

In this case it is Jael who lures Sisera into her tent and then drives a tent stake through his head. The illumination by Jackson vividly

Death of Sisera

JUDGES 5:1-31
She struck Sisera a blow. (5:26b)

AND·THERE·WAS·SISERA· ·LYING·DEAD·

portrays Jael with her tent stake and mallet, as well as the fallen Sisera, warriors climbing Mt. Tabor, and the flames of battle. The pattern from the Egyptian frieze forms the tent over Jael.

Chapter 5, the verse account of this story, has the classic elements of a ballad. It is not unlike the much later French and British ballads telling the stories of knights or the ancient Greek songs of the *Iliad* that recount great battles. It begins with a declaration that it is a song of praise to the Lord, describes the scene, and invites others to retell the story. These verses sing the account of the battle and move on to the story of Jael, "most blessed of women" for delivering Israel from its enemy Sisera. It imagines another woman, the mother of Sisera, waiting for her son to return from battle and realizing that he will not come home, that his troops have been routed. It is a beautiful piece of poetry inserted in the otherwise narrative account.

This illumination is the first of five small panels inserted into small places left on the pages of vellum when the text was written as long as nine years before. These five build up to the *Judges Anthology* page, when all is chaos and, as the text on that page says, "all the people did what was right in their own eyes." These five stories show the rise and fall of the judges, particularly the battles and conquests as they try to solidify a kingdom for Israel. Donald Jackson used thematic elements, including the striped element here to suggest a tent, pieces of the scarab pattern suggesting the pull of Egypt and Egypt's gods, and the fire of ongoing conflagration and battle. On another frieze in an Egyptian tomb, he found images of Egyptians in battle against African forces that he used to show the defeat of the Philistines. He continued with these figures in the illuminations *Story of Samson* and *Cities in Flames*.

❡ *Does this story surprise you? How does it fit or challenge your understanding of the Old Testament?*

then come and take refuge in my shade;
but if not, let fire come out of the bramble
and devour the cedars of Lebanon.

Death of Abimelech

JUDGES 9:22-57
Abimelech ruled over Israel
three years. (9:22)

What do you think would be the advantage or
disadvantage of being led by a judge instead of a king?

The story of Abimelech raises an important question at this point in the history of Israel: What is the role of monarchy? The tribes the Israelites are fighting against all seem to be ruled by kings. In the previous chapter, Abimelech's father, Gideon, is asked by the people to become their king. He answers, "I will not rule over you, and my son will not rule over you; the Lord will rule over you" (8:23). However, Gideon does make an idol for the people out of their loot, in the same way that Aaron collected jewelry to make the golden calf in the desert, and although he is a good judge and his time is blessed, he sets up the misery of Abimelech's time.

Abimelech is not only the youngest of Gideon's sons but also the son of a concubine and therefore not a direct heir. He incites his mother's family to back him in an overthrow of his brothers and kills all but the youngest of the seventy legitimate heirs. One thing to notice in the account is how it breaks completely from the earlier formulas. Where is the Lord? Abimelech makes himself king, and the people follow. God will intervene to avenge the death of the seventy through the "lords of Shechem" (9:23), but that is the only time God appears in this account. And, without God on his side, the very people who put Abimelech in power will now rise against him and overthrow him.

Of course, the people of Shechem are no friends of the Lord. In the end, God brings about destruction on both sides. What is also telling is that "when the Israelites saw that Abimelech was dead, they all went home" (9:56). The kingship has no depth, and unlike the situation with the good judges, where God raised up another leader to guide, the people are without a leader and seemingly without hope. They do seem to learn their lesson, however, and they return to depending on good judges, Tola and Jair, experiencing forty-five years of peace.

Notice that this illumination has no bars of gold running through it. All is chaos, fire and death. The cedars of Lebanon, which feed the fire Abimelech sets on the Tower of Shechem, are depicted on the right side of the illumination.

❧ Read the parable of the trees in Judges 9:7-15. What kind of predictor is this of Abimelech's reign?

How do you interpret the white, red, and gold figures in this illumination?

The story of the sacrifice of Jephthah's daughter reads like a Greek tragedy. Jephthah makes a vow that if the Lord gives him victory over the Ammonites, he will give as a burnt offering the first person to greet him after his return from battle. Probably he was hoping one of his servants would be first to greet him, but instead it is his daughter, who rushes out to meet him "with timbrels and dancing" (11:34).

Now Jephthah has a terrible choice. Should he fulfill his vow and sacrifice his daughter, his only child? It is the daughter herself—unnamed throughout the account—who urges him to fulfill his vow. She is permitted first to wander for two months, lamenting her virginity. We can take her virginity as a symbol of the unfulfilled promise of a life of marriage and

Burning of Jephthah's Daughter

JUDGES 11:29-40

My father, if you have opened your mouth to the Lord, do to me according to what has gone out of your mouth.
(11:36)

BURNING OF JEPHTHAH'S DAUGHTER

offspring. Furthermore, we are told that after her death "there arose an Israelite custom that for four days every year the daughters of Israel would go out to lament the daughter of Jephthah" (11:40). The verb translated as "lament" in this verse is translated elsewhere as "sing, tell, recite."[1]

Aside from Isaac, who was spared, Jephthah's daughter is the only story of an Israelite offered as a burnt sacrifice in the Bible, though the prophets constantly rail against the people who fall into that heinous sin.

The illumination depicts several aspects of this story. Notice how it breaks the frame at the top and bottom. The whole illumination forms an altar.

◀ *Do you know any stories from other cultures that are similar to this one?*

[1] Victor P. Hamilton, *Handbook on the Historical Books* (Grand Rapids, MI: Baker Academic, 2001), 146.

THE ART OF THE SAINT JOHN'S BIBLE

What kind of hero is Samson? How is he similar or different from the heroes we have seen before in these books?

Samson is a great and colorful hero of the Historical Books. Samson is called to deliver (one meaning of the title "judge") the Israelites from the Philistines, who have held them captive for forty years following the introductory and by now familiar verse, "The Israelites again did what was evil in the sight of the Lord" (13:1).

The story of Samson is also familiar in its elements. It begins with a barren woman, identified only as "the wife of Manoah." An angel of the Lord tells her that she will bear a son and that she should not cut his hair. He also tells her not to drink strong drink or eat unclean fruit. She takes the message to her husband, and although he immediately believes, he also wants to see the representative of the Lord with his own eyes. But it is only through his wife that he is brought to this messenger. There is something in the instructions and the dynamic that might make us think of Adam and Eve, and this story has the same elemental, mythical feel. Obey and be blessed. When they see the angel rise with the burnt offering, Manoah fears they will be killed by God, but his wife reassures him. If nothing else, the story demonstrates how confused they are about God and their relationship with God. This is how so many of the stories of salvation begin in the Historical Books. It is probably very akin to how people felt after the exile when they encountered the Lord God in the book of the law and the rabbinical tradition.

There are many tales in these short chapters about Samson, but the illumination in *The Saint John's Bible* focuses on two elements: the angel's visit to the wife of Manoah and the destruction of the palace. On the left, in gold, we see the figure of the angel of the Lord who appeared to the barren woman and told her she would have a child. The angel seems engulfed in orange flame—it could be that this is a depiction of the angel rising with the burnt offering. This part of the illumination is richly colored, suggesting the favor bestowed upon Samson. However, it is also interwoven with

Story of Samson

JUDGES 13–16
It is he who shall begin to deliver Israel from the hand of the Philistines. (13:5)

ing at our hands, or shown us all these things, or now announced to us such things as these." ❧ The woman bore a son, and named him Samson. The boy grew, and the LORD blessed him.²⁵ The spirit of the LORD began to stir him in Mahaneh-dan, between Zorah and Eshtaol.

14 Once Samson went down to Timnah, and at Timnah he saw a Philistine woman. ²Then he came up, and told his father & mother, "I saw a Philistine woman at Timnah; now get her for me as my wife."³ But his father & mother said to him, "Is there not a woman among your kin, or among all our people, that you must go to take a wife from the uncircumcised Philistines?" But Samson said to his father, "Get her for me, because she pleases me."⁴ His father and mother did not know that this was from the LORD; for he was seeking a pretext to act against the Philistines. At that time the Philistines had dominion over Israel. ⁵ Then Samson went down with his father and mother to Timnah. When he came to the vineyards of Timnah, suddenly a young lion roared at him.⁶ The spirit of the LORD rushed on him, and he tore the lion apart barehanded as one might tear apart a kid. But he did not tell his father or his mother what he had done.⁷ Then he went down and talked with the woman, and she pleased Samson.⁸ After a while he returned to marry her, and he turned aside to see the carcass of the lion, and there was a swarm of bees in the body of the lion, and honey.⁹ He scraped it out into his hands, and went on, eating as he went. When he came to his father & mother, he gave some to them, and they ate it. But he did not tell them that he had taken the honey from the carcass of the lion. ❧ His father went down to the woman, and Samson made a feast there as the young men were accustomed to do.¹¹ When the people saw him, they brought thirty companions to be with him.¹² Samson said to them, "Let me now put a riddle to you. If you can explain it to me within the seven days of the feast, and find it out, then I will give you thirty linen garments and thirty festal garments.¹³ But if you cannot explain it to me, then you shall give me thirty linen garments and thirty festal garments." So they said to him, "Ask your riddle;

ᵃ Cn: Heb *my*
ᵇ Gk Syr: Heb *vineyards*
ᶜ Heb *shocks*
ᵈ Gk Tg Vg: Heb *lacks* and

let us hear it."¹⁴ He said to them,
"Out of the eater came something to eat.
Out of the strong came something sweet."
But for three days they could not explain the riddle.¹⁵ ❧ On the fourth day they said to Samson's wife, "Coax your husband to explain the riddle to us or we will burn you and your father's house with fire. Have you invited us here to impoverish us?"¹⁶ So Samson's wife wept before him, saying, "You hate me; you do not really love me. You have asked a riddle of my people, but you have not explained it to me." He said to her, "Look, I have not told my father or my mother. Why should I tell you?"¹⁷ She wept before him the seven days that their feast lasted; and because she nagged him, on the seventh day he told her. Then she explained the riddle to her people.¹⁸ The men of the town said to him on the seventh day before the sun went down,
"What is sweeter than honey?
What is stronger than a lion?"
And he said to them,
"If you had not plowed with my heifer,
you would not have found out my riddle."
¹⁹ Then the spirit of the LORD rushed on him, and he went down to Ashkelon. He killed thirty men of the town, took their spoil, and gave the festal garments to those who had explained the riddle. In hot anger he went back to his father's house.²⁰ And Samson's wife was given to his companion, who had been his best man.

15 After a while, at the time of the wheat harvest, Samson went to visit his wife, bringing along a kid. He said, "I want to go into my wife's room." But her father would not allow him to go in.² Her father said, "I was sure that you had rejected her; so I gave her to your companion. Is not her younger sister prettier than she? Why not take her instead?"³ Samson said to them, "This time, when I do mischief to the Philistines, I will be without blame."⁴ So Samson went and caught three hundred foxes, and took some torches; and he turned the foxes tail to tail, and put a torch between each pair of tails.⁵ When he had set fire to the torches, he let the foxes go into the standing grain of the Philistines, & burned up the shocks and the standing grain, as well as the vineyards & olive groves.⁶ Then the Philistines asked, "Who has done this?" And they said, "Samson, the son-in-law of the Timnite, because he has taken Samson's wife and given her to his companion." So the Philistines came up and burned her and her father.⁷ Samson said to them, "If this is what you do, I swear I will not stop until I have taken revenge on you."⁸ He

'LET·ME·DIE·WITH·THE·PHILISTINES'

the Egyptian elements we've seen before. In fact, the depiction of the warrior bodies, representing the Philistines, comes from Egyptian frescos. The frescos are actually made on wet plaster on walls, and Donald Jackson said that the originals look like batik. They illustrate battle scenes and remind us that this story is part of a long history of stories about conquest and battles.

Samson seems to have been born to a single purpose: to punish the Philistines. In a variety of episodes, he wreaks havoc on them. He seems close to nature and reminiscent of the companion of Gilgamesh, Enkidu, who was a wild man, close to nature and possessed of great strength. In the horizontal part of this illumination that interrupts the text on the page, we see an image of Samson, the blue figure, with his hair grown back and his hands spread, pushing down the columns of the palace. Again in stylized fashion, we see the death of the Philistines among the broken columns.

Donald Jackson has continued the theme across the page, making the initial *A* of chapter 15 out of the columns and scattering a few at the bottom of the page with the motto, "Let me die with the Philistines" (16:30). Unlike other heroes we've encountered so far, Samson dies, as it were, in battle. His death is treated heroically, not as punishment for disobedience or a turn from God. The illumination shares many elements with the panels that precede it in Judges, all building up to the *Judges Anthology*.

◀ *There are so many stories packed into the account of Samson. Focusing on another aspect—his strength, his relationship to nature, or his relationship with women—how might you illuminate the passage?*

Cities in Flames

JUDGES 20

And there was the whole city going up in smoke toward the sky! (20:40)

What do this story and illumination tell us about the nature of violence?

The *Cities in Flames* illumination depicts a real low point for Israel. The story told in Judges 19 is of a Levite, a member of the priestly tribe of Israel, seeking shelter overnight in the Benjaminite city of Gibeah. While there, members of the tribe of Benjamin attack the house. He gives them his concubine, who is raped mercilessly throughout the night. In the morning she makes her way to the doorstep and dies. The Levite takes her body home and sends it in twelve pieces throughout the twelve tribal areas of Israel.

Chapter 20 tells what happens in the aftermath of this crime. By the end, the tribe of Benjamin is almost completely wiped out. What makes this episode stand out from the other acts of violence in these books is the fact that it is internal to Israel. Israel has sinned against itself.

What marks this illumination is the presence of a contemporary person, a young man or maybe a child. This person is a representative of the cities still in flames in the Middle East. Is he Israeli? Palestinian? He is definitely a representative of the currently divided area, where people fight against people who are close neighbors. It is representative of a place where people still do not live as brothers and cities still burn. Although it is tempting to find parallels to the current violence in Israel throughout *Historical Books*, this is the only reference to the current Israeli/Palestinian conflict in the volume.

◀ *What were your initial thoughts about the figure of the boy in this illumination? Why do you think it's so powerful in this context?*

THE ART OF THE SAINT JOHN'S BIBLE

Israel." But the Benjaminites would not listen to their kinsfolk, the Israelites." The Benjaminites came together out of the towns to Gibeah, to go out to battle against the Israelites." On that day the Benjaminites mustered twenty-six thousand armed men from their towns, besides the inhabitants of Gibeah." Of all this force, there were seven hundred picked men who were left-handed; every one could sling a stone at a hair, and not miss. And the Israelites, apart from Benjamin, mustered four hundred thousand armed men, all of them warriors. ¶ The Israelites proceeded to go up to Bethel, where they inquired of God, "Which of us shall go up first to battle against the Benjaminites?" And the LORD answered, "Judah shall go up first." ¶ Then the Israelites got up in the morning, and encamped against Gibeah." The Israelites went out to battle against Benjamin; and the Israelites drew up the battle line against them at Gibeah." The Benjaminites came out of Gibeah, and struck down on that day twenty-two thousand of the Israelites." The Israelites went up & wept before the LORD until the evening; and they inquired of the LORD, "Shall we again draw near to battle against our kinsfolk the Benjaminites?" And the LORD said, "Go up against them."" The Israelites took courage, and again formed the battle line in the same place where they had formed it on the first day." So the Israelites advanced against the Benjaminites the second day." Benjamin moved out against them from Gibeah the second day, and struck down eighteen thousand of the Israelites, all of them armed men." Then all the Israelites, the whole army, went back to Bethel and wept, sitting there before the LORD; they fasted that day until evening. Then they offered burnt offerings and sacrifices of well-being before the LORD." And the Israelites inquired of the LORD [for the ark of the covenant of God was there in those days, and Phinehas son of Eleazar, son of Aaron, ministered before it in those days], saying, "Shall we go out once more to battle against our kinsfolk the Benjaminites, or shall we desist?" The LORD answered, "Go up, for tomorrow I will give them into your hand."" So Israel stationed men in ambush around Gibeah. Then the Israelites went up against the Benjaminites on the third day, and set themselves in array against Gibeah, as before. ¶ When the Benjaminites went out against the army, they were drawn away from the city. As before they began to inflict casualties on the troops, along the main roads, one of which goes up to Bethel and the other to Gibeah, as well as in the open country, killing about thirty men of Israel." The Benjaminites thought, "They are being routed before us, as previously." But the Israelites said, "Let us retreat & draw them away from the city toward the roads."" The main body of the Israelites drew back its battle line to Baal-tamar, while those Israelites who were in ambush rushed out of their place west of Geba." There came against Gibeah ten thousand picked men out of all Israel, and the battle was fierce. But the Benjaminites did not realize that disaster was close upon them. ¶ The LORD defeated Benjamin before Israel; and the Israelites destroyed twenty-five thousand one hundred men of Benjamin that day, all of them armed. ¶ Then the Benjaminites saw that they were defeated. ¶ The Israelites gave ground to Benjamin, because they trusted to the troops in ambush that they had stationed against Gibeah." The troops in ambush rushed quickly upon Gibeah. Then they put the whole city to the sword." Now the agreement between the main body of Israel and the men in ambush was that when they sent up a cloud of smoke out of the city "the main body of Israel should turn in battle. But Benjamin had begun to inflict casualties on the Israelites, killing about thirty of them; so they thought, "Surely they are defeated before us, as in the first battle."" But when the cloud, a column of smoke, began to rise out of the city, the Benjaminites looked behind them— and there was the whole city going up in smoke toward the sky!" Then the main body of Israel turned, and the Benjaminites were dismayed, for they saw that disaster was close upon them." Therefore they turned away from the Israelites in the direction of the wilderness; but the battle overtook them, and those who came out of the city were slaughtering them in between." Cutting down the Benjaminites, they pursued them from Nohah and trod them down as far as a place east of Gibeah." Eighteen thousand Benjaminites fell, all of them courageous fighters, "when they turned and fled toward the wilderness to the rock of Rimmon; five thousand of them were cut down on the main roads, and they were pursued as far as Gidom, and two thousand of them were slain." So all who fell that day of Benjamin were twenty-five thousand arms-bearing men, all of them courageous fighters." But six hundred turned and fled toward the wilderness to the rock of Rimmon, and remained at the rock of Rimmon for four months." Meanwhile, the Israelites turned back against the Benjaminites, and put them to the sword - the city, the people, the animals, and all that remained. Also the remaining towns they set on fire.

IN THOSE DAYS THERE WAS NO KING IN ISRAEL.

Verses 22 and 23 are transposed
Gk, Vg: Heb on the plain
This sentence is continued by verse 44.
Compare Vg and some Gk Mss: Heb cities
Compare Syr: Meaning of Heb uncertain
Gk: Heb surrounding
Gk: Heb pursued them at their resting place

AND·THERE·WAS·THE·WHOLE·
·CITY·GOING·UP·IN·SMOKE·
·TOWARD·THE·SKY·

CITIES IN FLAMES

HISTORICAL BOOKS

Judges Anthology

In those days there was no king in Israel; all the people did what was right in their own eyes. (21:25)

How would you describe this illumination? What story does it tell of the age of judges?

The final verse of Judges (21:25) sets us up for what is to come next (after a brief interlude with the story of Ruth). The people of Israel have not come together under the judges, and now God will give them kings.

ALL • THE PEOPLE • DID WHAT • WAS RIGHT • IN THEIR • OWN EYES

JUDGES ANTHOLOGY

THE ART OF THE SAINT JOHN'S BIBLE

Meanwhile, what can we say (or see) about this period of the judges? The illumination here has thick black bars throughout, and narrow bands of gold. There is rising and descending, climbing and falling. There are flames. At the top, wild dogs devour the people. At the base of the illumination, more wild dogs devour the people and arrows pierce them. There is blood and fire and, above all, chaos. There is no sense in this illumination of progress or stability, of growth and transformation. Three golden calf idols emerge at various places in the illumination, which is bordered on the right by hieroglyphics. The Israelites may have asserted themselves militarily, but they have not asserted themselves culturally or unified around a single culture. They are still, in a way, slaves to the old ways. Their future at this point, despite living in the land of Canaan, is far from certain. It is not clear if they will ever do what is right in the eyes of the Lord. It is not certain if they will make their stamp on this place and become a people.

After completing this illumination, Donald Jackson returned to add a final layer, the black batons. We can see them as the opposite of the gold and silver batons suggesting divine presence and wisdom, showing the ongoing bad choices of the Israelites. Jackson suggests that here the gold wedges, showing clearly God's continued presence with God's people, are "sort of scurrying around, almost like divine sheep dogs, trying to pull all these people together, while they're all defying it, going their own way, and still surrounded by the symbols of their yearning for the foreign gods." It is the good-bye to the Egyptian chapter before the Israelites move toward the era of prophets and kings.

◀ *Why do you think the people rejected rule by judges? How might kings be better—or not?*

Ruth and Naomi and Ruth the Gleaner

RUTH 1:16-18 / RUTH 2:2-23

Where you go, I will go.
(1:16)

Let me go to the field and glean among the ears of grain, behind someone in whose sight I may find favor.
(2:2)

What strikes you as important about the story of Ruth and Naomi? Do we see examples of their loyalty and love in the world today?

The book of Ruth is like an oasis for readers of *Historical Books*. It is similar to encountering the Song of Solomon in *Wisdom Books* after the hard moral wrangling of Job, Proverbs, and Ecclesiastes. Let us not forget there is love in the world, as well as kindness and kinship. After the accounts of judges and the ongoing captivity and redemption of the Israelites, let us focus our minds for a moment on the story of a woman and her mother-in-law. They are not kings or judges—both are widows. Let us consider how a foreign woman, a Moabite, contributed to the line of David.

We should also realize that it is only in the Christian canon that the book of Ruth appears in this place in the Old Testament. In the Jewish canon it is in a final section known as the Writings, along with the Song of Solomon. Since Ruth is the grandmother of King David, the book of Ruth makes a fine bridge to 1 Samuel where the reader first encounters the noteworthy monarch.

The illumination *Ruth and Naomi* by Suzanne Moore is reminiscent of another of her illuminations, *Praise of Wisdom* (Sir 24). Again we see Moore's love of arcs of color, of movement and images that seem to dance on the page. In their original inks on vellum, the color and movement are even more stunning than in the reproduction books. Again we see an emphasis on fertility and the stamped motif that appears in all seven volumes of *The Saint John's Bible*, perhaps most prominent in the illumination of the *Loaves and Fishes* (Mark 6). Donald Jackson often refers to this motif as "sacred geometry." The term, which can be used to describe measurements used for a religious building or some of the mathematical formulas and proportions found in nature (in leaves, shells, etc.), is used by Jackson to suggest a sort of cosmic order to the universe. Here it seems to reflect a sign of God's favor and God's miraculous provision for the two widows in this story.

The image of Ruth and Naomi also has echoes of the

portrait of Mary and Martha in the *Luke Anthology* (Luke 10). That illumination also showed the backs of two women with their gaze fixed ahead. In the case of Martha and Mary, they listened to Jesus telling the parables. Mary sat and listened, while Martha stood in her apron with her hands on her hips, perhaps impatient. In the image of Ruth and Naomi, they are seated side by side, looking out to their future. They are dressed in similar headdresses and flowing clothing—who can say which one is the foreigner? In Moab, it would have been Naomi who would have been the presumed outsider, a widow dependent on the households of her sons. Their love for each other unites the two women, and Ruth follows Naomi back to the land of Judah.

Two widows are not better than one when it comes to providing for themselves. But it is clear that without Ruth, Naomi's prospects would have been quite dim. Ruth takes on the dangerous task of gleaning, walking behind the harvesters to pick up the meager grain left behind. It seems she might be able to provide the two of them with food this way during the harvest, but it's unclear how she will continue to provide after the harvest is over. Also, mention is made of the dangers of gleaning and the strong possibility of being "bothered" or mistreated by the men in the fields.

The story of Ruth's love for her mother-in-law and also, presumably, Ruth's beauty, catch the eye of Boaz. Through her marriage to him, she is able to keep the land in her first husband's name, in effect perpetuating Naomi's line. Two widows—one a foreigner, the lowest in rank in the area—find favor with the Lord and are rescued. The story of Ruth is a glimpse of the kingdom, of what God has in mind for Israel, a success story. Boaz acts rightly toward her, and it is a happily-ever-after story.

The illumination of *Ruth the Gleaner* particularly reflects the movement in the story from famine, barrenness, and isolation in Moab to plenitude, fruitfulness, and community in Bethlehem, that famous city. They arrive at the start of the harvest and find generosity from Boaz. The marriage results in a son, Obed, who is named by all the women in the community! The swirling image at Ruth's center in this illumination is more than a basket of grain. It seems to speak to the abundance and fertility at the center of her being, an extension of her swirling skirts. Barrenness and God's promises will play a role in the next story we consider, that of Hannah, and they are ultimately seen in the story of Mary, the mother of Jesus, and her cousin Elizabeth, the mother of John the Baptist. The parallels are rich.

It is true that the Israelites often did what was evil in the sight of the Lord. But through a single line of people, including this Moabite woman mentioned in the genealogy of Jesus that opens the New Testament, God's plan was carried through.

The book of Ruth concludes with a special text treatment by Donald Jackson. Above the text treatment are seven stars of David. Beneath it is another representation of a menorah. The stars can be seen as flames on the menorah candles or simply as an extension of the motif. The treatment itself is of the genealogy, the women naming Ruth's son Obed, and the line into which he fits—from Perez, son of Judah by Tamar, to Obed, father of Jesse, the father of King David. In this way, this unusual story provides the bridge from the age of the judges to the age of kings.

The book of Ruth stands as a witness for inclusivity. The writer wishes to make the point that Israel's greatest king, David, was the grandson of a Moabite woman. For most of their history, Moabites were enemies of Israel.

◖ *Which figure do you think is Ruth, and which is Naomi in the illumination? Why?*

2

Now Naomi had a kinsman on her husband's side, a prominent rich man, of the family of Elimelech, whose name was Boaz. And Ruth the Moabite said to Naomi, "Let me go to the field & glean among the ears of grain, behind someone in whose sight I may find favor." She said to her, "Go, my daughter." So she went. She came & gleaned in the field behind the reapers. As it happened, she came to the part of the field belonging to Boaz, who was of the family of Elimelech. Just then Boaz came from Bethlehem. He said to the reapers, "The LORD be with you." They answered, "The LORD bless you." Then Boaz said to his servant who was in charge of the reapers, "To whom does this young woman belong?" The servant who was in charge of the reapers answered, "She is the Moabite who came back with Naomi from the country of Moab." She said, "Please, let me glean and gather among the sheaves behind the reapers." So she came, and she has been on her feet from early this morning until now, without resting even for a moment." Then Boaz said to Ruth, "Now listen, my daughter, do not go to glean in another field or leave this one, but keep close to my young women. Keep your eyes on the field that is being reaped, and follow behind them. I have ordered the young men not to bother you. If you get thirsty, go to the vessels & drink from what the young men have drawn." Then she fell prostrate, with her face to the ground, and said to him, "Why have I found favor in your sight, that you should take notice of me, when I am a foreigner?" But Boaz answered her, "All that you have done for your mother-in-law since the death of your husband has been fully told me, and how you left your father and mother and your native land and came to a people that you did not know before. May the LORD reward you for your deeds, and may you have a full reward from the LORD, the God of Israel, under whose wings you have come for refuge!" Then she said, "May I continue to find favor in your sight, my lord, for you have comforted me & spoken kindly to your servant, even though I am not one of your servants." At mealtime Boaz said to her, "Come here, and eat some of this bread, and dip your morsel in the sour wine." So she sat beside the reapers, and he heaped up for her some parched grain. She ate until she was satisfied, and she had some left over. When she got up to glean, Boaz instructed his young men, "Let her glean even among the standing sheaves, and do not reproach her. You must also pull out some handfuls for her from the bundles, and leave them for her to glean, and do not rebuke her." So she gleaned in the field until evening. Then she beat out what she had gleaned, and it was about an ephah of barley.

She picked it up and came into the town, and her mother-in-law saw how much she had gleaned. Then she took out and gave her what was left over after she herself had been satisfied. Her mother-in-law said to her, "Where did you glean today? And where have you worked? Blessed be the man who took notice of you." So she told her mother-in-law with whom she had worked, and said, "The name of the man with whom I worked today is Boaz." Then Naomi said to her daughter-in-law, "Blessed be he by the LORD, whose kindness has not forsaken the living or the dead!" Naomi also said to her, "The man is a relative of ours, one of our nearest kin." Then Ruth the Moabite said, "He even said to me, 'Stay close by my servants, until they have finished all my harvest.'" Naomi said to Ruth, her daughter-in-law, "It is better, my daughter, that you go out with his young women, otherwise you might be bothered in another field." So she stayed close to the young women of Boaz, gleaning until the end of the barley & wheat harvests; and she lived with her mother-in-law.

Compare Gk. Vg: Meaning of Heb uncertain
Or rest with the sight to redeem

רות

RUTH THE GLEANER

HISTORICAL BOOKS

Hannah's Prayer

1 SAMUEL 1:11; 2:1-10

My heart exults in the Lord.
(2:1)

What similarities do you see between Hannah's prayer (1 Sam 2:1-10) and the Magnificat (Luke 2:46-55)?

The book of Samuel begins with the story of Hannah, another barren woman, and her two prayers. Both of her prayers are significant, although it is the second that is most remembered and most often discussed. The illumination depicts both prayers, showing Hannah approaching God with a lament and her public exultation of gratitude.

The first prayer is a prayer that comes directly from her heart, out of her anguish over not being able to have a child. It has been made clear that her inability to have children has not caused her any problems with her husband, who loves her and gives her a "double portion," trying to compensate for her loss. It is true that the other wife, Peninnah, harasses her, and that her general status would be less because she hasn't given her husband an heir. This status is emphasized by the fact that she goes to the temple without anything to sacrifice or any official standing. There she "presented herself before the Lord" directly, and she offers this heartfelt prayer, depicted in the first half of the illumination: "O Lord of hosts, if only you will look on the misery of your servant, and remember me, and not forget your servant, but will give to your servant a male child, then I will set him before you as a nazirite until the day of his death. He shall drink neither wine nor intoxicants, and no razor shall touch his head" (1:11).

No sooner has she mouthed this prayer than the priest, Eli, accuses her of being drunk herself. This only emphasizes what a rare thing it is for a woman, or anyone, to pray like this at the temple, outside the rituals of sacrifice and petition through the priest. When she tells him her situation, he blesses her, and she goes away satisfied—with faith that her prayer will be answered.

And when it is, she sings a prayer of gratitude to the Lord. "My heart exults in the Lord," begins her prayer in chapter 2. This song hearkens back to the song of Deborah in Judges 5, and also by association back to the song of the women of Israel along the banks of the River Jordan after the destruction of Pharaoh and his men (Exod 15:20-21). The theme is that "there is no Rock like our God" (2:2) a deliverer who sweeps away any enemies and raises up the lowly. He looks with favor on the humble and those in distress and offers them riches and freedom from their misery. In this way, Hannah's prayer of gratitude goes beyond thankfulness for the birth of a child. As the illumination emphasizes, "I rejoice in my victory." Her triumph is likened to triumph in battle. This prayer song is another beautiful poem, one that could take its place beside any of the psalms.

Usually, however, Hannah's prayer is not seen as an extension of those women's prayers that have come before but is recognized for its resonance with the *Magnificat*, Mary's prayer in Luke 1:46-55. Like Hannah, Mary has "found favor" with God and identifies herself as a lowly servant who has been exalted by God.

Are you starting to recognize the work of Thomas Ingmire? There are similarities in this treatment to *Beatitudes* and to his treatments in the book of Job, as well as to *Messianic Predictions* in Isaiah. The illumination pairs the two prayers, both of them cries to the Lord. First she cries out of her misery—the black panel of the illumination. The ghostly text speaks to her humility and her lack of power in the temple. But because "the Lord remembered her" (1:19), she also rejoices in the birth of her son, Samuel, whom she returns to the service of God. Like *Messianic Predictions*, this is a public prayer, bold as trumpets.

◖ *Both Samson and Samuel are given to the temple as nazirites. However, they couldn't be more different! Keep this in mind as you read more about Samuel and consider what this tells us about God's choice of people to save and lead Israel.*

HANNAH'S PRAYER

Call of Samuel

I SAMUEL 3:1-18

Speak, Lord, for your servant is listening. (3:9)

Do you feel, or have you ever felt, called by God?

If only we all heard God's call as clearly as Samuel.

We know that Samuel is given into a corrupt temple where the sons of the priest Eli take the lion's share of the people's sacrifices and consort with the women who serve at the temple. As the NRSV translates it, "The sons of Eli were scoundrels" (2:12).

Despite all the emphasis in that society on heirs and birth order, when a family goes bad, God is quite capable of raising up a just leader or, in this case, calling a just prophet. In fact, we learn that there have not been many prophecies from this temple precisely because Eli's sons show such contempt for the Lord, and their father is incapable or unwilling to restrain them.

God calls Samuel, Hannah's son the nazirite. In the dark of night, as Samuel sleeps near the ark of the covenant, God calls him in a voice as clear and loud as that of Eli sleeping next door. In fact, since Samuel has not heard God's voice before, he goes three times to Eli's chamber, assuming he is the one who has called him. Finally Eli figures out what is happening and in-

CALL OF SAMUEL

structs Samuel to answer, "Speak, Lord, for your servant is listening." When Samuel does this, the Lord reveals himself and his plan to Samuel and instructs Samuel to bring the bad news to Eli—his family is about to be destroyed.

The illumination by Hazel Dolby emphasizes the nature of the call. In strips seemingly folded back and forth, the name of Samuel called in the dark night by God fills the space from top to bottom. God's word comes down, and Samuel's attention goes up, until the nature of what is happening becomes clear. Random letters are accented in gold foil, as Samuel learns what it means to hear God's voice, to recognize God in the simple language that wakes him up again and again.

This illumination also resonates with 3:19-20: "As Samuel grew up, the Lord was with him and let none of his words fall to the ground. And all Israel from Dan to Beer-sheba knew that Samuel was a trustworthy prophet of the Lord." The words here, seemingly folded on a single strip, do not fall to the ground but retain their crispness and clarity even as they traverse the spaces of heaven and earth.

This page is also marked by an error—a line left out by the scribe and recognized only when the scribe reached the end of the column and found it too short. In previous volumes, such errors have been "corrected" by ingenious illustrations, such as a bee cranking a pulley system in Wisdom 7 and a bird lifting the line into place in *Sower and the Seed* (Mark 4), and later a lemur will mark the spot for another missed line in 2 Chronicles. But here the treatment is simple, so as not to distract from the illumination, and the ornament, such as it is, is in keeping with the illumination. A gold leaf diamond and a simple line point to the place where the line was omitted, and a simple blue box, accompanied by a matching diamond, marks the line to be inserted by the reader in that place.

❧ *Samuel is the last of the judges, the one who will appoint Saul as the first king of Israel. Having gone through these stories, what have you learned about the role of judges?*

Is Saul a hero? Is he a tragic hero? How do you interpret Saul's character throughout his story?

As Samuel's story begins with a shake-up of the lineage of the priests, so Saul and his sons will not be heir to the kingship of Israel. The story of King Saul takes up more than two-thirds of the book of Samuel. But Saul is still only a transition to the true kingship, that of King David. It is from the house of David, not the house of Saul, that God will send the Savior and Redeemer. The prophets all proclaim this truth. Saul plays his role in the cycle of Israel as the people struggle with their relationship with God here in an earthly kingdom.

It is in part the failure of Samuel's own sons to be good judges that leads the people of Israel to beg him for a king. We begin the story of the illumination *Saul Anthology* with a text treatment in the margins of chapter 9. "And the Lord said to Samuel, 'Listen to the voice of the people in all that they say to you; for they have not rejected you, but they have rejected me from being king over them'" (8:7).

Saul is chosen by God; he is as handsome as any hero and from the lowliest of the twelve tribes, the tribe of Benjamin. This time Samuel anoints a king, not a judge, to deliver the people from the Philistines. He lets the people know in no uncertain terms that they have failed by not recognizing that God is their king but insisting on an earthly ruler. Still, despite this weakness on the part of the Israelites, Samuel and God will continue to be on their side. But the Israelites are warned: a king cannot save them, only God. If their king fails to follow God's commandments, the king will fall.

And in the very next story, in the first major challenge to Saul, he does indeed break the Lord's command. Although he has been told to wait for Samuel to offer the sacrifice that will bless their battle, Saul becomes impatient as the men start to leave, and he offers the sacrifice himself. But he is no priest, and this is not his role. To usurp the role of the anointed priest and to ignore God's command is serious. And, of course, no sooner has Saul done this thing than

Samuel shows up. (Haven't many of us suffered the consequences of impatience like this?) As the marginal text announces, "Samuel said to Saul, 'You have done foolishly; you have not kept the commandment of the Lord your God'" (13:13). In that one move, Saul lost the kingdom and sealed his own fate and that of his sons, who will perish at the end of the book of Samuel and be disgraced.

Almost immediately we meet David, the true king and the challenger to Saul's throne. He, too, is of most humble origins (remember the foreigner Ruth and her son, Obed?). His is a hero's story that rivals any in literature. David slays the giant Goliath with his slingshot; he is rescued from the lion and the bear. He is a beautiful shepherd who plays songs to the Lord on his lyre. And the women sing, "Saul has killed his thousands, and David his ten thousands" (18:7), a curse to Saul's ears as dangerous as the pronouncement of any mirror on a wall in a fairy tale.

From very early on, Saul pursues David to kill him. And we have the story of the great friendship between David and Jonathan, Saul's son, who protects David, makes a covenant with him, and does not seek the kingship over his relationship with David. Again, the themes are clear: loyalty to God and God's chosen one is to be treasured. Victory goes to the faithful. Saul, who depends on his own power instead of the Lord, is ultimately vanquished and driven to an ignoble fate. Finally accepting the consequences, he falls on his own sword.

This illumination uses the three colors—gold, green, and

SAUL ANTHOLOGY

purple—emphasized in *Historical Books*. The focus is on Saul's kingship, and by using a single column, the illumination reflects the hierarchy of God's kingdom, the realm of priests and prophets, and finally the realm of kings. As we see, the heavenly kingdom is beautiful, and the crown of golden archways at the top is suggestive of heavenly mansions. Israel is favored, but the story is always complex. The green realm demonstrates the presence of Samuel, who guides Israel and advises Saul throughout Saul's reign. The text in the margin of the illumination is the final words of Samuel in chapter 28. In this astonishing passage, Samuel speaks from the dead, through a medium, to tell Saul yet again that his kingship has been handed over by God to David. His words are in green with gold caps, suggestive of his place now after death and of the power of his prophecy.

Finally, there is the realm of purple, Saul's kingship, also shot through with gold. We see the presence of a prayer shawl with dangling fringes but also with the Egyptian motif. There are occasional flames, the warring nature of his kingship, and in the shadow of the prayer shawl, a skull. Saul's skull is separated from his body by the Philistines, and his body is placed on the wall until the men of Israel take them down, burn them, and bury their remains beneath the tamarisk tree in Jabesh. A tree stands above the skull in the illumination, suggestive of the tamarisk and also of the young monarchy taking root in Israel. The book closes with the men of Israel beginning a seven-day fast, the next stage in a cycle that always ends with repentance and an appeal to God for deliverance.

◀ *How might you have chosen to illuminate the story of King Saul? What elements of the story do you think are most important?*

What similarities do you see between this illumination and Hannah's Prayer at the opening of 1 Samuel?

1 Samuel began with Hannah's prayer to the Lord expressing her sorrow. 2 Samuel begins with David mourning the deaths of his beloved friend Jonathan and of King Saul. Again we have an illumination by Thomas Ingmire. This time it depicts the song, again in vertical panels, and shows David's multiple emotions, such as the anger that drives him to kill the Amalekite; the public line of the song that will be passed down throughout the ages, "How the mighty have fallen!"; and his more personal grief over Jonathan's death, an expression of distress that seems a shadow engraved on the page.

In this single, compact illumination, Ingmire seems to capture all the emotion of this moment, both for the people of Israel and for David personally. The king is dead. The people are vanquished by the Philistines—and so, too, is his beloved brother Jonathan.

What do we make, if anything, of the left-hand side of this illumination? We can almost make out words, but the letter forms are disrupted. Maybe it is representative of David's rage at the Amalekite who brought him the news, not only because he witnessed Jonathan's and Saul's deaths but also because he drove his own sword into Saul. The man brought the crown and armlet to the rightful heir, David, and no doubt expected some reward for his actions. David reminds him that Saul was "the Lord's anointed" (1:14). In his statement and in his ordering the man's death, which seems unduly harsh, David nonetheless sides with the Lord and seems to forgive Saul, establishing again that his ambition was to serve, not to overthrow Saul's kingdom.

The song in verses 19-27 praises not only Jonathan but also Saul and calls for collective mourning by Israel for both men. David's character has been ascending in the last half of 1 Samuel, and he is fully worthy of the kingship here.

❧ *What has been your experience with public or private grief?*

David's Lament (How the Mighty Have Fallen)

2 SAMUEL 1:19-27
How the mighty have fallen! (1:19)

I Will Raise Up Your Offspring

2 SAMUEL 7:12

I will not take my steadfast love from [your offspring], as I took it from Saul, whom I put away from before you. Your house and your kingdom shall be made sure forever before me; your throne shall be established forever. (7:15-16)

To the covenant with Abraham and the covenant with Moses is now added a third, the covenant with David. This verse is messianic and as such is embraced by the Christian church as a prediction of Jesus, who will come from the line of David as the Redeemer.

The text treatment by Sally Mae Joseph is done in all capitals and in purples, reflecting again this time of the kings. The Lord is making this promise not with an individual (as in the Abrahamic covenant) or with the remnant wandering in the desert (as in the Mosaic covenant) but with those who will inhabit the kingdom of God. This kingdom is explored throughout the New Testament, where it is again seen as something in the future, an ideal. In Jewish tradition, the text underscores the Davidic line for the life of the people of Israel. When the Messiah comes, he will usher in an eternal reign of peace and prosperity in this world.

2 SAMUEL 7:12

What elements might you choose to do an illumination of the reign of David?

How to depict the reign of David, shepherd hero, giant slayer, king and warrior, psalmist, the one who brought the ark of the covenant to Jerusalem, the one through whom God will establish the everlasting kingdom? This was a problem for the artists.

In this illumination, Jackson has simplified the entire story to a depiction of a vision of Israel in David's time and placed it in the context of the larger story of *The Saint John's Bible*. He has begun with seven panels, echoing the seven panels of *Creation*. David's kingship is a significant restoration of the establishment of God's kingdom. The clearest images in the illumination are the gold stamped archways. We've seen this stamp used repeatedly in *The Saint John's Bible*, and in fact it was used on the carpet page for this volume, before the opening of the book of Joshua. Its source, according to Donald Jackson, is the arches of the Cathedral of Santiago de Compostela. This Spanish cathedral is the destination point for pilgrims on the Way of St. James, a pilgrimage that brings people annually along various routes across Europe. The spires at the top of the panels are also reminiscent of the spires of this cathedral. But the top appears to be both cathedral and fortress, symbolic of God's protection. People seek God in sacred spaces, and David is at the center of this human longing—bringing the ark at last to its destination in Jerusalem. The Divine is present in this city, but it must still be sought. It is hard to tell if the gold permeates or is only at the edges and above the chaos of the city.

The other major parallel for this illumination is to the frontispiece of *Psalms*. The *Psalms* frontispiece is also in panels, reminiscent of scrolls, crowned with menorah lights instead of the spires at the top of these archway panels. That piece features similar color and movement, which we may read as David's joy and song. The opening verses of Psalm 18 are inscribed in the margin of the previous page:

David Anthology and Tent Detail from David Anthology

1 SAMUEL 16–2 SAMUEL 24 / 2 SAMUEL 6:17

They brought in the ark of the Lord, and set it in its place, inside the tent that David had pitched for it; and David offered burnt offerings and offerings of well-being before the Lord. (2 Sam 6:17)

"The Lord is my rock, my fortress and my deliverer." This psalm is also found, with a few slight alterations, in 2 Samuel 22. It is sometimes referred to as "The Song of David," David's response to his victory over Saul and all his enemies. Here David declares, "For this I will extol you, O Lord, among the nations, and sing praises to your name. He is a tower of salvation for his king, and shows steadfast love to his anointed, to David and his descendents forever" (2 Sam 22:50-51).

That verse also illustrates David's significant place between two other illuminations built on the seven-branched menorah: *Abraham and Sarah* in Genesis and the *Genealogy of Christ* frontispiece of Matthew's Gospel. With the seven panels topped with gold we have a faint echo of the menorah and the sense of David's place in the covenant story of Israel. God has made a covenant with David, as with Abraham, that will be ultimately fulfilled in the birth of Jesus.

The detail on the previous page suggests that the arch we see throughout is also symbolic of the ark. It is the holy of holies, a gate that must be passed through to be close to God. The tent itself is merely a veil and certainly not as substantial as the hoped-for temple. Here it is pulled aside to reveal God's dwelling place.

◀ *How do you experience God's presence in sacred spaces? How might you depict your own experience with finding where God resides?*

THE ART OF THE SAINT JOHN'S BIBLE

שמואל ב

TENT DETAIL FROM DAVID ANTHOLOGY

HISTORICAL BOOKS

45

Army Ant Workers and Grasshopper

At the end of 2 Samuel, we find the first of Chris Tomlin's insect illustrations in this volume. Throughout *The Saint John's Bible*, Tomlin has provided illustrations drawn from the natural world. Perhaps most striking is the monarch butterfly in Mark's Gospel, shown in three stages: caterpillar, chrysalis, and butterfly.

When considering how to depict and acknowledge the violence in *Historical Books*, one approach was to reflect how this violence goes on throughout the natural world. The relentlessness of the cycle of life, the battles between predator and prey, become beautiful in Chris Tomlin's detailed illustrations. Note the echoes between the actions of real armies and real peoples in these pages and the insects depicted from here until the end of the volume.

They are most commonly inserted in the space at the end of a book, but some appear in the margins. Their placement is not meant to correspond to any particular passage or book but rather to provide ornamentation and another visual thematic element for *Historical Books*.

THE ART OF THE SAINT JOHN'S BIBLE

Guide to the insect illustrations of Chris Tomlin:

2 Samuel 24	Army Ant Workers and Grasshopper
2 Kings 16	Imperial Scorpion and Arizona Bark Scorpion
1 Chronicles 25	Leafcutter Ants
2 Chronicles 27	Praying Mantis and Banded Damselfly, both United States
2 Chronicles 36	Harlequin Beetle (*Acrocinus longimanus*) South America
Tobit 14	Wasps
Judith 16	Monarch Butterfly Being Eaten by Whip Spider
1 Maccabees 4	Gold Beetle (*Chrysina resplendens*) and Silver Beetle (*Chrysina bates*), both Central America
1 Maccabees 11	Glasswing Butterfly (*Greta oto*) and Black Widow Spider (*Latrodectus mactans*)
2 Maccabees 7	Painted Lady Butterfly (*Vanessa cardui*) and Caterpillars, United Kingdom
2 Maccabees 15	Chameleon

Wisdom of Solomon

I KINGS 3:16-28

And they stood in awe of the king, because they perceived that the wisdom of God was in him, to execute justice. (3:28)

WISDOM OF SOLOMON

How would you define wisdom? Can you think of any examples where someone demonstrated wisdom?

In 1 Kings 2:9, Solomon asks God, "Give your servant therefore an understanding mind to govern your people, able to discern between good and evil; for who can govern this your great people?" Wisdom is privileged in a king, more than might. It's a refreshing break from the battles and "striking down" we've been reading.

This simple, abstract illumination by Hazel Dolby gets to the heart of Solomon's wisdom. We are told the famous case of the two women with the single live baby. One of them is lying about whether or not the child is hers, and the other one is ruthless enough to take another woman's baby. Still, there is nothing arbitrary about Solomon's judgment. He decrees what at first is a "fair" but completely ridiculous— unwise—decision. Cut the baby in half and give half to each woman. This follows a cold logic, but of course it wouldn't work with a baby! It does, however, expose the ruthless woman who stole the baby and reveal the woman who is the baby's actual mother.

In the illumination, a light divides the darkness like a sword. This sword is made of gold and silver, used throughout *The Saint John's Bible* to suggest the presence of the divine (gold) and wisdom (silver). The highlighted verse in the margin also uses that great verb, "execute." Solomon's wisdom and justice are swift, and he is able to take right action immediately. How often have we seen unwise rulers, in these books and in our own time, rush to wrong judgment and bring about great harm rather than justice?

How does this image of the temple compare to that found in Ezekiel 40?

David was the keeper of the ark, and he brought the ark to Jerusalem. However, the ark remained in a tent during his reign. It is his son Solomon who builds the temple, fulfilling the ambitions of the people of Israel to have a permanent kingdom and a central place to worship Yahweh.

Chapters 5–8 go into great detail about the plans, furnishings, and building of the temple. There is so much detail that over time people have built models of it. Isaac Newton made extensive drawings of it, believing it followed a "sacred geometry" revealed to Solomon. There are definite similarities, although they are minimal, between the architectural look of Donald Jackson's various images of the temple and Isaac Newton's drawings.

The illumination here is a version of the illumination first made by Donald Jackson for *Vision of the New Temple* in Ezekiel. Whereas that illumination seems to pulse with visionary energy and is permeated by the rainbow motif that is found throughout *Prophets*, this one is more like an architectural drawing. There is still the complex, delicate gold maze, hinting at the mystery of approaching God. While in no way meant to accurately depict the scriptural instructions, this illumination suggests the solidity of a human-made place.

The emphasis is on the elements of the temple, including the two cherubim, the gold box that represents the ark's resting place in the holy of holies, and the gates and arches on all four sides. However, Donald Jackson has preserved everywhere the aspect of mystery, drawing always on the vision of the temple in Ezekiel. The cherubim in the smoke-filled chamber possess the characteristics of the creatures in *Vision at the Chebar* (Ezek 1). We can see the elaborate wings and the human faces modeled on funereal art. The labyrinth from the vision is also in this image.

The primary color here is purple, suggesting the majesty of the kingdom united by David and consolidated under

Solomon's Temple

I KINGS 8:1-66

I have built you an exalted house. (8:13)

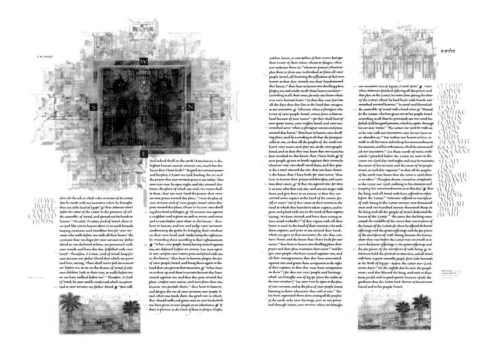

Solomon. For the first time, Israel's God has a temple and Israel's people have their king and a center for worship. This is the height of the kingdom of Israel on earth—it is as close to an earthly paradise as humans can come. Solomon's prayer, inscribed in the margin, celebrates this right relationship with God: "O Lord, God of Israel, there is no God like you in heaven above or on earth beneath, keeping covenant and steadfast love for your servants who walk before you with all their heart" (8:23).

The rainbow theme is more pronounced in the details on the two pages. Here we see that idealized, dreamlike vision of the kingdom, with palm trees and golden archways. The temple is only part of the vision realized—the ideal kingdom is yet to be experienced.

By the end of 1 Kings, however, the kingdom of David will be in collapse. First it will be separated into northern

THE ART OF THE SAINT JOHN'S BIBLE

and southern kingdoms, and by the end of 2 Kings, both kingdoms will fall, the temple will be destroyed, and the people will be in exile. At the time of Ezekiel, the temple and promise of a kingdom will become more apocalyptic, a vision of a perfect, restored future.

❧ *What is a place that has great significance to you? How might you represent it in a drawing, highlighting certain elements and its meaning?*

After the Fire

I KINGS 19:4-18

And after the fire a sound of sheer silence. (19:12)

The passage illuminated here is one of the most beautiful accounts in the Old Testament of an encounter with God. Elijah, God's prophet, has escaped Jezebel and has been fleeing and hiding for forty days. Finally, he rests overnight in a cave on Mount Horeb. A voice tells him to go outside the cave because God will be passing by.

Where is God? How is God to be perceived?

We are told that first there was "a great wind, so strong that it was splitting mountains and breaking rocks in pieces," but "the Lord was not in the wind." After that comes an earthquake, followed by a fire, but the Lord is not in either of these. Finally, there is "a sound of sheer silence." Elijah, here depicted in green, the color of the prophets, wraps his face and goes out to meet the Lord in the silence.

In the illumination, we see a steep wall of chaos, including fire and earthquake. We also see the green figure of Elijah with his face covered by his mantle to shield himself from the glory of God. His posture is one of awe and reverence. To the side stand the two angels in white, looking over him. Notice the look of the stone on which Elijah stands. Donald Jackson's brother, who does stone carving, enjoys the beauty of stone in which fossils are embedded, and he loaned polished pieces of stone with fossil traces to Jackson. He used these as the model for this decorative element to give, he said, the sense of the story embedded in the stone.

In the actual illumination, the silver bars that depict the silence are much more subtle than in the reproduction. They are masked by the grey tones in the page and can take you by surprise. The glory is there, embedded in the page, but we must be still and attentive to witness it.

❧ *The words "awe" and "fear of God" are often used interchangeably. Can you describe an experience of awe?*

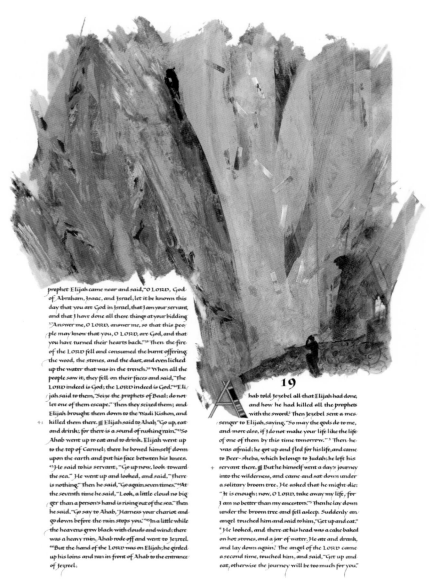

prophet Elijah came near and said, "O LORD, God of Abraham, Isaac, and Israel, let it be known this day that you are God in Israel, that I am your servant, and that I have done all these things at your bidding. ³⁷Answer me, O LORD, answer me, so that this people may know that you, O LORD, are God, and that you have turned their hearts back." ³⁸Then the fire of the LORD fell and consumed the burnt offering, the wood, the stones, and the dust, and even licked up the water that was in the trench. ³⁹When all the people saw it, they fell on their faces and said, "The LORD indeed is God; the LORD indeed is God." ⁴⁰Elijah said to them, "Seize the prophets of Baal; do not let one of them escape." Then they seized them; and Elijah brought them down to the Wadi Kishon, and killed them there. ⁴¹ Elijah said to Ahab, "Go up, eat and drink; for there is a sound of rushing rain." ⁴²So Ahab went up to eat and to drink. Elijah went up to the top of Carmel; there he bowed himself down upon the earth and put his face between his knees. ⁴³He said to his servant, "Go up now, look toward the sea." He went up and looked, and said, "There is nothing." Then he said, "Go again seven times." ⁴⁴At the seventh time he said, "Look, a little cloud no bigger than a person's hand is rising out of the sea." Then he said, "Go say to Ahab, 'Harness your chariot and go down before the rain stops you.'" ⁴⁵In a little while the heavens grew black with clouds and wind; there was a heavy rain. Ahab rode off and went to Jezreel. ⁴⁶But the hand of the LORD was on Elijah; he girded up his loins and ran in front of Ahab to the entrance of Jezreel.

19

Ahab told Jezebel all that Elijah had done, and how he had killed all the prophets with the sword. ²Then Jezebel sent a messenger to Elijah, saying, "So may the gods do to me, and more also, if I do not make your life like the life of one of them by this time tomorrow." ³Then he was afraid; he got up and fled for his life, and came to Beer-sheba, which belongs to Judah; he left his servant there. ⁴But he himself went a day's journey into the wilderness, and came and sat down under a solitary broom tree. He asked that he might die: "It is enough; now, O LORD, take away my life, for I am no better than my ancestors." ⁵Then he lay down under the broom tree and fell asleep. Suddenly an angel touched him and said to him, "Get up and eat." ⁶He looked, and there at his head was a cake baked on hot stones, and a jar of water. He ate and drank, and lay down again. ⁷The angel of the LORD came a second time, touched him, and said, "Get up and eat, otherwise the journey will be too much for you."

AND AFTER THE FIRE
A SOUND OF SHEER SILENCE

AFTER THE FIRE

Elijah and the Fiery Chariot

2 KINGS 2:1-14

Please let me inherit a double share of your spirit. (2:9)

How is color used here to tell the story?

The two figures in this illumination, drawn by the icon painter Aidan Hart, are the prophets Elisha and Elijah. Although we think of the story of Elijah and the fiery chariot as one of God's triumph, we can tell by the look on Elisha's face that he is worried.

In the Scripture passage, Elijah and Elisha are journeying. Elijah asks Elisha three times to stop and wait, but Elisha insists on following Elijah to the end of his journey. The three points of the journey are Bethel, Jericho, and the Jordan. In a way, he is retracing the steps back to where we last saw Moses.

They pass through Bethel, where the ark of the covenant containing the Ten Commandments was housed, where Jacob received the name Israel, and a place that is mentioned in Ezra and Nehemiah as existing after the time of exile. Next they stop at Jericho, site of the famous first battle by Joshua when the Israelites entered the Promised Land. Finally they cross the Jordan, and Elijah parts the waters with his mantle, reminding us of Moses parting the Red Sea so that the Israelites could escape Pharaoh.

After they cross the Jordan, Elisha asks Elijah to leave him a "double portion" of Elijah's spirit. Elijah throws down his mantle as he is being taken up to heaven in the chariot, a sign of this outpouring. This event is paralleled twice in the Scriptures: first when Moses says he must disappear before Joshua, his successor, will receive his power, and then in the New Testament when Jesus says he will send his Spirit after he ascends to heaven. In all three cases, there is no "body" to be found on earth, although it is presumed that Moses dies and his tomb is hidden. The apostles see Jesus ascend, which is followed by Pentecost, the outpouring of the Holy Spirit when they begin testifying in many languages to the people assembled in Jerusalem (Acts 1–2).

In this illumination, we see many elements of the story. At the top left are the groups of prophets waiting to see what God will do. Elisha, saddened by the loss of his predecessor and grabbing hold of his own destiny, looks to Elijah being transported to heaven amid fire and chariot wheels. The connections between the book of the prophet Ezekiel and these stories of Elijah continue s. The chariot wheels are based on the same image of wheels used in *Vision at the Chebar* in Ezekiel 1. However, these chariot wheels don't have the addition of "eyes" that were incorporated into the stamp for Ezekiel's vision.

At the top center is the arch, ever-present in *Historical Books* as the arches of the kingdom and God's ongoing covenant to raise up a people. And below are fish, reeds, and river, suggesting the River Jordan, which the two prophets have crossed to reach this place. The colors are also quite intentionally used here—the purple of the earthly kingdom, the green of prophecy and priesthood, and the gold of God's heaven to which they aspire.

◖ *Why do you think the chariot was "fiery"?*

ELIJAH AND THE FIERY CHARIOT

Elisha and the Six Miracles

2 KINGS 4–6

What do these miracles say about the role of the prophet in Israel?

Elijah performed miracles, and so does Elisha. We can look at Elisha's miracles to see what kind of prophet he is and what his role among the people is. What is noticeable is that people come to him for basic needs: for food, money to pay their debts, health for their children, a cure for leprosy, and the means for building shelter. When the situation seems hopeless, Elisha has the power to meet their needs. He intervenes in the lives of the people in times of dire need and restores them.

In this illumination we have another depiction of Elisha by Aidan Hart. Elisha is wearing Elijah's mantle, and he looks more confident here than we have seen him in the

ELISHA AND THE SIX MIRACLES

THE ART OF THE SAINT JOHN'S BIBLE

past illuminations. He is also in green, the color of priests and prophets. The use of a transparent wash of color seems to embed him in the panels, making him part of the events.

The illumination is divided into six panels depicting the miracles. Again they are topped by archways. The miracles are gateways to a vision of heaven, and each panel becomes a portal through which the love of God flows down.

In the first panel we see depictions of bread, because Elisha feeds the multitude on a few loaves of barley. This panel parallels the illumination *Loaves and Fishes* in Mark's Gospel, right down to the background of colored squares and gold stamped filigree. This miracle is twinned to another of Elisha's miracles, the purification of the poisoned pot of stew by throwing a handful of flour into it.

The second panel depicts the jugs of overflowing oil that benefitted the widow and her son. Elisha provides these as a means for getting the widow out of debt. However, the miracle also resonates with Jesus turning water to wine at Cana (John 2:1-11).

The third and fourth panels depict Elisha's healing ministry. After first making it possible that the Shunammite woman will have a son, he later returns to her house and, because of her faith, raises her son from the dead. This story has the closest parallel to Jesus' healing ministry. The quote written across the illumination is actually words of Jesus, "Do not fear, only believe" (Mark 5:36). These are the words that Jesus speaks to Jairus, the official from the synagogue, who came to Jesus to ask that he heal his daughter. When Jairus is told on the way that his daughter is dead, Jesus speaks these words, and encountering the mourners, he says, "The child is not dead but sleeping" (Mark 5:39). He takes the girl by the hand and raises her up.

Next, Elisha encounters Namaan, an Aramite commander of the enemy's army. Namaan seeks him out because he has leprosy, and his servant, an Israelite captive, has said the prophet would cure him. When Elisha sends word that Namaan should just wash himself in the Jordan seven times and he will be clean, Namaan is furious. He wanted to see the great prophet and feel the power of the Lord bestowed on him with great fanfare. Again, this resonates with what people wanted and expected of Jesus in his ministry—dramatic shows of power. Finally, Namaan does what he has been told, is healed, and turns to worship only Yahweh.

The illumination here also reprises a theme from *Gospels and Acts*, the first volume of *The Saint John's Bible* to be completed. In the illumination *Peter's Confession* in the Gospel of Matthew, Donald Jackson included an image of the AIDS virus as seen under a microscope in his vision of the underworld. Here we have a microscopic representation of leprosy, an image that was also used in the *Vision of the Son of Man* illumination in the book of Daniel.

Finally, we see the ax floating on the waters of the Jordan. The last miracle depicted here is of Elisha providing for a prophet a means to build his house when he loses his ax head in the river. When Elisha throws a stick near the place where the ax went under, it floats to the top and the prophet can lift it out. Again, there is a familiarity with Jesus' miracles on the water, especially providing fish for the fishermen who fished without luck all night long.

Also like Jesus, these miracles address the needs of a wide range of people: a widow, Elisha's hungry followers, a wealthy woman, an enemy commander, and a prophet. It is not surprising that in the story of Jesus in Matthew's Gospel—depicted in *Peter's Confession*—when Jesus asks, "Who do people say that I am?" the answer is, "Some say John the Baptist, but others Elijah, and still others Jeremiah or one of the prophets" (Matt 16:14).

◀ *What is the relationship like between Elisha and the people who experience his miracles?*

THE ART OF THE SAINT JOHN'S BIBLE

When the king heard the words of the book of the law, he tore his clothes. (22:11)

Suzanne Moore is behind this stunning illumination that closes out the official Hebrew history of Israel, before we move on to later, Greek texts. As we can see, things end in a rather mixed fashion. Josiah is a good king and restores the Law to Israel. However, it is too late for the kingdom, though Josiah himself will die in peace, as the prophetess Huldah proclaims.

Josiah is the final king before the southern kingdom of Judah falls (the northern kingdom of Israel had fallen to the Assyrians about one hundred years earlier) and the people are taken into Exile. So this will be the end of the cycle of rescue, disobedience, conquest, and obedience that we've seen played out again and again throughout the reign of the judges and the kings.

What is perhaps most notable in the account of Josiah is how far he is from knowledge of the Law handed down by Moses. He sends instructions for money brought to the temple to be given to the caretakers to repair the temple. We can only imagine what this means—where has the money been going until this time? Why has the temple been allowed to fall into disrepair? It speaks of corruption and of neglect of both the temple and God.

Josiah's servant returns from his errand with "the book of the law" given to him by the high priest (22:8-10). No one seems to recognize this book or its contents. King Josiah hears it read for the first time and grasps its meaning. Josiah responds to the reading of the Law by tearing his clothes in repentance. He needs someone to interpret this book for him, and the prophetess Huldah, identified as the "keeper of the wardrobe," a married woman living in Jerusalem, gives the prophecy that the kingdom will soon fall and only Josiah, who has repented, will be spared. Josiah will die in peace before the fall of his kingdom.

This illumination, then, depicts the Law one more time. As only a calligrapher could do, Moore makes great beauty

The Prophetess Huldah and Scroll Detail

2 KINGS 22:1-20

2 KINGS 23:1-3

out of letter forms. The primary image is that of a quill, from which unrolls an image of a scroll. For this illumination, Moore used fragments of sacred texts in multiple languages, including letters from Deuteronomy in the Dead Sea Scrolls.

Again we find the imagery of archways, this time gates in gold and blue. The source of this image is the double archway of one of Huldah's Gates, now partially blocked by a medieval tower, at the Temple Mount in Jerusalem. The gate once provided a passageway to the top of the Temple Mount, but over time the gates were walled up, and people now use a different entrance. Here the gates seem to have more to do with access to the celestial kingdom, the perfect kingdom that becomes the focus after the exile and that is predicted in this text.

The illumination carries over to the next page, with an image viewing the scroll from above. This abstract image again points forward to a time when God's kingdom will be realized in perfect form. This image can be compared with Suzanne Moore's illumination of *The Last Judgment* of Matthew 24–25. How can we, readers of a book, hearers of the Law and of Jesus' parables, grasp what the kingdom will be like?

We are leaving the account of the earthly kingdom of the people of Israel, but the people aren't left hopeless. Those reading this history from exile will recognize the pattern, and they will also recognize God's endless forgiveness when the people repent. What they must do is follow the Law given to them by Moses, worship their God as they have been instructed, and keep the commandments. They need to keep the book close to them and not forget what it says.

Again, this story makes us think about what it means that the Law, and this history, is written. What are we to make of it? What are we to learn from it? We must not forget the story of God's loving relationship to the people and the call to follow God and trust God, and we must keep the story close to our hearts so that we won't be led astray.

Before we leave these pages, note the decoration on the previous page with the notes for 2 Kings 20–21. Beneath the notes, hidden in the design, are the letters *D* and *R*. It was

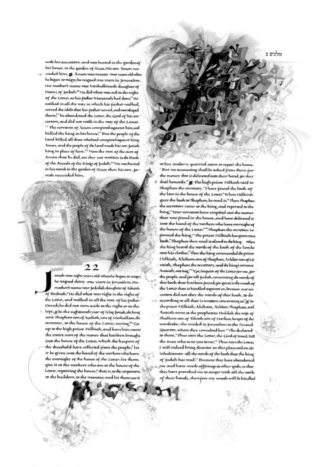

during the time Suzanne Moore was working on this illumination that Brother Dietrich Reinhart died of melanoma.
Brother Dietrich, a monk of Saint John's Abbey and president of Saint John's University for seventeen years, was
president of the university when *The Saint John's Bible* was
commissioned and a champion of the project. It is appropriate that his initials are inscribed here in the context of the
image of a scroll and a vision of God's perfect kingdom.

❧ *What history does your family pass on from generation to
generation? Why is it important?*

1 Chronicles and 2 Chronicles

In terms of illuminations, we sort of leapfrog over 1 Chronicles and 2 Chronicles, which are what they sound like: a retelling of the history of the Israelites from Adam to the exile, in brief form. They are an important part of *Historical Books*. They are punctuated in *The Saint John's Bible* by several of Chris Tomlin's beautiful, marginal insects. At 2 Chronicles 11 you will also find the ringtailed lemur that marks a correction to the text.

The Chronicles and the books that follow them also mark a different perspective to the history of Israel. They were written after the exiles had returned to Judah, and the purpose of Chronicles is not to tell a history of Israel but to contribute to the restoration and building up of the Jewish nation. The Chronicles are not full of warning and violence like the books we've read so far. The characters are not complex. Good kings are without flaw, and bad kings are completely evil. You won't find Bathsheba in the Chronicles because she does not make King David look good.

These books attempt to provide hope for a people still living under Persian rule. They affirm the identity of the Lord's people, who can find hope for the future in their identity and in the faith of their ancestors, particularly David and Solomon.

SCROLL DETAIL

THE ART OF THE SAINT JOHN'S BIBLE

The project of restoring Israel and calling the people together as a nation and as a people who are faithful to God deepens in the books of Ezra and Nehemiah. In the book of Ezra, the temple is restored. In the book of Nehemiah, the wall of Jerusalem is rebuilt. After considering an illumination in the book of Nehemiah, we will consider the story of Queen Esther.

The deuterocanonical books of the Additions to Esther, Tobit, and 1 and 2 Maccabees are what the name implies, a "second" or "secondary" canon to the Catholic Bible. The Greek version of the Old Testament contains them, while the Hebrew version of the Old Testament does not. The Protestant traditions follow the Hebrew, whereas Catholic, Greek, and other denominations use the Greek version. This situation explains why some Bibles contain these books but others do not.

Square before the Watergate

NEHEMIAH 8:1-12

For the joy of the Lord is your strength. (8:10)

Nehemiah is a faithful Jewish layman. He is an important member of the Persian King Artaxerxes's staff, and it is actually the king who makes it possible for him to carry out his calling. His book is told in the first person, drawn from his memoirs, and that in itself adds another layer to the variety of these historical books. He tells the story of how he rebuilt the walls of Jerusalem, joining forces with the priest Ezra who had rebuilt the temple. Together they offer the people of Jerusalem a way to be restored after exile and to unite as a single people. It has been generations since they have practiced their faith in their own land. Again, it is the book of the law, a record of what God said to them through Moses, that makes continuity possible.

This illumination by Hazel Dolby, as so many illuminations in *The Saint John's Bible*, makes use of abstraction to tell a theological story. On a field of gold, she has set up a pattern of interlocking diamonds, but it is far from complete. In fact, many of the pieces are outside the border. They are still scattered in the margin and on the next page.

When the wall and its gates are completed, Nehemiah says, "The city was wide and large, but the people within it were few and no houses had been built" (7:4). He finds the book of the genealogy of those who had come back first, and he calls the people back inside the walls to settle. This is the context in which

SQUARE BEFORE THE WATERGATE

THE ART OF THE SAINT JOHN'S BIBLE

the story depicted in this illumination takes place. The people are gathered in the square, and the book of the Law is read aloud to them. Not only do they hear the words; there are also scholarly interpreters present to explain to the people what they are hearing. This is a great parallel to what many "people of the book" do to this day—they gather to hear their sacred texts read aloud and interpreted. It is also an important feature of what is called second temple Judaism. After exile, the Jews rely on inspired teachers to interpret the word of God as found in the Scriptures. Their interpretations are collected in rabbinical literature and the Talmud.

Once the book of the Law has been read and interpreted, the people are instructed to rejoice and feast. Their natural inclination is to mourn like Josiah and tear their clothes. There will be time for confession, but this is not the day. On this day, the people are instructed to rejoice because God is with them.

Hazel Dolby's illumination is a depiction of the restoration taking place and of the joy that is spreading throughout the kingdom. It begins in the center with gold and purple and extends throughout the square. In fact, it breaks the boundary of the square, reaching to gather in all the people. Many see in this illumination God's power and authority, as well as joyfulness punctuated by areas of quiet reverence. Dolby avoided strong patterns as she worked with the squares and triangles. The heart of this illumination is the embodiment of the quotation "For the joy of the Lord is your strength" (8:10). As the celebration expands, the people gain strength to move forward.

◁ *Does this illumination make you feel joyful? How else might you depict the spread of joy?*

If you have never read the book of Esther, you are in for a treat. Like the earlier deuterocanonical text Tobit, this piece of historical fiction reads like a fairy tale or melodrama. It is the story of an orphan girl among the exiled people who wins favor in the king's harem and becomes queen. It is the story of a pompous and treacherous official who sets out to destroy the queen's people and how she and her uncle, with the help of a foreign king, turn the tables on him and save the people of Israel.

The illumination of Esther by Donald Jackson celebrates first and foremost Esther's dual identity. On the right, she is a natural beauty, a Jewish woman, crowned by the menorah and a pattern that parallels the mantle of Elijah. But the left side shows her also as the queen of Babylon, chosen from among all the beauties of the empire to be the king's wife.

In the opening of the book of Esther, we are told that King Ahasuerus "ruled over one hundred twenty-seven provinces from India to Ethiopia." The book tells of the king's wealth at great length and seems to revel in the accounts of his banquets, the costuming and perfuming of his potential wives, and the power of his golden scepter and signet ring. This excess is contrasted to Esther, who is quoted in the margin saying, "You know that I hate the splendor of the wicked" (14:15). Esther goes to the king with only the basics, although we are led to believe other prospective princesses used every means at their disposal to increase their beauty and attract the king's attention.

If the face of Queen Esther looks familiar, it is for good reason. Donald Jackson based the image on a portrait of Adele Bloch-Bauer by Gustav Klimt. She was Klimt's patroness, married to a wealthy, older man. As Jackson says, the image nods at the fact that "t'were always so," that such marriages are known throughout history. But Jackson was also taken with the enormity of what Queen Esther stands to lose if her rescue mission doesn't work and with her ambivalence about her own situation. He has focused on her vulnerability and discomfort with her position in the marginal quotes.

that I will prepare for them, and then I will do as the
king has said." ¶ Haman went out that day happy
and in good spirits. But when Haman saw Mordecai
in the king's gate, and observed that he neither rose
nor trembled before him, he was infuriated with
Mordecai; nevertheless Haman restrained himself
and went home. Then he sent & called for his friends
& his wife Zeresh, and Haman recounted to them
the splendor of his riches, the number of his sons,
all the promotions with which the king had honored
him, and how he had advanced him above the officials and the ministers of the king." Haman added,
"Even Queen Esther let no one but myself come with
the king to the banquet that she prepared. Tomor-

ESTHER

From the very first illuminations in the book
of Genesis, Jackson has reveled in using period
sources and drawing on textiles for some of the
rich imagery in his pieces. Here in the illumination of Esther, Jackson layers images of the opu-
lence as well as the integrity of Queen Esther.
Although they are not based on the period in
this story, they are taken from pieces in the region that are marks of royalty and weddings.

Esther's queenship is marked by finery and
"cosmetic" treatments, crowned by a gold
figure of the lion of Babylon and by rich Persian
rugs. The images on the left side of the illumination are inspired by Turkmen (Afghani) traditional bridal gifts and ancient Persian gold arti-
facts such as coins, jewelry, and textiles.

The other striking feature of this illumination is the hanged man. This figure, Haman,
who attempts to destroy the Jews and finds
himself destroyed, wears a rather contempo-
rary-looking tunic and has sad, limply hanging
slippers. If the image makes us uncomfortable,
that is as it should be. Here Donald Jackson looks straight at
the violence of the accounts we have read throughout this
volume. No matter how treacherous the hanged man has
been, we should reflect on our reaction to him. *The Saint
John's Bible* was written between 1999 and 2011, a period
that saw the United States and European allies engaged in
wars in the Middle East following the terrorist attacks on
September 11, 2001. As the project of writing the Bible
drew to a close, *Historical Books*, published in 2010, confronted the readers and the artists with their weariness over
the violence of the past decade and their countries' partici-
pation in it. The image of Haman is based on images of
public executions in Saudi Arabia.

◖ *The Jewish holiday of Purim is based on the story of Esther.
What can you find out about this holiday and how it is celebrated?*

Where does the history of Israel end? For *The Saint John's Bible*, it ends with a foreshadowing of the Christian story of redemption. Sally Mae Joseph has written a text treatment of a passage from 2 Maccabees, the final book in this volume, that lays out the themes of the Historical Books and points toward a greater restoration of the kingdom through resurrection of the dead.

Historically speaking, the Historical Books take us up to the year 134 B.C.E. The final two books, 1 and 2 Maccabees, tell the story of Mattathias the Hasmonean and his sons John, Simon, Judas, Eleazar, and Jonathan Maccabeus. This family defends Judaism against Greek influence during the time of the Greek Empire. The Maccabees repel the attempted invasions of Jerusalem by Greeks Antiochus and Appolonius and defend the Law and practices like circumcision. In 2 Maccabees, the struggle is seen more as a struggle between traditional Jews in the countryside, who have names like those of the heroes above, and Jews who have been heavily influenced by the Greeks, who have Greek names like Jason and Menelaus, and who are supported by Greek leaders like Antiochus and Appolonius.

Both books are available only in Greek manuscripts, although 1 Maccabees was originally written in Hebrew. For this reason, they are part of the deuterocanon and are included in Catholic and Orthodox Bibles but not in Protestant or Jewish collections of the Old Testament literature. As biblical studies become more and more ecumenical, the deuterocanon is sometimes included in other translations, but collected as a group and placed between the Old and New Testaments. In *The Saint John's Bible* the books appear according to their placement in the Catholic version of the Old Testament.

Historical Books closes, then, with a few more adventure accounts and with the ongoing struggle to build up Israel and maintain a civil society committed to the law of Moses and true to Yahweh, worshiping no other gods. Like 2 Chronicles and the first-person account of Nehemiah, one of the delights of 2 Maccabees is the way the author

And They Turned to Supplication

2 MACCABEES 12:42-45

³⁷In the language of their ancestors he raised the battle cry, with hymns; then he charged against Gorgias's troops when they were not expecting it, and put them to flight. ¶ Then Judas assembled his army and went to the city of Adullam. As the seventh day was coming on, they purified themselves according ³⁸ to the custom, and kept the sabbath there. ¶ On the ³⁹ next day, as had now become necessary, Judas and his men went to take up the bodies of the fallen and to bring them back to lie with their kindred in the sepulchres of their ancestors.⁴⁰ Then under the tunic of each one of the dead they found sacred tokens of the idols of Jamnia, which the law forbids the Jews to wear. And it became clear to all that this was the reason these men had fallen.⁴¹ So they all blessed the ways of the Lord, the righteous judge, who reveals

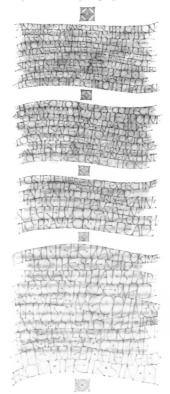

[*] 163 B.C.
¹¹ Or the scene of the things that had been done

the things that are hidden;⁴² and they turned to supplication, praying that the sin that had been committed might be wholly blotted out. The noble Judas exhorted the people to keep themselves free from sin, for they had seen with their own eyes what had happened as the result of the sin of those who had fallen.⁴³ He also took up a collection, man by man, to the amount of two thousand drachmas of silver, and sent it to Jerusalem to provide for a sin offering. In doing this he acted very well & honorably, taking account of the resurrection.⁴⁴ For if he were not expecting that those who had fallen would rise again, it would have been superfluous and foolish to pray for the dead.⁴⁵ But if he was looking to the splendid reward that is laid up for those who fall asleep in godliness, it was a holy and pious thought. Therefore he made atonement for the dead, so that they might be delivered from their sin.

13

In the one hundred forty-ninth year word came to Judas and his men that Antiochus Eupator was coming with a great army against Judea, ² and with him Lysias, his guardian, who had charge of the government. Each of them had a Greek force of one hundred ten thousand infantry, five thousand three hundred cavalry, twenty-two elephants, and three hundred chariots armed with scythes. ³ ¶ Menelaus also joined them and with utter hypocrisy urged Antiochus on, not for the sake of his country's welfare, but because he thought that he would be established in office.⁴ But the King of kings aroused the anger of Antiochus against the scoundrel; and when Lysias informed him that this man was to blame for all the trouble, he ordered them to take him to Berea and to put him to death by the method that is customary in that place.⁵ For there is a tower there, fifty cubits high, full of ashes, and it has a rim running around it that on all sides inclines precipitously into the ashes. ⁶ There they all push to destruction anyone guilty of sacrilege or notorious for other crimes. ⁷ By such a fate it came about that Menelaus the lawbreaker died, without even burial in the earth. ⁸ And this was eminently just; because he had committed many sins against the altar whose fire and ashes were holy, he met his death in ashes. ¶ The ⁹ king with barbarous arrogance was coming to show the Jews things far worse than those that had been done in his father's time.¹⁰ But when Judas heard of this, he ordered the people to call upon the Lord day and night, now if ever to help those who were on the point of being deprived of the law and their country and the holy temple;¹¹ and not to let the people who had just begun to revive fall into the hands reveals himself on the page. The author can be said to have a "purple pen," writing at times in exaggerated detail and striving for heightened emotional responses from the reader.

If you turn to the very end of 2 Maccabees, you will see that this author has trouble finding a proper ending to his story. We might sympathize, as the Historical Books seem a very long account of people who took a very long time to learn what seems like a simple lesson (and of course, it is uncertain whether it has been or can ever be learned). The author writes:

> This, then, is how matters turned out with Nicanor, and from that time the city has been in possession of the Hebrews. So I will here end my story. If it is well told and to the point, that is what I myself desired; if it is poorly done and mediocre, that was the best I could do. For just as it is harmful to drink wine alone, or, again, to drink water alone, while wine mixed with water is sweet and delicious and enhances one's enjoyment, so also the style of the story delights the ears of those who read the work. And here will be the end. (15:37-38)

Given such a playful and colorful ending, Donald Jackson could not resist including one more image. So, at the end of this volume you will find a colorful chameleon by Chris Tomlin about to put an end to a very innocuous-looking fly.

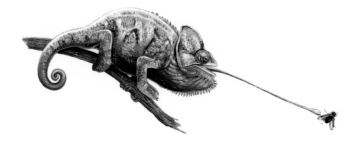

CHAMELEON

LETTERS AND REVELATION

WE NOW TURN our attention to *Letters and Revelation*. If you've been reading *The Saint John's Bible* or these books as they've been published, it's been a long time since we've been in the New Testament. In fact, *Gospels and Acts* was the first volume completed, and now we have arrived at the last.

Because of the order in which *The Saint John's Bible* was completed, we find ourselves now jumping from the end of *Historical Books*, volume 2 in the series, to volume 7, *Letters and Revelation*. In terms of our reading, we move from a time when the people of Israel were rebuilding the temple in Jerusalem and their vision of God's kingdom had moved from a literal kingdom on earth to an idealized vision of the kingdom, to the time following the life, death, and resurrection of Jesus, the beginning of the Christian church.

In some ways, this is a great way to take up these volumes. We are still engaged with the people of God and their central questions: "Who is God?" and "What is God's relationship to humanity?" If Jesus is the Son of God, sent by God as our Redeemer, crucified, and risen—and promising to come again in glory—then how are we to live as God's people?

These central questions are taken up by Paul and the other letter writers as they engage with people in churches throughout the Greek and Roman world. They provide us with the core of early Christian theology, a theology that has been taken up and lived out—and that has resulted in more than a few schisms over the past two millennia.

Raymond E. Brown, in his central work *An Introduction to the New Testament*, considers Paul's theology through a series of questions. One of them is: "What is the theological center of Paul's theology?" He identifies a number of themes identified by theologians, including (1) "justification by faith," (2) "the antithesis between human flesh and the divine Spirit," (3) human experience of salvation through the revelation of faith, (4) "the Christ-event as the consummation and end of history," and (5) sanctification through Christ.[1] The Reformation was in part about the inter-

[1] Raymond E. Brown, SS, *An Introduction to the New Testament* (New York: Doubleday, 1997), 440.

pretation of Paul's writings on these and other issues. In the end, the whole Christian church has reformed, and recent ecumenical efforts show that on the question of Paul's theology there is a great deal of commonality. The doctrinal differences on issues of justification and sanctification aren't as divisive as they once were.

The Committee on Illumination and Text (CIT) chose passages to be highlighted in the letters that reflect major points of Christian theology, including those listed above. Unlike the text passages in the margins of *Historical Books*—which emphasize the ongoing cycle of turning to God, victory, turning from God, and punishment—there is no single story in the letters. The CIT aimed to put the letters in the context, however, of fulfillment of the eschatological vision, the fulfillment of creation and history in Christ. The gospels proclaim the message of Christ; the letters work out that message in actual churches; and Revelation points to where that message is going, the establishment of God's kingdom.

As you read through the letters and consider Paul's reflections and directions to the churches, this book will attempt to give a bit broader context and situate the highlighted verses in the story of the church (ecclesiology) and Paul's message of God's love and grace. In the end, what is important to Paul is that through Christ, God gave the gift of salvation to all people independently of the directives of the Jewish Law.

Our response to these letters, then, is much like our response throughout the Old and New Testaments, to offer praise and gratitude to God for the mercy and grace offered us and to find ways to live that reflect that great gift of God's love for us.

As preparation, it might be a good idea to return to the book of Acts and the illumination *Life of Paul* as a starting place. Paul is the author of many of these letters, and it might help to know who he is and what his story is—a version of which is found in Acts 7:58–28:31—before reading the words attributed to him during his ministry.

Revelation is a book that takes up more specifically the question of eschatology, the end of history, the ultimate fulfillment of the promise of God's kingdom. It is an imaginative and literary masterpiece. It is also rooted in the ecclesiology of the early Christian church. That is to say, it is full of symbols and images related to what it means to be church. In fact, it is a letter of a very different sort written to "the seven churches." It brings together all the creative energy of the prophets, wisdom books, history, and gospels, as well as poetry and visions that project forward to a hope for the ultimate and permanent establishment of God's kingdom.

The Bible began in the book of Genesis with two visions of creation that laid out a vision of who God was in relationship to the cosmos and humanity. We end with a Christian vision of God's ongoing and permanent covenant with humanity through the church, made possible by the sacrifice of God's Son, Jesus. As you read Revelation through the illuminations of *The Saint John's Bible*, our hope is that you will see the references to other illuminations and be able to place the story it tells in the context of the Bible as a whole.

Carpet Page and Other Elements

Letters and Revelation begins with a carpet page, a blank page that sets the tone of the volume with a simple pattern. This page is meant to be a rest for the eye as the reader moves from one part of the Bible to another. Here Donald Jackson used a stamp based on a length of woven cotton from the Karachi jail in the Sindh region of Pakistan (ca. 1880). Originally, Sally Mae Joseph made a line drawing from the textile design for use on carpet pages at the end of each gospel in *Gospels and Acts*. It was also used in the border of *The Resurrection* (John 20:1-23). Parts of the stamp were sanded down to make the pattern more subtle on the carpet pages in *Gospels and Acts*. In its use throughout the letters, Jackson wanted the same motif as in the gospels but did not sand down the pattern. The carpet pages throughout *The Saint John's Bible* have also introduced a motif for each volume. Here we find a motif that connects the gospels and the letters, but with more color. We will see the motif repeated throughout the letters, woven into the decorative elements for the text treatments. A lovely use of it is on the pages of the second and third letters of John and the Letter of Jude, where the motif is laid like a piece of lace at the bottom of each brief text.

The book titles for each letter, painted by Donald Jackson, are richly colored and written in gold.

The initial capitals in *Letters and Revelation* are handled somewhat differently than in other volumes. In the past, Jackson has enjoyed creating unique initial capitals for each chapter in a book. However, to give unity to the letters and to preserve the simple freshness of the genre, Jackson created one alphabet for the initial capitals and used that throughout. The letter forms don't change, but the colors reflect the individual spreads, often picking up on the text treatments or illuminations.

Similarly, Jackson designed one alphabet and a standard decorative treatment to use in all thirteen text treatments he did in *Letters*. Many of his treatments are of quite long passages, and space was limited. For his text treatments, Jackson chose a hand that, although sophisticated, is direct. He wanted it to capture the spontaneous nature of writing a letter.

There are eighteen text treatments in all in *Letters*, the other five done by calligraphers Thomas Ingmire (1 Cor 11:23-26; 1 Cor 13:1-3), Hazel Dolby (Eph 5:8, 14), and Suzanne Moore (Phil 2:5-11; Heb 8:10).

There is one other element to note on these opening pages, namely

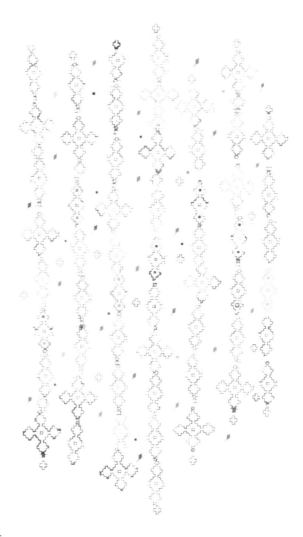

CARPET PAGE

the Benedictine cross in the margin. We have seen these throughout *The Saint John's Bible* to reference places that the Rule of Benedict quotes Scripture. You will see many of them in the margins of *Letters*, as St. Benedict incorporates Paul's and other writers' teaching into his rule of life for monastic communities.

THE ART OF THE SAINT JOHN'S BIBLE

Romans is the longest letter in the New Testament and perhaps the most developed in terms of its theological discussion. Interpretation of this letter's key points on grace and salvation has also been at the heart of the major split in Western Christianity, the Reformation. Because it has so many key ideas in it, this letter has the largest number of text treatments. It also has a major illumination. If at one time interpretations of Romans were the reason for division within Christianity, today they can be the reason for unity and mutual growth.

There are only three illuminations in *Letters*, and these are *Fulfillment of Creation*, (Rom 8:1-39), *At the Last Trumpet* (1 Cor 15:50-58), and *Harrowing of Hell* (1 Pet 3:18–4:11). As you can see even from the titles, these three emphasize the place of the letters in the eschatological movement of the New Testament, the movement toward the fulfillment of God's plan. The New Testament books dealing with the early Christian church, from the first chapter of Acts and the ascension of Christ, tell the story of looking forward to Christ's return and the fulfillment of the promise of unification with God and the establishment of God's perfect kingdom.

As Paul lived and moved among the churches, he advised the early Christians on life in community and interpreted the message of Jesus. The message was, first and foremost, one of salvation for those who have faith.

Much like Matthew's Gospel appealed to a Jewish Christian community, Paul's Letter to the Romans is conscious of the Jewish character of the church in Rome, in which there were also Gentiles.

Paul explains justification through faith by citing the example of Abraham. Paul points to Abraham as one who believed God's promise to him and acted accordingly. In this argument, Paul proclaims the possibility of forgiveness of sins and justification before God for everyone, not just the people of Israel. He also claims the Old Testament story of the people of God for all Christians, a single story that began with Abraham and was opened to all through the death and resurrection of Jesus Christ.

For What Does the Scripture Say and For This Reason It Depends on Faith

ROMANS 4:3

ROMANS 4:16-17

The importance of this, says Paul, is that justification is a gift from God. No one can "boast" or put himself or herself above others. No one can earn this gift that is given freely by God. Rather, it is bestowed on all as an act of God's grace.

Whereas in the *Historical Books* volume the text treatments appear in the margins, taking a back seat to the illuminations of the stories, in *Letters* the words of Paul and the other authors are central. The eighteen passages chosen for special treatment by the Committee on Illumination and Text emphasize key elements of Christian theology. Despite the conflicts and disputes, these passages have been the source of hope and joy for millennia.

ROMANS 4:3 AND ROMANS 4:16–17

THE ART OF THE SAINT JOHN'S BIBLE

The decorated cross at the top of Romans 5 is a version of the cross at the end of the genealogy that opens the Gospel of Matthew. That genealogy traces Jesus's origins all the way back to Abraham, an important connection for the early Christian community. In this cross in Romans, Donald Jackson has ornamented it with the gold stamp used in the carpet page for *Letters*. In this way he has connected the work of the gospels and Paul's letters in guiding the emerging Christian communities.

ROMANS 5:1–21

Paul continues his argument about salvation in this passage. Salvation has come through God's grace, through the single action of Christ's death and resurrection, and this salvation is available to all. People have lived under the sin of Adam's transgression, and now they live under the salvation gained by Christ's sacrifice.

This passage is often cited as being one of the sources for the doctrine of original sin and how Christ has reclaimed the universe from that sin.

*For the creation waits with
eager longing for the
revealing of the children of
God. (8:19)*

*What are the key points in this long passage that stand
out to you as you read? Do you see them explored in the
illumination?*

In Romans 8:1-39, the apostle Paul declares the Good News:
through the sacrifice of Jesus Christ, God has once and for
all reconciled humanity, fulfilled the covenant, and demonstrated the power and aim of God's love—to bring all of creation into communion with God. There will be no more exile,
for the Spirit of God dwells within believers. There is no separation between the love of God and those who have faith.

When Paul speaks of "death" here, he does not mean literal death but a state of being that negates life. The life that
comes through Christ is life the way creation was meant to
be. As Paul says in the opening of chapter 6, "Just as Christ
was raised from the dead by the glory of the Father, so we
too might walk in newness of life" (6:4). The Roman Christians to whom this letter was written knew better than anyone that the "freedom" they received through grace, and
the "enslavement" to Christ, was neither a free pass to licen-
tious living nor the promise of immediate joy and freedom
on earth. Their reward was more likely to be persecution by
the Romans and possibly a martyr's death.

In this way, Paul pointed forward to the fulfillment of
God's vision on a larger scale. What is the reward for believing
in God? God will count it as righteousness. We will be sanc-
tified and receive the gift of eternal life. "The wages of sin are
death, but the free gift of God is eternal life in Christ Jesus our
Lord" (6:23). This illumination links Paul's words about the
"free gift of God" with the richness of this gift; now, through
Christ, creation is reconciled to God completely. Nothing can
separate us from the love of Christ (see 8:38-39).

Thomas Ingmire references quantum physics, astronomy,
and computer science in this illumination. He was fascinated
by the way that quantum physics "reduces everything to one
thing, pure energy." The digital world, too, by reducing
everything to zeros and ones, unifies our perception. Ingmire
began with an image from the Hubble telescope that shows

a star in the shape of a cross. He added graphs, equations, and plot points that relate to the way scientists measure distances to individual stars.

At the bottom of the illumination is an echo of the *Creation* illumination from Genesis. We would do well to keep this image in mind for all the illuminations in *Letters and Revelation*.

The creation narrative in Genesis tells us why God creates. God creates out of goodness and love, bringing order to chaos. That creation is incomplete, however, and sin enters the picture.

The passion, death, and resurrection of Jesus Christ re-creates creation. In this illumination, the stars, the cosmos, and the echoes of the seven days of creation all proclaim that from the chaos of Christ's death and the glory of his resurrection, new life—eternal life—becomes the norm. It is a new order that unites us to God so completely that there can be no more separation.

◀ *How do the elements of this illumination communicate the fulfillment of Creation?*

FULFILLMENT OF CREATION

Chris Tomlin's Nature Illustrations

Once again, nature illustrator Chris Tomlin has graced the margins and open spaces of this volume with his insects and flowers. Unlike the destructive insect life we saw in *Historical Books*, the insects and plant life in *Letters* are hopeful and bright. They return us to the New Testament marginal illustrations of *Gospels and Acts*. They are the harbingers of spring and summer in Minnesota and Wales, although some, like the little butterfly in First Corinthians, are dramatic and even exotic. Here is where you can find them:

1 Corinthians 2–3	Black and White Butterfly (*Nemoptera bipernis*)
2 Corinthians 7	Bee Decoration (Generic Bee, Honey Bee Inspired)
Galatians 3:23-29	Common Butterfly (*Polygonia c-album*)
Colossians 1	Common Blue Butterfly (*Polyommatus icarus*) on Buddleia Flowers
Hebrews 1	Dragonfly on Yorkshire Fog Grass, *Holcus ianatus*

THE ART OF THE SAINT JOHN'S BIBLE

This final text treatment in the Letter to the Romans takes up again the relationship of faith to the Jews and Gentiles. Throughout their history, particularly in the Historical Books leading up to the exile but continuing into the time of the second temple, the Jewish people's fidelity to God has been shaky. We have read the cycles of obedience and disobedience. But we have also read the ongoing cycle of God's forgiveness, mercy, and love for the people. Throughout their checkered past, God has always preserved "a remnant," be it Noah and his family, those who return from exile and continue practicing in the Diaspora, or Esther's family.

What is new, Paul says, is that God's love and salvation has been extended to the Gentiles. He compares Christian Gentiles to the wild branches grafted onto an olive tree.

But If Some of the Branches Were Broken Off

ROMANS 11:17-24

This page draws attention to *The Saint John's Bible* as an arti-fact handwritten by calligraphers. All six calligraphers were present in Wales when this page was ready to be written, and they decided to split it up. It is the only page where all six cal-ligraphers contributed to the same body of text, although there are many examples of pages where multiple calligra-phers contributed various elements. The calligraphers were all trained in the single script used for *The Saint John's Bible*; nevertheless, each developed his or her own idiosyncrasies, including differences in descenders and some capital letters. However, on this page it is nearly impossible to tell where the work of one calligrapher ends and another begins. Hon-oring the work of those who went before, each calligrapher closely "stuck to the script" and wrote his or her passage uniformly, contributing to the unity of the page. It's a great tribute to the team.

Then, in the second column, Donald Jackson himself omit-ted a line! As with others in *The Saint John's Bible*, this line is a particularly important one. (Or perhaps they only seem that way when they are highlighted by being omitted.) The passage is 1 Corinthians 11:23-26, where Paul recounts the Last Supper event that is the source of the Christian practice of Eucharist.

Because of the fragility of the vellum, the work of all the calligraphers on the page, and the work already completed on the other side of the sheet (there is significant show-through on this page from Thomas Ingmire's text treatment for 1 Corinthians 11:23-26), there was no possibility of "erasing" or starting over. The solution, as with other omit-ted lines, was to write it at the bottom and show where it be-longs in the text. Hoping not to distract, the correction is made as simply as possible, a delicate box and line pointing to the space where the text belongs.

Finally, the bar at the bottom of the page contains the calligrapher's mark of each of the six scribes who worked on the project. These marks are like seals, artist's signatures with which the calligraphers identify their work. The marks belong, left to right, to Sally Mae Joseph, Angela Swan, Sue Hufton, Brian Simpson, Susan Leiper, and Donald Jackson.

rifice, they sacrifice to demons and not to God. I do
not want you to be partners with demons.²¹ You cannot drink the cup of the Lord and the cup of demons.
You cannot partake of the table of the Lord and the
table of demons. ²²Or are we provoking the Lord to
jealousy? Are we stronger than he? ■ "All things
are lawful," but not all things are beneficial. "All things
are lawful," but not all things build up.²⁴ Do not seek
your own advantage, but that of the other.²⁵ Eat whatever is sold in the meat market without raising any
question on the ground of conscience,²⁶ for "the earth
and its fullness are the Lord's."²⁷ If an unbeliever invites you to a meal and you are disposed to go, eat
whatever is set before you without raising any question on the ground of conscience. ²⁸ But if someone
says to you, "This has been offered in sacrifice," then
do not eat it, out of consideration for the one who
informed you, & for the sake of conscience—²⁹ I mean
the other's conscience, not your own. For why should
my liberty be subject to the judgment of someone
else's conscience? ³⁰ If I partake with thankfulness,
why should I be denounced because of that for which
I give thanks? ³¹ So, whether you eat or drink, or
whatever you do, do everything for the glory of God.
³²Give no offense to Jews or to Greeks or to the church
of God,³³ just as I try to please everyone in everything I do, not seeking my own advantage, but that
11 of many, so that they may be saved. ¹ Be imitators
of me, as I am of Christ.

² ■ I commend you because you remember me in
everything & maintain the traditions just as I handed
them on to you.³ But I want you to understand that
Christ is the head of every man, and the husband
is the head of his wife, and God is the head of Christ.
⁴ Any man who prays or prophesies with something
on his head disgraces his head,⁵ but any woman who
prays or prophesies with her head unveiled disgraces
her head—it is one and the same thing as having her
head shaved. ⁶ For if a woman will not veil herself,
then she should cut off her hair; but if it is disgraceful
for a woman to have her hair cut off or to be shaved,
she should wear a veil. For a man ought not to have
his head veiled, since he is the image & reflection
of God; but woman is the reflection of man. ⁸ Indeed,
man was not made from woman, but woman from
man.⁹ Neither was man created for the sake of woman, but woman for the sake of man. ¹⁰ For this reason
a woman ought to have a symbol of authority on
her head, because of the angels. ¹¹ Nevertheless,
in the Lord woman is not independent of man or
man independent of woman. ¹² For just as woman
came from man, so man comes through woman; but
all things come from God. ¹³ Judge for yourselves: is

it proper for a woman to pray to God with her head
unveiled ?¹⁴ Does not nature itself teach you that if
a man wears long hair, it is degrading to him, ¹⁵ but
if a woman has long hair, it is her glory? For her hair
is given to her for a covering.¹⁶ But if anyone is disposed to be contentious—we have no such custom,
nor do the churches of God. ■ Now in the following instructions I do not commend you, because
when you come together it is not for the better but
for the worse. ¹⁸ For, to begin with, when you come
together as a church, I hear that there are divisions
among you; and to some extent I believe it. ¹⁹ Indeed,
there have to be factions among you, for only so will
it become clear who among you are genuine. ²⁰ When
you come together, it is not really to eat the Lord's
supper.²¹ For when the time comes to eat, each of
you goes ahead with your own supper, and one goes
hungry and another becomes drunk.²² What! Do
you not have homes to eat and drink in? Or do you
show contempt for the church of God & humiliate
those who have nothing? What should I say to you?
Should I commend you? In this matter I do not commend you! ■ For I received from the Lord what I
also handed on to you, that the Lord Jesus on the
night when he was betrayed took a loaf of bread,
²⁴ and when he had given thanks, he broke it and
said, "This is my body that is for you. Do this in remembrance of me." ²⁵ In the same way he took the
cup also, after supper, saying, "This cup is the new
covenant in my blood. Do this, as often as you drink
it, in remembrance of me." ²⁶ For as often as you eat
this bread & drink the cup, you proclaim the Lord's
death until he comes. ■ Whoever, therefore, eats the
bread or drinks the cup of the Lord in an unworthy
manner will be answerable for the body and blood
of the Lord. ²⁸ Examine yourselves, and only then
eat of the bread and drink of the cup.² For all who
eat and drink without discerning the body, eat &
drink judgment against themselves. For this reason
many of you are weak and ill, and some have died.
³¹ But if we judged ourselves, we would not be judged.
³²But when we are judged by the Lord, we are dis-
ciplined so that we may not be condemned along
with the world. ³³ So then, my brothers and sisters,
when you come together to eat, wait for one another.
³⁴If you are hungry, eat at home, so that when you
come together, it will not be for your condemnation.
About the other things I will give instructions when
I come.

it, in remembrance of me."²⁶ For as often as you eat

For I Received from the Lord

I CORINTHIANS 11:23-26

FOR I RECEIVED
FROM THE LORD

The church at Corinth, comprised of diverse, multiethnic Greek Christians, had a lot of problems. Paul wrote more to this community than to any other, and he advised them, sometimes harshly, on issues ranging from behavior to church practices.

Paul's letters are ecclesial and liturgical as well as theological. They address concrete questions about how to be church, both how to live together (ecclesial) and how to worship together (liturgical). The passage highlighted in this text treatment by Thomas Ingmire is in the context of a longer discussion about how to worship together. Early Christian communities met in people's homes to share the eucharistic meal, a reenactment of the Last Supper, which was itself a Passover meal shared between Jesus Christ and his disciples.

In Corinth, the church was not celebrating the Eucharistic meal in the manner that was expected. Rather than gathering together and sharing bread and wine regardless of station in life, there were some who were holding a private, separate meal before the gathering, to which only a chosen few, those with the most status, were invited. At this meal, meat was being served that was part of sacrifices to other gods.

Paul instructs them by giving them liturgical language that reminds the participants of the significance of the eucharistic meal. Some form of this text, either as Paul has recorded it here or as it is found in the gospels of Matthew, Mark, and Luke, is used in virtually all Christian traditions during their celebration of the Eucharist. *The Saint John's Bible* also features an illumination of the words of consecration found in Luke 22:14-20.

THE ART OF THE SAINT JOHN'S BIBLE

This text treatment is the final piece we will see in *The Saint John's Bible* by Thomas Ingmire. It is in two parts that convey Paul's specific style of instruction. Paul's words are bold and sometimes absolute. In the first part of the illumination Paul questions the purpose of any gifts of the Spirit if they are not joined to love. The black text jangles down the right-hand column. Although it is the first part of the passage, the placement on the page makes it feel strident and out of place. It is separated from the well-known litany that begins "Love is patient; love is kind."

Often referred to as the Hymn of Love, this litany is a popular reading at wedding ceremonies. It enumerates the qualities of love and its importance among the values. Ingmire has matched it to the lettering of the passage on the previous page, this time beginning with text saturated in color and moving down the page to more simple text. He also has made a rainbow of the body of the hymn. Packed into the space is some of the most eloquent language in Paul's letters.

Several hymns that Paul has woven into his letters are given special treatment in this volume. These hymns are natural occasions for text treatments, emphasizing the liturgical nature of these letters. The words are probably variations on hymns that were sung by early Christian communities. Paul worshiped with these communities, broke bread with them, baptized them, and also sang hymns of praise to God with them. Other hymns that receive special treatment in this volume are found at Ephesians 5:14, Philippians 2:5-11, and Colossians 1:15-20.

IF I SPEAK IN THE TONGUES OF MORTALS

What surprises you about this illumination?

Before ending this first letter to the Corinthians, Paul points forward again to the final hope of Christians. The sting of death on the previous page is transposed against the soft patterning and words—"we will be changed," the promise of resurrection. It is similar to the illumination *Fulfillment of Creation*, which transposed "the wages of sin are death" with the Good News of eternal life.

Hazel Dolby created this illumination and saw in the passage a connection to her earlier illumination *Square before the Watergate* in Nehemiah. As the image in Nehemiah united the people returning from exile, so does this image, with its focus on geometric patterning, suggest an ingathering and transformation in Christ. Here is the ultimate cohesion and unity, with lines of gold suggesting Christ's light.

Dolby wanted to continue the illumination into the book heading for 2 Corinthians by providing the background. She felt it would further emphasize the movement from bottom to top and from right to left of the transformation. Donald Jackson agreed, and so Dolby painted the background for the book title, and Jackson returned later to add the lettering in gold.

◖ *How would you represent this passage in 1 Corinthians in an image?*

Paul writes to the Christians in Galatia during a time of unrest. These churches have turned away from Paul's teaching of relying on Christ's passion, death, and resurrection for salvation. In this fiery, passionate letter, Paul offers a strong argument to make his point. So we have this compact passage of six verses in which we find key statements by Paul on the role of faith in justification and on the centrality of faith.

Paul's specific ministry was to the Gentiles, which is why he traveled through Galatia in the first place. His vision is of a new community where Gentile and Jew, slave and free, and male and female are united by faith in Jesus. As we saw in the text treatments of Romans 4, his focus on the genealogy from Abraham through Christ opens salvation to all through the death and resurrection of Jesus.

Now before Faith Came

GALATIANS 3:23-29

NOW BEFORE FAITH CAME WE WERE IMPRISONED & GUARDED UNDER THE LAW UNTIL FAITH WOULD BE REVEALED. THEREFORE THE LAW WAS OUR DISCIPLINARIAN UNTIL CHRIST CAME, SO THAT WE MIGHT BE JUSTIFIED BY FAITH. BUT NOW THAT FAITH HAS COME, WE ARE NO LONGER SUBJECT TO A DISCIPLINARIAN, FOR IN CHRIST JESUS YOU ARE ALL CHILDREN OF GOD THROUGH FAITH. AS MANY OF YOU AS WERE BAPTIZED INTO CHRIST HAVE CLOTHED YOURSELVES WITH CHRIST. THERE IS NO LONGER JEW OR GREEK, THERE IS NO LONGER SLAVE OR FREE, THERE IS NO LONGER MALE AND FEMALE: FOR ALL OF YOU ARE ONE IN CHRIST JESUS. AND IF YOU BELONG TO CHRIST, THEN YOU ARE ABRAHAM'S OFFSPRING, HEIRS ACCORDING TO THE PROMISE.

NOW BEFORE FAITH CAME

There Is One Body and One Spirit and For Once You Were Darkness

EPHESIANS 4:4–6
EPHESIANS 5:8, 14

These text treatments by Hazel Dolby again emphasize the message of unity and salvation for all. Complemented by the gold and purple initial caps and verse markers, the treatments bookend the spread with their light.

The "bookends" serve another purpose here, inviting us to do more than read the highlighted passages. When reading Paul's letters, which are for the most part brief, it is good to dig into the full text. It is best not to rely on a single verse or small group of verses to convey the whole meaning of the letter.

EPHESIANS 4:4–6

This letter is ecclesial, as Paul instructs the Ephesians to "lead a life worthy of the calling to which you have been called" (4:1). As we read the letter to the Ephesians, we learn more about what it means to "live in the light" as members of one body in Christ.

THE ART OF THE SAINT JOHN'S BIBLE

This passage is another example of a hymn in Paul's letters. The text treatment by Suzanne Moore weaves the words "Christ," "Jesus," and "Lord" in fourteen languages into the English translation of the hymn. The hymn itself probably has its origins in earlier Christian hymns. We hear the references to Adam and the Suffering Servant, Old Testament passages that the early Christian community would have seen as prefiguring Christ. It is possible that Paul learned this hymn after his conversion and taught it to the Philippians and other communities as he traveled. An interesting way to experience this hymn is to read it along with the *Suffering Servant* illumination at Isaiah 53 in the *Prophets* volume.

This hymn has two quite beautiful and balanced parts. The first half describes Jesus' position as God who emptied himself and became human, humbled and "obedient to the point of death—even death on a cross" (2:8). The second half turns to resurrection, the position attained by Christ above all and a salvation extended to all people, so that everyone "should confess that Jesus Christ is Lord, to the glory of God the Father" (2:11).

The opening invitation, "Let the same mind be in you that was in Christ Jesus" (2:5), invites the church to share in Jesus' crucifixion and in so doing also share in the resurrection.

Are you seeing a pattern in these letters yet? Paul continuously balances death and resurrection, darkness and light, as he invites the early Christians to live in hope and celebrate the gift of Christ's love in very difficult times.

And Every Tongue Should Confess

PHILIPPIANS 2:5-11

PHILIPPIANS 2:5-11

Index of languages:

English	Lord
Greek	Christ
French	Jesus
Armenian	Lord
Japanese	Christ
Vietnamese	Jesus
Coptic	Jesus
German	Lord
Coptic	Christ
Portuguese	Christ
Chinese	Lord
Italian	Lord
Russian	Jesus
Korean	Lord
Ethiopian	Jesus

THE ART OF THE SAINT JOHN'S BIBLE

HE IS THE IMAGE OF THE
INVISIBLE GOD, THE FIRSTBORN
OF ALL CREATION; FOR IN HIM
ALL THINGS IN HEAVEN AND
ON EARTH WERE CREATED,
THINGS VISIBLE AND INVISIBLE,
WHETHER THRONES OR
DOMINIONS OR RULERS OR
POWERS ALL THINGS HAVE
BEEN CREATED THROUGH HIM

At the opening of Colossians we find yet another hymn, much like the one in Philippians 2:6-11. This hymn also arranges itself into two parts. This time the first names Jesus Christ as the firstborn of creation in (or by) whom all was created. Rather than the Suffering Servant, the Old Testament parallel here is Wisdom, found in the *Wisdom Books* illumination *Seven Pillars of Wisdom* (Prov 8:22–9:6).

Again, the second part of the hymn turns to resurrection. As Jesus is the firstborn of creation, he is also "the firstborn from the dead" (1:18). The hymn stresses again the major points of Jesus' role in creation, the church, and salvation. He is the head of "the body, the church" (1:18) and has reconciled "all things . . . through the blood of his cross" (1:20).

Donald Jackson has written this treatment, and it is worth noting the beauty of the text, the evenness of the execution that, by this final volume, we may be taking for granted. These passages, written after the rest of the text on the page is complete, are less planned and more spontaneous than the daily work of calligraphy in the body of the text. The calligrapher here has to see the line and the whole passage and make decisions, keeping things readable and fresh as the passage unfolds.

The letters to the Thessalonians were written very close together in the early days of Paul's ministry. The story of
Paul's stay in Macedonia and Thessalonica is told in Acts 16
and 17. The visit was so successful for Paul and his partners,
Silas and Timothy, that they were pretty quickly and contin-
ually run out of town. They left behind a fervent church
that was very focused on the Second Coming—so excited, it
seems, that they were neglecting work and the demands of
ordinary life and just waiting.

Paul's teaching in these two letters outlines a vision of
the Second Coming that has become popularized as the
Rapture and Last Judgment.

Certainly, the early Christians believed the end of time

and establishment of God's permanent kingdom, either in "the skies" or on earth, was imminent. Throughout time, different communities have continued to feel they had identified the date Christ would return, and they check out of life in that belief. Most recently, billboards across America proclaimed that May 21, 2011, would be the date that believers would be "taken up" and disappear. Many who believed this went into debt and stopped paying bills, believing the rapture would bring an end to earthly obligations.

The idea that the rapture would involve only a select few is rather recent and not part of church tradition. Paul is talking about the end times, which must be kept within context of all of Paul's writings. All creation is saved. In addition, Christians must always remember what Jesus answers when asked about the end of the world: "But about that day or hour no one knows, neither the angels in heaven, nor the Son, but only the Father" (Mark 13:32).

Paul offers this image of the end times as a source of encouragement, the promise that there will come a time when "we will be with the Lord forever" (1 Thess 4:17). He follows up immediately with the warning that "you yourselves know very well that the day of the Lord will come like a thief in the night" (5:2). His recommendation is that they keep aware and live in the light of salvation.

In his second letter to the Thessalonians, Paul further clarifies. The message that Christ will return is not an excuse for idleness or lawlessness. They are to live in community following Paul's example. "Anyone unwilling to work should not eat" (3:10).

Seeing it starkly on the page as a text treatment by Donald Jackson, one cannot help but think of the monastic community who commissioned this book. *Ora et Labora*, prayer and work, is a key principle of Benedictine living. Only the infirm and elderly are relieved from the work of keeping the community going.

This Is the Covenant

HEBREWS 8:10

Suzanne Moore painted this text treatment, revisiting the theme of covenant we have followed from the Pentateuch through the gospels. In quoting Jeremiah 31:31-34, the author of the letter to the Hebrews uses the Old Testament prophet to make the point that Jesus is "the mediator of a better covenant, which has been enacted through better promises" (8:6).

THIS IS THE COVENANT

THE ART OF THE SAINT JOHN'S BIBLE

HEBREWS 11:1

This brief text treatment by Donald Jackson focuses the reader's attention on the centrality of faith and the hopefulness of these letters in claiming the promise of eternal life.

This famous verse defining faith is followed by a list of examples of Old Testament figures who exhibited faith and a recounting of the heroic acts and deliverance made possible through faith. Chapter 12 completes the discussion with the claim that Jesus is "the pioneer and perfecter of our faith, who for the sake of the joy that was set before him endured the cross, disregarding its shame, and has taken his seat at the right hand of the throne of God" (12:2). As with so many letters to the early Christian communities, this one exhorts them to follow the example of Christ in the assurance of the gift of eternal life. Again, there is a strong association with the Rule of Benedict and these verses. The Prologue of the Rule ends with these words: "We shall through patience share in the sufferings of Christ that we may deserve also to share in his kingdom."

What Good Is It My
Brothers and Sisters,
But the Wisdom
from Above Is First
Pure, and Are Any
among You Suffering?

JAMES 2:14-17
JAMES 3:17-18
JAMES 5:13-16

Into James's letter are packed three text treatments, all written by Donald Jackson. This brief letter has also been the source of much controversy. Martin Luther felt its author's teachings were in conflict with Paul, particularly claiming that it privileged works over faith.

However, the letter, and particularly these highlighted passages, is full of good instruction for those looking for advice on how to live in the life and light described by Paul. Also, there are a great number of parallels between the letter of James and the Sermon on the Mount in Matthew 5.

It is helpful to begin by noticing the Benedictine cross in the margin at verse 2:13, just before the first highlighted passage. This verse is found in chapter 64 of the Rule of Benedict, the chapter on the role of abbot. It is not difficult to see how showing mercy and refraining from judgment would be important to any kind of community life. This verse is in a paragraph in the Rule that begins, "Once in office, the abbot must keep constantly in mind the nature of the burden he has received, and remember to whom he will have *to give an account of his stewardship* (Luke 16:2). Let him recognize that his goal must be profit for the monks, not preeminence for himself" (RB 64.7-8; emphasis in original). As we read the text treatments in James, we realize the importance of acting on our faith and remaining the servants of all. The abbot serves God by showing love to the brothers, just as we serve God in the ways we show love to one another.

JAMES 2:14-17

The verses in the first text treatment are at the heart of the controversy over faith and works, but one must read beyond the first verse! Read as a whole, the passage sounds like Paul himself talking about the one who speaks in tongues but has no love, or the great teacher who lacks wisdom. It also hearkens back to those Thessalonians who refused to work because they believed the return of Christ was so imminent. It is a call to social justice, the heart of the commandment in Matthew 28 to feed and clothe the poor, which hearkens back to the prophet Micah's instruction to "do justice" (Mic 6:8) or even further back to Leviticus 19 and the direction to care for the widow, the orphan, the poor, and the alien.

The second passage, James 3:17-18, draws attention to the fruits of wisdom, namely peace, mercy, gentleness, and truthful living. Again, what you believe and what you do should be in harmony.

Finally, James 5:13-16 gives another model of Christian life in community. The members of the church are to serve one another, confess to one another, anoint one another, and pray with and for one another.

These three passages deepen our understanding of what life in Christ (that very life that has been the subject of Paul's letters) looks like. As a Bible commissioned by a Benedictine community striving to live together as witnesses to the Good News of Christ, these text treatments have even greater resonance.

I PETER 3:18–4:11

The harrowing of hell is the traditional name used to describe the redemption of all the people who died before Jesus Christ's incarnation in time. In eternity there is no time; Christ's redemption is for all.

In this illumination, we see yet another depiction of the conclusion of history and the movement toward fulfillment of God's kingdom that is at the heart of the letters. For the illumination, Suzanne Moore revisited three of her earlier works for *The Saint John's Bible: Calming of the Storm* (Matt 8:23-27), *The Last Judgment* (Matt 24–25), and *Demands of Social Justice* (Amos 3–4). Although all three of these previous works use darkness, chaos, and fragmentation to depict the brokenness of the relationship between God and humanity, the most direct parallels to the current illumination are the two from Matthew's Gospel.

HARROWING OF HELL

On the left side, Moore said the images "grew unconsciously from other illuminations I have painted." Her inspiration was the "living hell" of Guernica that she used in *The Last Judgment* but also more recent hellish tragedies, including Hurricane Katrina and the large-scale devastation of Haiti by an earthquake.

Contrasted to this darkness are the soaring images of paradise. As in her earlier pieces, Moore uses Gothic architecture symbolizing the church, the stamp referred to

THE ART OF THE SAINT JOHN'S BIBLE

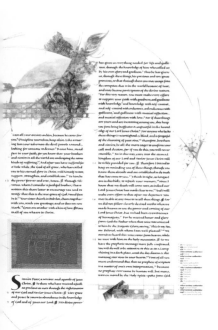

throughout *The Saint John's Bible* as "sacred geometry," and an image of plant life. "My definition of eternity would have to include a garden," Moore said, "an aesthetic, three-dimensional place, rich with growth and potential." In the openness of the right side of the page, she also invites the viewer to enjoy the possibilities and to "fill in the blank with her / his own definitions of the afterlife."

Notice also the reference to the Rule of Benedict in the margin. 1 Peter 4:11 is found in chapter 57 of the Rule of Benedict, the chapter on artists in the monastery. In this way it is significant to *The Saint John's Bible*, where all the art is meant to give glory to God. This verse also serves as a primary motto and prayer of all Benedictines to this day: "That in all things, God may be glorified" (RB 57.9). This motto is built into the brickwork of the original monastic enclosure of Saint John's Abbey, signified by the Latin initials IOGD (*in omnibus glorificetur Deus*).

Beloved, Let Us Love One Another

I JOHN 4:7-12

The central truth of Christianity—namely, God's love expressed through the life, death, and resurrection of his Son, Jesus Christ, and what it means for Christian life—is eloquently expressed in this final text treatment. We encounter it in *The Saint John's Bible* just before turning to the book of Revelation, wedged between *Harrowing of Hell* and the vivid accounts of the Apocalypse! It can serve as a reminder that these letters concern not just a future promise but also instruction on Christian life in all times.

Looking in the margins, we see two Benedictine crosses marking references found in the Rule of Benedict. 1 John 4:1 is found in chapter 58 about receiving new candidates. In that context, the treatment of those seeking entry to the monastery might seem contrary to Benedictine hospitality, but in reality, being a member of a religious community requires perseverance and a spiritual maturity that are best tested early.

The second reference, 1 John 4:18, is found in chapter 7 of the Rule of Benedict at the close of the long discussion on the twelve steps of humility. The passage reads:

> Now, therefore, after ascending all these steps of humility, the monk will quickly arrive at that *perfect love* of God which *casts out fear* (1 John 4:18). Through this love, all that he once performed with dread, he will now begin to observe without effort, as though naturally, from habit, no longer out of fear of hell, but out of love for Christ, good habit and delight in virtue. All this the Lord will by the Holy Spirit graciously manifest in his workman now cleansed of vices and sins." (RB 7.67–70; emphasis in original)

Again, the verses of this text treatment in *The Saint John's Bible* emphasize God's love and the saving action of Christ's sacrifice. The result of this love, the goal of Christians, should be to love one another. "If we love one another, God lives in us, and his love is perfected in us" (4:12).

Reread the vision of the Son of Man in Daniel 7:9-14. What similarities do you see to this vision?

The book of Revelation was written and illuminated entirely by Donald Jackson. He is the scribe of the book and also provided all the visual elements. Although it doesn't have the scale of some other books of the Bible, it certainly has the scope. As the culmination of *The Saint John's Bible* project, the book of Revelation draws on many elements found in previous books of the Bible. The Committee on Illumination and Text (CIT) encouraged Jackson to employ these elements in his effort to bring unity to these pages.

REVELATION 1:1-20

"I am the Alpha and the Omega," says the Lord God, who is and who was and who is to come, the Almighty. (1:8)

And what a grand opportunity it is! Jackson said in this book that he "turned the volume up full blast," and there is both a richness and intensity to the images and colors. Using the seven colors of the spectrum as in *Prophets*, he hoped "to express the fundamental unity of the visions with roots of imagery in the Old Testament."

Jackson began by laying down color backgrounds, working on all eight spreads at once. Because of that, you will see the shifts in tone even on the two pages without illuminations, through the colors of the capitals and verse markers. You will also notice the expansiveness of the illuminations, which are not isolated on parts of pages or confined to columns but spill even onto the margins.

Such is the case with this first spread, which includes the elaborate book heading, incipit, and a multipaneled illumination. Because Donald Jackson wrote all of Revelation, he was able here and there to adjust the text and space the illuminations accordingly.

The primary reference in this illumination is to the prophecy of the Son of Man in the book of Daniel. The central image of these pages reprises the image of the Son of Man from the *Prophets* volume of *The Saint John's Bible*. The lampstands are taken from the illumination *Vision of Isaiah*, where the prophet Isaiah witnessed God seated on a throne surrounded by lampstands.

Both images have a rich liturgical feel. For this opening

illumination of Revelation, the CIT suggested that Donald Jackson recreate the feel of an ornate, incense-filled church. The Revelation to John was written to be proclaimed at churches throughout Asia Minor, and as such it is a liturgical book. You will notice the artwork has a liturgical feel to it throughout, especially in these first spreads and the final illumination, *The Great Amen.*

In addition to the visual images from *Prophets*, Jackson used the stamp he made from a textile covered with mirrors that was used for the tree of life in *Wisdom Books* (see Sirach carpet page). We also see here the fish that have been used throughout, most notably in *Loaves and Fishes* (Mark 6:33-44).

REVELATION INCIPIT
WITH THE SON OF MAN

For marginal quotations, Jackson wrote the verse, "'I am the Alpha and the Omega,' says the Lord God" (1:13). He added another verse that describes the state John was in as he received and wrote the letter. As John describes, "I was in the Spirit" (1:10). The verse announces that what we are reading is not a literal experience. As in the visions of the Old Testament prophets, the language is often that of approximation and comparison. I saw "something like . . . ," says John, just as the prophet Ezekiel grasped at language to describe the creatures in his *Vision at the Chebar*. The state of the seer/prophet is also a basis for the enhanced color and imagery that is to come.

Letter to the Seven Churches with the Heavenly Choir

REVELATION 2:1–5:14

Let anyone who has an ear listen to what the Spirit is saying to the churches. (3:22)

Which of these messages to the churches resonates with you? What message of hope do these letters offer?

Although Revelation is certainly treated as an "open letter" to all churches, it was written specifically to seven churches in the western section of Asia Minor. Just like the other letters in the New Testament, these brief letters offer exhortations, warnings, and correction. The problems that the churches were facing in the first century are also recognizable from the letters by Paul and others: false teaching, persecution, and complacency.

As biblical scholar Raymond E. Brown points out in his *An Introduction to the New Testament*:

LETTERS TO THE SEVEN CHURCHES WITH THE HEAVENLY CHOIR

> Most modern readers who know something about Revelation think of persecution as the only issue addressed and consequently reinterpret the book in the light of threatening situations today. The struggle against complacency may be much more applicable to modern Christianity. The false teaching is very conditioned by the first century in one way (eating meat offered to idols), and yet the underlying issue of Christians conforming in an unprincipled way to the surrounding society remains a very current problem.[1]

It is important to recognize the first-century context of this book, as well as its genre, that of apocalyptic and escha-

[1] Raymond E. Brown, SS, *An Introduction to the New Testament* (New York: Doubleday, 1997), 782.

tological literature, and not to read it literally or apply it haphazardly to our own time. The illumination balances the modern and ancient contexts with imagery and color.

The churches are vivid, painted in the rainbow colors of the vision. They are adorned with crosses that suggest a variety of cultural traditions. We also see the seven lampstands. At the bottom is a golden calf representing the casting out of idol worship as well as its presence as a threat. The churches are still surrounded by the pagan cults, and the church at Thyatira is specifically criticized for eating food sacrificed to idols (2:20).

Among the doorways of the churches is the golden archway we have seen throughout *The Saint John's Bible*. It is, significantly, stamped on *Vision of the New Temple* in Ezekiel, but also in the detail of the tent image in *David Anthology* in *Historical Books*. You'll also find it, in black, in *Life of Paul* in the book of Acts. All these things—temple, ark, church—will be unified and perfected by the action of this vision.

Following the letters to the churches, the dramatic action of the vision begins. Forming an informal central panel in this illumination is the slain lamb standing atop the scroll with its seven seals. The lamb is the source of hope for the churches, called forth as the only one worthy to open the scroll and usher in the cosmic battle.

Finally, Donald Jackson has painted banners to depict the

triumphant song of the heavenly choir in chapter 4. The words "Holy, Holy, Holy" are written in Syriac, Greek, and Latin, along with a Greek Orthodox cross and the cross used by the Benedictines of Saint John's Abbey. Again, this hymn has resonance with *Vision of Isaiah*, in which the heavenly choir also sang "Holy, Holy, Holy," a prayer that became one of the earliest pieces of Christian liturgy. In fact, the whole passage describing the elders and angels worshiping God on the throne owes much to the prophetic visions of Ezekiel, Daniel, and Isaiah.

Looking at this piece as a whole, we might be struck by the liturgical feel of the images. In many American Christian churches in recent decades, the sanctuaries have been adorned with brightly colored banners, often depicting the lamb (though not with seven eyes and seven horns!) and words of praise to God. Just as the elders in the vision fully participate in this surreal liturgy, prostrating themselves and "casting their crowns before the throne" (4:10), this illumination invites us to enter in and praise God with our full being.

Of course, the banners here also have a military feel. This panel sets up the movement to the battle depicted in the next two spreads. When the lamb opens the seals, havoc will break out, beginning the final battle between good and evil, as the world descends into chaos. However, we already know what side will win, and at the center of the restoration will be the lamb that was slain.

What are your associations with the image of the four horsemen of the Apocalypse?

Perhaps no image from Revelation has so entered the popular consciousness as the four horsemen of the Apocalypse. When the lamb, depicted on the left side of the illumination, breaks the first four seals, the four horses and their riders are released: the white horse of conquering war, the red horse of violence, the black horse of famine, and the green horse of death. The horses in this illumination display their banners: bow, sword, scales, and skull and crossbones.

REVELATION 6:1-8
*Then I saw the Lamb open
one of the seven seals. (6:1)*

The horses are not alone in this vision—it is a catalog of fearful dark imagery: locusts and pestilence, earthquakes and black clouds, the bodies of slaughtered armies, a bloody moon, and displaced mountains. It is a portrait of environmental, human, and cosmic destruction.

Again, Donald Jackson has brought his modern sensibility to the image, as well as his imagination. He began with images of modern-day cavalry, hulking black tanks coming from both directions.

Jackson doesn't find locusts very scary, so instead he painted in praying mantis figures. The figures from Ezekiel's *Vision at the Chebar* (Ezek 1:1–3:27) are here: the frightening faces and the eagle and lion heads. There are other frightening and frightened eyes emerging from the dark, fiery, bloody landscape. At the center, the bright blue and red swirling soup is made up of microscope images of modern diseases. Down the right side are the bodies, falling and drowned, that appeared in the opening illumination of *Historical Books, Joshua Anthology,* an image of conquest.

Also included in this illumination are images of oil rigs and towers. These images have a twofold resonance for Donald Jackson, given our contemporary context. First, there is the great damage being done to the land in the millennia of human exploitation of natural resources. We blight the land and oceans with powerful rigs for extracting resources. Also, wars often find their root cause in access to these resources. Whether it is war in the Middle East or

famine, displacement, and war in Africa, oil is often at the heart of the conflict.

Jackson was also completing these pages as Japan struggled to contain and manage the nuclear disaster at its nuclear power plant in Fukushima following the powerful earthquake and tsunami in March 2011. Conscious of the text proclaiming that there was nowhere to hide from this destruction, not even in caves or under the earth (6:15), Jackson was struck by the invisible and pervasive destructive force of radiation. People fled the disaster, but where can we hide from nuclear fallout? To the image he added the triangular signs used to warn of radiation and, in the upper left, a single nuclear tower.

The presence of the divine is also there in the batons sprinkled across the image. However, these are not made of gold leaf or platinum as in other volumes of *The Saint John's Bible*. In Revelation, Jackson used holographic foil. This foil is not a single color but more textured and mirrorlike, reflecting a rainbow of color. It suited his vision of Revelation perfectly, providing a shimmering surface that doesn't always come across in the reproductions. Here it suggests not so much the presence of the divine as the surreal nature of the vision.

❦ *Donald Jackson has substituted some contemporary images for the ones in John's vision. What images might you add to this depiction of a world descending into chaos?*

Woman and the Dragon and The Cosmic Battle

REVELATION 12:1-17

A great portent appeared in heaven: a woman clothed with the sun, with the moon under her feet, and on her head a crown of twelve stars. (12:1)

What do you see in the image of the woman that relates to the story of salvation that unfolds throughout the Bible?

A great narrative plays out in these seventeen verses of chapter 12. Donald Jackson made these notes on the action:

· The woman appears, pregnant (in heaven).
· The dragon appears (in heaven).
· The child is snatched away and taken to God.
· The woman flees.
· The devil is vanquished and hurled to the earth by St. Michael.
· The devil makes war on earth and pursues the woman.
· She is flown to safety by the two wings of a great eagle.

The elements of the story are depicted in two illuminations covering four pages. At their center is the image of the woman and the dragon. The woman is richly clothed, wearing the headdress we saw in the illumination *Esther* in *Historical Books*. The fabric of her clothing includes a reprise of the fabric design on Mary Magdelene's cloak in *The Resurrection* (John 20:1-23). However, the woman is not Esther, Mary Magdalene, Wisdom Woman, or Eve. Neither is she the Virgin Mary or the church exclusively. Rather, she is all the faithful women of our text, and more particular to the allegory in Revelation, she is both Mary and the church. The crown of stars, a reprise of the wisdom tree stamp, surrounds her head. The moon, made of holographic foil, is at her feet. She holds her pregnant belly and looks anxious. Just as Mary gave birth to Christ at a dangerous time in history, so too does the church make Christ present for all times and places.

In the bottom half of the illumination we see the dragon. As depicted by Donald Jackson, the dragon's many faces include human faces with a number of expressions. He meant these to suggest masks and the presence of the evil in all of us. "Do we wear masks behind which parts of ourselves are hidden?" he asks. The devil also has the face of the ten-horned monster from the book of Daniel. Again, this vision has a lot in common with Daniel's vision of the Son of Man. Finally, we see a reprise of Chris Tomlin's snake from Genesis, "that ancient serpent, who is called the Devil and Satan, deceiver of the whole world" (12:9). The gold lance of St. Michael descends across the image, impaling one of the devil's heads.

Another important piece of the drama is found in the upper left hand corner, next to chapter 9. Explained by the marginal text, "But her child was snatched away and taken to God and to his throne" (12:5), we find a reprise of the image of the Son of Man from Daniel 7 in *Prophets*. Included in the image is a gold cross, clearly identifying this Son of Man. Separated by two pages from the action between the woman and the dragon, the Son of Man has taken his place on the throne of heaven. This image and its placement have special resonance with the apocalyptic moment the first-century Christians held closely. The story unfolding in Revelation is outside of time because, by his death and resurrection, Jesus has already accomplished the victory.

WOMAN AND
THE DRAGON

Turning the page, we find a continuation of the narrative in the illumination *The Cosmic Battle*. The devil descends to earth and pursues the woman in war. However, she escapes, represented by the rich fabric of her dress and wings on the right-hand page.

The devil in the form of a snake fills the left half of the illumination. "His angels" are represented here by the praying mantis figures we saw in *The Four Horsemen of the Apocalypse*. The black insects are fitting minions of the devil and blend with the figures of black tanks rolling across the landscape. For the landscape, Donald Jackson used aerial photos of farm fields and also images of a small modern city.

Note how the colors shift slightly in the image of the woman taking flight. Rather than the blue, black, and green of the cosmic battle scene, we see the deep lilac beginning to dominate and the harmonious fields of color. Already the mood is shifting, preparing us for the depiction of the new Jerusalem, the resolution of the battle to renewed creation.

◀ *Where do you see hope in these verses and in the illumination?*

Vision of the
New Jerusalem

REVELATION 21:1–22:5

"See, I am making all things new." (21:5)

What elements from other illuminations do you recognize in this one?

The great vision finds resolution in this image of the new Jerusalem, God's city descending from heaven to earth. It is, like so many prophetic images, full of metaphors. The description reminds us of the rebuilding of Jerusalem after exile in Ezra and Nehemiah. As with the various images of the temple, a tree and a river are present. And, in fact, this passage in Scripture reminds us of the instructions for building and rebuilding the temple. However, as John writes, "I saw no temple in the city, for its temple is the Lord God the Almighty and the Lamb"

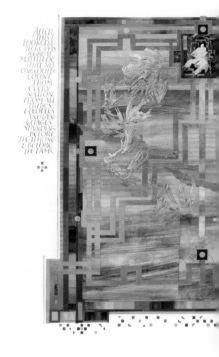

VISION OF THE NEW JERUSALEM

(21:22). In fact, this illumination is a place we might expect to see that gold archway repeated. But it is not here. The Son of Man on the throne inhabits the city.

To capture the images in this passage, Donald Jackson began with his vibrant but more subdued palette of colors. The streets of gold resemble the gold pattern in *Vision of the Son of Man* found in Daniel. Still, the four gates remind us of the temple images. The space includes a triumphant chorus of angels, which are disembodied, more like birds or butterflies than other winged creatures we've seen.

The tree of life is connected to the city and its streets and bears gold leaves that will heal nations. However, it also

THE ART OF THE SAINT JOHN'S BIBLE

stands apart. The design for the tree was adapted from a second-century Chinese relief carving. Jackson said he "liked

its strength and sobriety in contrast to the radiant celebratory colors of the main New Jerusalem page." In his portrayal, the tree is "rooted" just as the New Jerusalem will be, not a vision of another realm but of a heaven on earth.

The final piece of this illumination was the reprise of the boxes in the lower margin. The design comes from Hazel Dolby's illumination *Square before the Watergate* in the book of Nehemiah.

The Committee on Illumination and Text requested that Donald include some image of the people, since the nations and people are so central to the Scripture passage. This is not an otherworldly ideal city but one that is fully inhabited. The people live there by the light reflected by the presence of God, and all good things transpire there. But how to show that in the illumination without adding a portrait of a crowd or something else that would disrupt the unity and simplicity of the vision? Jackson remembered Hazel Dolby's geometric representation of the people entering Jerusalem after the exile at the end of *Historical Books*. He added it to this illumination, where it shows the gathering in of the people, retains the unity that this is ultimately the story of the tribes of Israel, and complements rather than detracts from the vision of the city.

Finally, you will notice the two burnished crosses at the

bottom right of the page. On June 18, 2011, Donald and Mabel Jackson presented this illumination to the community of Saint John's Abbey and University in the Abbey Church in Collegeville, Minnesota. They processed with the folio during Evening Prayer as part of a celebration of the completion of *The Saint John's Bible*. Abbot John Klassen, OSB, of Saint John's Abbey and Father Robert Koopmann, OSB, president of Saint John's University, placed the folio on the altar and burnished the two gold Benedictine crosses. This ritual follows a tradition in Judaism whereby the final mark on a new scroll is made by the one who commissioned the work.

THE GREAT AMEN

The book of Revelation in *The Saint John's Bible* doesn't end with the vision of the new Jerusalem but with a final illumination that ties together the book and again draws attention to its liturgical nature. The colors and text mirror the book title and incipit. Behind this banner of text is a layer from *Vision of the New Jerusalem*. Angels circle a cross, the symbol of salvation.

Notice also the gold voiceprint just above the base of the cross. Voiceprints like these were a regular feature in the *Psalms* volume of *The Saint John's Bible*. There they captured the sacred chant from multiple traditions, including the *schola* of Saint John's Abbey chanting psalms as part of their daily prayer. For this final illumination, Donald Jackson asked Father Robert Koopmann, OSB, president of Saint John's University and an accomplished pianist, if there was a selection of some joyous piece of piano music that could be captured and used in the final illumination. Father Bob recommended a celebratory segment of "Adoro te Devote" from his recording *Sacred Improvisations*. Although it is faint on the page, it provides another connection to liturgy and the prayer of the church.

The Saint John's Bible comes to an end with a great Amen and with the hope of Christians, "Come, Lord Jesus!" In liturgy, in our life together as Christians, as we strive to enact justice and mercy within the order of creation, we celebrate and sing.

◀ *How has this consideration of the book of Revelation changed any preconceptions you had?*

The Great Amen

REVELATION 22:20-21
Come, Lord Jesus! (22:20)

2 Kings 16

1 Chronicles 25

2 Chronicles 11

1 Maccabees 11

1 Corinthians
2–3

Tobit 14

Hebrews 1

Colossians 1

sons, has borne him."¹⁶Then Naomi took the child
and laid him in her bosom, and became his nurse.
¹⁷The women of the neighborhood gave him a name,
saying, "A son has been born to Naomi." They named
him Obed; he became the father of Jesse, the father

18 of David. ¶ Now these are the descendants of Perez:
Perez became the father of Hezron,¹⁹Hezron of Ram,
Ram of Amminadab,²⁰Amminadab of Nahshon,
Nahshon of Salmon,²¹Salmon of Boaz, Boaz of Obed,
²²Obed of Jesse, and Jesse of David.

¹⁷ THE WOMEN OF THE
NEIGHBORHOOD
GAVE HIM A NAME,
SAYING, "A SON HAS
BEEN BORN TO NAOMI."
THEY NAMED HIM
OBED; HE BECAME THE
FATHER OF JESSE, THE
FATHER OF DAVID.'

¹⁸ 'NOW THESE ARE THE
DESCENDANTS OF PEREZ:
PEREZ BECAME THE FA-
THER OF HEZRON, HEZ-
RON OF RAM, RAM OF
AMMINADAB, AMMIN-
ADAB OF NAHSHON,
NAHSHON OF SALMON,

²¹ SALMON OF BOAZ, BOAZ
OF OBED, OBED OF JESSE,
AND JESSE OF DAVID

I
SAMUEL

There was a certain man of Ramathaim, a
Zuphite from the hill country of Ephraim,
whose name was Elkanah son of Jeroham
son of Elihu son of Tohu son of Zuph, an Ephraimite.
²He had two wives; the name of the one was Hannah,
and the name of the other Peninnah. Peninnah had
children, but Hannah had no children. ¶ Now this
man used to go up year by year from his town to worship and to sacrifice to the LORD of hosts at Shiloh,
where the two sons of Eli, Hophni & Phinehas, were
priests of the LORD. ⁴On the day when Elkanah sacrificed, he would give portions to his wife Peninnah
and all her sons & daughters;⁵ but to Hannah he
gave a double portion, because he loved her, though
the LORD had closed her womb.⁶ Her rival used to
provoke her severely, to irritate her, because the LORD
had closed her womb. ⁷So it went on year by year;
as often as she went up to the house of the LORD,
she used to provoke her. Therefore Hannah wept
and would not eat.⁸ Her husband Elkanah said to
her, "Hannah, why do you weep? Why do you not
eat? Why is your heart sad? Am I not more to you
than ten sons?" ¶ After they had eaten and drunk
at Shiloh, Hannah rose & presented herself before
the LORD. Now Eli the priest was sitting on the seat
beside the doorpost of the temple of the LORD.¹⁰She
was deeply distressed & prayed to the LORD, and
wept bitterly.¹¹She made this vow: O LORD of hosts,
if only you will look on the misery of your servant,
and remember me, and not forget your servant, but
will give to your servant a male child, then I will set
him before you as a nazirite until the day of his death.
He shall drink neither wine nor intoxicants, and

12 no razor shall touch his head." ¶ As she continued
praying before the LORD, Eli observed her mouth.

a Compare Gk and
1 Chr 6.35-36: Heb
Ramathaim-zophim
b Syr: Meaning of Heb
uncertain
c Gk: Heb lacks and
presented herself before
the LORD
d That is one appointed or
one consecrated
e Gk Compare Gk Q MS
1.32: MT then I will dedi-
cate him to the LORD all the
days of his life

Excerpts from Joshua 24:8-14 They fought with you, and I handed them over to you, and you took possession of their land. . . . I sent the hornet ahead of you, which drove out before you the two kings of the Amorites; it was not by your sword or by your bow. I gave you a land on which you had not labored, and towns that you had not built, and you live in them; you eat the fruit of vineyards and oliveyards that you did not plant. "Now therefore revere the Lord, and serve him in sincerity and faithfulness." *Donald Jackson*

(Found in the margins of the book of Joshua)

Judges 2:11 Then the Israelites did what was evil in the sight of the Lord.

Judges 4:1 The Israelites again did what was evil in the sight of the Lord, after Ehid died.

Judges 6:1 The Israelites did what was evil in the sight of the Lord.

Judges 8:34 The Israelites did not remember the Lord their God, who had rescued them.

Judges 10:6 The Israelites again did what was evil in the sight of the Lord.

Judges 13:1 The Israelites again did what was evil in the sight of the Lord.

Judges 18:1 In those days there was no king in Israel.

Judges 21:25 In those days there was no king in Israel.

Judges 2:18-20 Whenever the Lord raised up judges for them, the Lord was with the judge, and he delivered them from the hand of their enemies all the days of the judge; for the Lord would be moved to pity by their groaning because of those who persecuted and oppressed them. But whenever the judge died, they would relapse and behave worse than their ancestors, following other gods, worshiping them and bowing down to them. They would not drop any of their practices or their stubborn ways. So the anger of the Lord was kindled against Israel.

(Found at the end of the Book of Judges)

All text treatments in the book of Judges are by *Donald Jackson*

AND
THE LORD
SAID
TO
SAMUEL,
"LISTEN
TO THE
VOICE OF
THE
PEOPLE
IN ALL
THAT
THEY SAY
TO YOU;
FOR
THEY
HAVE NOT
REJECTED
YOU.
BUT THEY
HAVE
REJECTED
ME,
FROM
BEING
KING
OVER
THEM."

8:7

I SAMUEL 8:7

Ruth 4:17-21 The women of the neighborhood gave him a name, saying, "A son has been born to Naomi." They named him Obed; he became the father of Jesse, the father of David. Now these are the descendants of Perez: Perez became the father of Hezron, Hezron of Ram, Ram of Amminadab, Amminadab of Nahshon, Nahshon of Salmon, Salmon of Boaz, Boaz of Obed, Obed of Jesse, and Jesse of David.   *Donald Jackson*

1 Samuel 8:7 And the Lord said to Samuel, "Listen to the voice of the people in all that they say to you; for they have not rejected you, but they have rejected me from being king over them."

1 Samuel 13:13 Samuel said to Saul, "You have done foolishly." (13:13)

1 Samuel 13:13 "You have not kept the commandment of the Lord your God."   (found at 1 Sam 16)

1 Samuel 17:37 David said, "The Lord, who saved me from the paw of the lion and from the paw of the bear, will save me from the hand of this Philistine."

1 Samuel 28:15 Saul answered, "I am in great distress, for the Philistines are warring against me and God has turned away from me and answers me no more."

1 Samuel 28:17-18 "The Lord has done to you just as he spoke by me; for the Lord has torn the kingdom out of your hand, and given it to your neighbor, David. Because you did not obey the voice of the Lord."   (Found at 1 Sam 31)

All text treatments in the book of 1 Samuel are by *Donald Jackson*

2 Samuel 12:13 David said to Nathan, "I have sinned against the Lord."   *Donald Jackson*

2 Maccabees 12:42-45 And they turned to supplication, praying that the sin that had been committed might be wholly blotted out. The noble Judas exhorted the people to keep themselves free from sin, for they had seen with their own eyes what had happened as the result of the sin of those who had fallen. He also took up a collection, man by man, to the amount of two thousand drachmas of silver, and sent it to Jerusalem to provide for a sin offering. In doing this he acted very well and honorably, taking account of the resurrection. For if he were not expecting that those who had fallen would rise again, it would have been superfluous and foolish to pray for the dead. But if he was looking to the splendid reward that is laid up for those who fall asleep in godliness, it was a holy and pious thought. Therefore he made atonement for the dead, so that they might be delivered from their sin.   *Sally Mae Joseph*

Romans 4:3 For what does the scripture say? "Abraham believed God, and it was reckoned to him as righteousness."   *Donald Jackson*

Romans 4:16-17 For this reason it depends on faith, in order that the promise may rest on grace and be guaranteed to all his descendants, not only to the adherents of the law but also to those who share the faith of Abraham (for he is the father of all of us, as it is written, "I have made you the father of many nations")—in the presence of the God in whom he believed, who gives life to the dead and calls into existence the things that do not exist.   *Donald Jackson*

2 MACCABEES 12:42-45

Romans 5:1-21 Therefore, since we are justified by faith, we have peace with God through our Lord Jesus Christ, through whom we have obtained access to this grace in which we stand; and we boast in our hope of sharing the glory of God. And not only that, but we also boast in our sufferings, knowing that suffering produces endurance, and endurance produces character, and character produces hope, and hope does not disappoint us, because God's love has been poured into our hearts through the Holy Spirit that has been given to us.

For while we were still weak, at the right time Christ died for the ungodly. Indeed, rarely will anyone die for a righteous person— though perhaps for a good person someone might actually dare to die. But God proves his love for us in that while we still were sinners Christ died for us. Much more surely then, now that we have been justified by his blood, will we be saved through him from the wrath of God. For if while we were enemies, we were reconciled to God through the death of his Son, much more surely, having been reconciled, will we be saved by his life. But more than that, we even boast in God through our Lord Jesus Christ, through whom we have now received reconciliation.

Therefore, just as sin came into the world through one man, and death came through sin, and so death spread to all because all have sinned— sin was indeed in the world before the law, but sin is not reckoned when there is no law. Yet death exercised dominion from Adam to Moses, even over those whose sins were not like the transgression of Adam, who is a type of the one who was to come.

But the free gift is not like the trespass. For if the many died through the one man's trespass, much more surely have the grace of God and the free gift in the grace of the one man, Jesus Christ, abounded for the many. And the free gift is not like the effect of the one man's sin. For the judgment following one trespass brought condemnation, but the free gift following many trespasses brings justification. If, because of the one man's trespass, death exercised dominion through that one, much more surely will those who receive the abundance of grace and the free gift of righteousness exercise dominion in life through the one man, Jesus Christ.

Therefore just as one man's trespass led to condemnation for all, so one man's act of righteousness leads to justification and life for all. For just as by the one man's disobedience the many were made sin-

ROMANS 5:1-21

THE ART OF THE SAINT JOHN'S BIBLE

ners, so by the one man's obedience the many will be made righteous. But law came in, with the result that the trespass multiplied;
but where sin increased, grace abounded all the more, so that, just as
sin exercised dominion in death, so grace might also exercise dominion through justification leading to eternal life through Jesus Christ
our Lord. *Donald Jackson*

Romans 6:22-23 But now that you have been freed from sin and enslaved
to God, the advantage you get is sanctification. The end is eternal life.
For the wages of sin is death, but the free gift of God is eternal life in
Christ Jesus our Lord. *Thomas Ingmire*

Romans 11:17-24 But if some of the branches were broken off, and you, a
wild olive shoot, were grafted in their place to share the rich root of
the olive tree, do not boast over the branches. If you do boast, remember that it is not you that support the root, but the root that supports
you. You will say, "Branches were broken off so that I might be grafted
in." That is true. They were broken off because of their unbelief, but
you stand only through faith. So do not become proud, but stand in
awe. For if God did not spare the natural branches, perhaps he will not
spare you. Note then the kindness and the severity of God: severity toward those who have fallen, but God's kindness toward you, provided
you continue in his kindness; otherwise you also will be cut off. And
even those of Israel, if they do not persist in unbelief, will be grafted in,
for God has the power to graft them in again. For if you have been cut
from what is by nature a wild olive tree and grafted, contrary to nature,
into a cultivated olive tree, how much more will these natural branches
be grafted back into their own olive tree. *Donald Jackson*

1 Corinthians 11:23-26 For I received from the Lord what I also handed on
to you, that the Lord Jesus on the night when he was betrayed took a
loaf of bread, and when he had given thanks, he broke it and said,
"This is my body that is for you. Do this in remembrance of me." In
the same way he took the cup also, after supper, saying, "This cup is
the new covenant in my blood. Do this, as often as you drink it, in remembrance of me." For as often as you eat this bread and drink the
cup, you proclaim the Lord's death until he comes. *Thomas Ingmire*

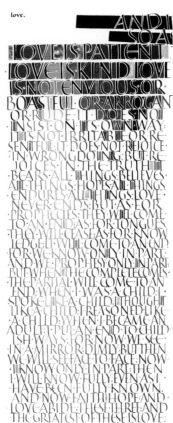

love.

1 Corinthians 13:1-13 If I speak in the tongues of mortals and of angels, but do not have love, I am a noisy gong or a clanging cymbal. And if I have prophetic powers, and understand all mysteries and all knowledge, and if I have all faith, so as to remove mountains, but do not have love, I am nothing. If I give away all my possessions, and if I hand over my body so that I may boast, but do not have love, I gain nothing. Love is patient; love is kind; love is not envious or boastful or arrogant or rude. It does not insist on its own way; it is not irritable or resentful; it does not rejoice in wrongdoing, but rejoices in the truth. It bears all things, believes all things, hopes all things, endures all things. Love never ends. But as for prophecies, they will come to an end; as for tongues, they will cease; as for knowledge, it will come to an end. For we know only in part, and we prophesy only in part; but when the complete comes, the partial will come to an end. When I was a child, I spoke like a child, I thought like a child, I reasoned like a child; when I became an adult, I put an end to childish ways. For now we see in a mirror, dimly, but then we will see face to face. Now I know only in part; then I will know fully, even as I have been fully known. And now faith, hope, and love abide, these three; and the greatest of these is love.

Thomas Ingmire

I CORINTHIANS 13:1-13

Galatians 3:23-29 Now before faith came, we were imprisoned and guarded under the law until faith would be revealed. Therefore the law was our disciplinarian until Christ came, so that we might be justified by faith. But now that faith has come, we are no longer subject to a disciplinarian, for in Christ Jesus you are all children of God through faith. As many of you as were baptized into Christ have clothed yourselves with Christ. There is no longer Jew or Greek, there is no longer slave or free, there is no longer male and female; for all of you are one in Christ Jesus. And if you belong to Christ, then you are Abraham's offspring, heirs according to the promise.

Donald Jackson

Ephesians 4:4-6 There is one body and one Spirit, just as you were called to the one hope of your calling, one Lord, one faith, one baptism, one God and Father of all, who is above all and through all and in all.   *Hazel Dolby*

those who are disobedient." Therefore do not be
associated with them." For once you were darkness,
but now in the Lord you are light. Live as children

FOR ONCE YOU WERE
DARKNESS BUT NOW IN THE LORD YOU ARE LIGHT LIVE AS
CHILDREN OF LIGHT · FOR EVERYTHING THAT BECOMES
VISIBLE IS LIGHT THEREFORE IT SAYS · SLEEPER AWAKE!
RISE FROM THE DEAD AND CHRIST WILL SHINE ON YOU·

Ephesians 5:8, 14 For once you were darkness, but now in the Lord you are light. Live as children of light . . . for everything that becomes visible is light. Therefore it says,

> "Sleeper, awake!
> Rise from the dead,
> and Christ will shine on you."   *Hazel Dolby*

Philippians 2:5-11 Let the same mind be in you that was in Christ Jesus,
who, though he was in the form of God,
did not regard equality with God
as something to be exploited,
but emptied himself,
taking the form of a slave,
being born in human likeness.
And being found in human form,
he humbled himself
and became obedient to the point of death—
even death on a cross.
Therefore God also highly exalted him
and gave him the name
that is above every name,
so that at the name of Jesus
every knee should bend,
in heaven and on earth and under the earth,
and every tongue should confess
that Jesus Christ is Lord,
to the glory of God the Father.   *Donald Jackson*

Colossians 1:15-20 He is the image of the invisible God, the firstborn of all creation; for in him all things in heaven and on earth were created, things visible and invisible, whether thrones or dominions or rulers or powers—all things have been created through him and for him. He himself is before all things, and in him all things hold together. He is the head of the body, the church; he is the beginning, the firstborn from the dead, so that he might come to have first place in everything. For in him all the fullness of God was pleased to dwell, and through him God was pleased to reconcile to himself all things, whether on earth or in heaven, by making peace through the blood of his cross.   *Donald Jackson*

I THESSALONIANS
4:16-18

1 Thessalonians 4:16-18 For the Lord himself, with a cry of command, with the archangel's call and with the sound of God's trumpet, will descend from heaven, and the dead in Christ will rise first. Then we who are alive, who are left, will be caught up in the clouds together with them to meet the Lord in the air; and so we will be with the Lord forever. Therefore encourage one another with these words.   *Donald Jackson*

2 Thessalonians 3:10 For even when we were with you, we gave you this command: Anyone unwilling to work should not eat. *Donald Jackson*

Hebrews 8:10 This is the covenant that I will make with the house of Israel
after those days, says the Lord:
I will put my laws in their minds,
and write them on their hearts,
and I will be their God,
and they shall be my people.   *Suzanne Moore*

Hebrews 11:1 Now faith is the assurance of things hoped for, the conviction of things not seen.   *Donald Jackson*

James 2:14-17 What good is it, my brothers and sisters, if you say you have faith but do not have works? Can faith save you? If a brother or sister is naked and lacks daily food, and one of you says to them, "Go in peace; keep warm and eat your fill," and yet you do not supply their bodily needs, what is the good of that? So faith by itself, if it has no works, is dead. *Donald Jackson*

James 3:17-18 But the wisdom from above is first pure, then peaceable, gentle, willing to yield, full of mercy and good fruits, without a trace of partiality or hypocrisy. And a harvest of righteousness is sown in peace for those who make peace. *Donald Jackson*

James 5:13-16 Are any among you suffering? They should pray. Are any cheerful? They should sing songs of praise. Are any among you sick? They should call for the elders of the church and have them pray over them, anointing them with oil in the name of the Lord. The prayer of faith will save the sick, and the Lord will raise them up; and anyone who has committed sins will be forgiven. Therefore confess your sins to one another, and pray for one another, so that you may be healed. The prayer of the righteous is powerful and effective. *Donald Jackson*

1 John 4:7-12 Beloved, let us love one another, because love is from God; everyone who loves is born of God and knows God. Whoever does not love does not know God, for God is love. God's love was revealed among us in this way: God sent his only Son into the world so that we might live through him. In this is love, not that we loved God but that he loved us and sent his Son to be the atoning sacrifice for our sins. Beloved, since God loved us so much, we also ought to love one another. No one has ever seen God; if we love one another, God lives in us, and his love is perfected in us. *Donald Jackson*

HEBREWS 11:1

Index of Artists

ILLUMINATORS

Donald Jackson (Artistic Director and Illuminator — Monmouthshire, Wales)

One of the world's leading calligraphers, Donald Jackson is the artistic director and illuminator of *The Saint John's Bible*. From his scriptorium in Wales he oversees scribes, artists, and craftsmen who work with him on the handwriting and illumination of this seven-volume, 1,150-page book. His studio/workshop is the only calligraphy atelier in the United Kingdom where artist calligraphers are still regularly employed as assistants, maintaining the highest traditions of this ancient art in a modern context.

From an early age Jackson sought to combine the use of the ancient techniques of the calligrapher's art with the imagery and spontaneous letter forms of his own time. As a teenager his first ambition was to be "The Queen's Scribe" and a close second was to inscribe and illuminate the Bible. His talents were soon recognized and his ambitions fulfilled.

At the age of twenty, while still a student himself, Jackson was appointed a visiting lecturer (professor) at the Camberwell College of Art, London. Within six years he became the youngest artist calligrapher chosen to take part in the Victoria and Albert Museum's first International Calligraphy Show after the war and was appointed a scribe to the Crown Office at the House of Lords. As a scribe to Her Majesty Queen Elizabeth II, he was responsible for the creation of official state documents. In conjunction with a wide range of other calligraphic projects he executed Historic Royal documents under The Great Seal and Royal Charters. In 1985 he was decorated by the Queen with the Medal of The Royal Victorian Order (MVO), which is awarded for personal services to the Sovereign.

Jackson is an elected Fellow and past Chairman of the prestigious Society of Scribes and Illuminators, and in 1997 was named Master of the six-hundred-year-old Guild of Scriveners of the city of London. His personally innovative work and inspirational teaching, together with books, a film series, and exhibitions in Europe, North America, Puerto Rico, Australia, and China, have led to his being widely acknowledged as a seminal influence on the growth of Western calligraphy over the past twenty-five years. In 1980 he wrote *The Story of Writing*, which has since been published in many editions and in seven languages. His thirty-year retrospective exhibition, *Painting With Words*, premiered at the Minneapolis Institute of Arts in Minneapolis, Minnesota, in August 1988 and traveled to thirteen museums and galleries.

Since the time of his first lectures in New York and Puerto Rico (1968), Donald Jackson has had a very stimulating influence on the growth of modern Western calligraphy in the United States through the many workshops and lectures he has given. It was the first of the International Assembly of Lettering Artists seminars, inspired by Jackson, that brought him to Saint John's Abbey and University for the first time in 1981. He has since attended and lectured at several other of these annual assemblies, including those held at Saint John's in 1984 and 1990. Jackson returned again to Saint John's in the summer of 1996 to serve as one of the keynote speakers at *Servi Textus: The Servants of the Text*, a symposium that included a calligraphy exhibition featuring Jackson's work along with that of other artists, many of whom were his past students and past associates of his atelier.

Interpretive illuminations, incipits, book titles, marginal, and special text treatments in these volumes are the work of Donald Jackson, unless otherwise noted below. Donald Jackson wrote and illuminated the entire book of Revelation.

Hazel Dolby (Illuminator — Hampshire, England)

Trained at Camberwell Art College, London, and later at the Roehampton Institute with Ann Camp, she is a Fellow of the Society of Scribes and Illuminators (FSSI). She is a lecturer at the University of Roehampton, teaching art and drawn and painted lettering, and teaches workshops in Europe and the United States. Her work is in various collections, including the Poole Museum and the Crafts Study Centre, London.

1 Samuel 3:1-18	Call of Samuel
1 Kings 3:16-28	Wisdom of Solomon
Nehemiah 8:1-12	Square before the Watergate
1 Corinthians 15:50-58	At the Last Trumpet
2 Corinthians	Book Heading (contribution to piece by Donald Jackson)
Ephesians 4:4-6	There Is One Body and One Spirit
Ephesians 5:8, 14	For Once You Were Darkness

Aidan Hart (Iconographer — Shropshire, Wales)

Studied in New Zealand, the United Kingdom, and Greece. He was a full-time sculptor in New Zealand before returning to the United Kingdom in 1983. Since then he has worked as a full-time iconographer. He is a member of the Orthodox Church, and his work is primarily panel icons but also includes church frescoes, illuminations on vellum, and carved work in stone and wood. His work is in collections in over fifteen countries of the world. He has contributed to numerous publications. He is visiting tutor at the Prince's School of Traditional Arts, London.

2 Kings 2:1-14	Elijah and the Fiery Chariot (collaboration with Donald Jackson)
2 Kings 4–6	Elisha and the Six Miracles (collaboration with Donald Jackson)

Thomas Ingmire (Illuminator — San Francisco, California)

Trained as a landscape architect at Ohio State University and University of California, Berkeley, before beginning the study of calligraphy and medieval painting techniques in the early 1970s. He is the first foreign member to be elected (in 1977) a Fellow of the Society of Scribes and Illuminators (FSSI). Ingmire teaches throughout the United States, Canada, Australia, Europe, Japan, and Hong Kong. He has exhibited widely in the United States. His work is in many public and private collections throughout the world, including the San Francisco Public Library's Special Collections; the Newberry Library, Chicago; and the Victoria and Albert Museum, London.

1 Samuel 1:11; 2:1-10	Hannah's Prayer
2 Samuel 1:19-27	David's Lament (How the Mighty Have Fallen)
Romans 6:22-23	But Now That You Have Been Freed from Sin
Romans 8:1-39	Fulfillment of Creation
1 Corinthians 11:23-26	For I Received from the Lord
1 Corinthians 13:1-13	If I Speak in the Tongues of Mortals

Sally Mae Joseph (Scribe/Illuminator and Senior Artistic Consultant — Sussex, England)

Studied illumination, calligraphy, and heraldry at Reigate School of Art and Design and calligraphy, applied lettering, and bookbinding at the Roehampton Institute, London. She is a Fellow of the Society of Scribes and Illuminators (FSSI). She has exhibited and lectured in Europe and the United States and has contributed articles to numerous publications.

She was a lecturer at Roehampton Institute from 1991 to 1993. Her work is in many public and private collections.

Suzanne Moore (Illuminator — Vashon Island, Washington)

Earned a BFA in printmaking and drawing at the University of Wisconsin–Eau Claire, followed by the study of lettering and book design. She began creating manuscript books in the early 1980s, and she melds traditional scribal techniques with contemporary aesthetics in her book work. Suzanne has taught and exhibited widely, and her books have been acquired for private and public collections in the United States and Europe, including the Pierpont Morgan Library, the Library of Congress, and the James S. Copley Library, La Jolla, California.

Chris Tomlin (Natural History Illustrator — London, England)

Trained at the Royal College of Art, London, studying natural history illustration. He has worked for Oxford University Press and the National Trust, as well as for other publishers. He also studies flora and fauna in the field on expeditions as far from home as Minnesota and Madagascar, where he has worked in the rainforest recording endangered species.

1 Maccabees 11	Glasswing Butterfly and Black Widow Spider
2 Maccabees 7	Painted Lady Butterfly and Caterpillars (UK)
2 Maccabees 15	Chameleon
1 Corinthians 2–3	Black and White Butterfly
2 Corinthians 7	Generic Bee (inspired by the honey bee)
Colossians 1	Common Blue Butterfly on Buddleia Flowers
Hebrews 1	Dragonflies on Yorkshire Fog Grass

SCRIBES

Sue Hufton (London, England)

Trained at the Roehampton Institute, London, studying calligraphy and bookbinding. She is a fellow of the Society of Scribes and Illuminators (FSSI). She is a lecturer at the University of Roehampton, teaching calligraphy and bookbinding. She teaches in Europe, Canada, and Australia and has led calligraphic retreats to Holy Island (Lindisfarne), United Kingdom. She is the editor of the SSI journal, *The Scribe*, and has contributed articles to other publications.

> *Historical Books* and *Letters* (prose text); English running heads in *Historical Books*

Donald Jackson (see biography above)

> *Letters and Revelation* (prose text); all capital letters; all book titles; all incipits; all titles of additions in *Esther*

Sally Mae Joseph (see biography above)

> *Historical Books* and *Letters* (prose text)

Susan Leiper (Edinburgh, Scotland)

Born and brought up in Glasgow, Scotland. She studied French at the University of St Andrews and history of art at the Courtauld Institute of Art in London. After calligraphy classes in Hong Kong and Edinburgh, Susie completed the Advanced Training Scheme with the Society of Scribes and Illuminators, of which she is now a Fellow (FSSI). She has undertaken commissions for major institutions, including the British Museum, the National Museums of Scotland, and the BBC, and she contributed to the *Great Book of Gaelic*. She also edits books on Chinese art, which is the main source of inspiration in her own work. She lives in Edinburgh with her husband and four children.

> *Historical Books* and *Letters* (prose text)

Brian Simpson (Leicestershire, England)

Studied calligraphy and heraldry (a fellow student of Donald Jackson) at Central School for Arts and Crafts, London, with Irene Wellington and Mervyn Oliver. He worked as a lettering artist and graphic designer for forty-nine years. Now he concentrates on calligraphy and heraldic art.

> *Historical Books* and *Letters* (prose text); all chapter numbers; all Greek running heads in *Historical Books*

Angela Swan (Abergavenny, Wales)

Studied calligraphy and bookbinding at the Roehampton Institute from 1985 to 1988. She was an assistant to Donald Jackson in Monmouth, Wales, for three years. Angela works as a freelance calligrapher. She teaches and exhibits in the United Kingdom and has contributed to various books and publications.

> *Historical Books* and *Letters* (prose text); English running heads in *Letters and Revelation*; all footnotes in the book of Revelation

Izzy Pludwinski (Jerusalem, Israel)

Started out as a certified religious scribe (*Sofer* STaM) and branched out to calligraphy and design. He studied at the Roehampton Institute, where he completed the certificate in calligraphy and design. He has taught in both London and Israel.

> All Hebrew running heads in *Historical Books*; consultant for all Hebrew writing

Other team members:

> *Mabel Jackson*: Partner
> *Rebecca Cherry, Rachel Collard, Jane Grayer*: Project Managers
> *Sarah Harris*: Studio Manager
> *Vin Godier*: Designer and IT Consultant; computer graphics
> *Sally Sargeant*: Proofreader

Michael Patella, OSB

Michael Patella, OSB, SSD, is both professor of New Testament at the School of Theology•Seminary of Saint John's University, Collegeville, and seminary rector. In addition to serving as chair of the Committee on Illumination and Text for *The Saint John's Bible*, he has written *The Death of Jesus: The Diabolical Force and the Ministering Angel* (Paris: Gabalda, 1999), *The Gospel according to Luke*, New Collegeville Bible Commentary Series (Collegeville, MN: Liturgical Press, 2005), *The Lord of the Cosmos: Mithras, Paul, and the Gospel of Mark* (New York: T&T Clark, 2006), and *Angels and Demons: A Christian Primer of the Spiritual World* (Collegeville, MN: Liturgical Press, 2012). He has been a frequent contributor to *The Bible Today* and is a member of the Catholic Biblical Association.

Susan Wood, SCL

Susan Wood, SCL, is a professor of theology at Marquette University, Milwaukee, Wisconsin. She taught in both the Theology Department and the School of Theology at Saint John's University for twelve years and was the associate dean of the School of Theology for five years. She earned her bachelor's degree at Saint Mary College in Leavenworth, Kansas, her master's degree at Middlebury College, Middlebury, Vermont, and her doctorate at Marquette University, Milwaukee, Wisconsin.

Columba Stewart, OSB

Columba Stewart, OSB, is the executive director of the Hill Museum & Manuscript Library (HMML), the home of *The Saint John's Bible*, where he has developed HMML's projects of manuscript digitization in the Middle East. Having served on the CIT and as curator of special collections before becoming director of HMML, he often speaks about how *The Saint John's Bible* expresses the vision for the book arts and religious culture at Saint John's University. Father Columba has published extensively on monastic topics and is a professor of monastic studies at Saint John's School of Theology. He received his bachelor's degree in history and literature from Harvard College, his master's degree in religious studies from Yale University, and his doctorate in theology from the University of Oxford.

Irene Nowell, OSB

Irene Nowell, OSB, is a Benedictine from Mount St. Scholastica in Atchison, Kansas, where she is the director of junior sisters. She is an adjunct professor of Scripture for the School of Theology at Saint John's University. Sister Irene received her bachelor's degree in music from Mount St. Scholastica College in Kansas and her master's degrees in German and theology from the Catholic University of America and Saint John's University. She holds a doctorate in biblical studies from the Catholic University of America.

Johanna Becker, OSB

A Benedictine potter, teacher, art historian, and Orientalist, Johanna Becker, OSB, combines these in the different facets of her work. As a teacher in the Art Department of the College of Saint Benedict and Saint John's University, she taught both studio classes (primarily ceramics) and art history, focusing for the past several years on the arts of Asia. As a specialist in Asian ceramics, particularly those of seventeenth-century Japan, she has done connoisseurship for public and private museums, published a book, *Karatsu Ware*, and written and lectured worldwide. Her art history classes benefit from the years she lived in Japan and her time spent in many Asian countries as an art researcher. Sister Johanna holds a bachelor of fine arts degree from the University of Colorado, a master of fine arts degree in studio art from Ohio State University, and a doctorate in art history from the University of Michigan. Although retired, she continues to teach Asian art history classes. She is a member of the Monastery of Saint Benedict, St. Joseph, Minnesota.

Nathanael Hauser, OSB

Nathanael Hauser, OSB, is an artist who works in egg tempera, enamel, calligraphy, and mosaic. While teaching art history as an associate professor at Saint John's University, he also taught calligraphy and the theology and practice of icon painting. Father Nathanael has undertaken commissions for churches, monastic communities, and private collections, creating icons, enameled crosses, calligraphy books, reliquaries, and Christmas crèches. His work and papers have been exhibited and presented in the United States and in Rome, Italy. Father Nathanael received his bachelor's degree in philosophy from St. John's Seminary College in Camarillo, California. He received his bachelor's degree in sacred theology from the Pontificio Ateneo di Sant'Anselmo, Rome, and his doctorate in classical and medieval art and archaeology from the University of Minnesota.

Alan Reed, OSB

Alan Reed, OSB, is the curator of art collections at the Hill Museum & Manuscript Library. He previously taught design and drawing in the joint Art Department of Saint John's University and the College of Saint Benedict for twenty-five years, and toward the end of that time he was chair of the department for six years. He has a bachelor's degree from Saint John's University in studio art, a master's in art education from the Rhode Island School of Design, and a master of fine arts from the University of Chicago in studio art and art theory.

Ellen Joyce

Ellen Joyce teaches medieval history at Beloit College in Beloit, Wisconsin. Her research interests are in the role of visions and dreams in medieval monastic culture. She also has a passion for the study of illuminated manuscripts and their production, and she often teaches courses on topics related to books and their readers in the Middle Ages. She served on the CIT while she was employed at the Hill Museum & Manuscript Library and teaching at Saint John's University. Dr. Joyce received her master's and doctorate degrees from the Centre for Medieval Studies at the University of Toronto and her undergraduate degree in humanities from Yale University.

Rosanne Keller

Rosanne Keller is a sculptor whose work is on permanent display throughout the United States and the United Kingdom. In 1993 she was commissioned to create a ceramic Buddha and eight ritual vessels for the private meditation room of His Holiness, the Dalai Lama. Her sculpture can be seen at St. Deiniol's Library and St. Bueno's Jesuit Retreat Center in Wales; Saint John's University and the St. Cloud Children's Home in Minnesota; Exeter Cathedral; Taizé, France; and on the campus of Texas Woman's University. She has published a book on pilgrimage, *Pilgrim in Time*, and a novel, *A Summer All Her Own*, as well as texts for literacy programs.

David Paul Lange, OSB

A monk, artist, and teacher, David Paul Lange, OSB, has been a member of the Art Department of Saint John's University and the College of Saint Benedict since 2001. He has a bachelor's degree from Saint Olaf College in philosophy and a master of fine arts in studio art from the University of Southern Illinois at Edwardsville. A sculptor by training, Brother David Paul also teaches modern contemporary art history and theory, drawing, and foundations.

Simon-Hòa Phan, OSB

Brother Simon-Hòa Phan is an associate professor of art at Saint John's University. He holds a bachelor of arts in philosophy (Saint John's Seminary, Camarillo), a bachelor of arts in Religious Studies (Louvain), a bachelor of fine arts in painting (Maryland Institute), and a master of fine arts in film and video (California Institute of the Arts). A member of the CIT since 2008, he served as artist advisor for the Bible Project.

Other members of the broader Saint John's community, including Susan Brix, Jerome Tupa, OSB, and David Cotter, OSB, have served at various times on the Committee for Illumination and Text.

At Saint John's University, the project is overseen by Michael Bush, Director, *The Saint John's Bible*, located at the Hill Museum & Manuscript Library.